D1462061

秀作ショップデザイン

物販店＆ショールーム

EXCELLENT SHOP DESIGNS Store & Showroom

秀作ショップデザイン

物販店&ショールーム

EXCELLENT SHOP DESIGNS Store & Showroom

PART 1 ファッション Fashion

PART 2 カルチュア & ホビー Culture & Hobby

目次

PART 3 リビング Living

PART 4 フード ＆ 和風の店 Foods & Japanese Style Shop

本書には、84年から86年に開店し、月刊「商店建築」に特集掲載された物販店にショールームを加えた82店舗を収録。
業種・業態で●ファッション(ファッション ブティックは除きましたが、ショールームは加えました)●カルチュア＆ホビー●リビング●フード＆和風の店の４部に分類し、写真と平面図、設計者による解説を加えて紹介しています。
ショールームも収録しましたので、各業種の店舗の企画・設計のデザインソースとして、また、業種・業態に分類しているので、デザインのスタイルブックとして拡く利用できます。
●ファッション(22)●カルチュア ＆ ホビー(20)●リビング(23)●フード＆和風の店(17)合計82店舗を収録いたしました。
巻末に店名索引を加えました。
解説の最後の(　　)内の数字は掲載号を表しています。
例(86-11)は､｢商店建築｣86年11月号掲載の意味です。

1988年３月
商店建築社

STORE & SHOWROOM

This book covers 82 shops, including showrooms, that opened between 1984 and 1986.
By type of business and mode of operation, they have been classified into four categories: • fashion (excluding fashion boutiques, but including showrooms) • culture & hobby • living • food/Japanese style shops. Each of them comes with photos, a plan and the designer's explanation.
Since showrooms were also covered, this book can be used widely either as a design source when planning and designing shops in various types of business, or as a design style book, since they are classified by type of business and mode of operation. A total of 82 shops were covered: • fashion (22) • culture & hobby (20) • living (23) • food/Japanese style shop (17)

March 1988

SHOTENKENCHIKU-SHA
Published by Shotenkenchiku-sha Co., Ltd.
7-22-36-2, Nishi-shinjuku, Shinjuku-ku, Tokyo, Japan

平面図の略号 Abbreviation

AC	Air Cleaner	エアクリーナー
AD	Air Duct	エアダクト
CT	Counter Table	カウンターテーブル
DS	Duct Space	ダクトスペース
DT	Display Table	ディスプレイテーブル
ENT	Entrance	出入口
EV	Elevator	エレベーター
FR	Fitting Room	フィッティングルーム
FRF	Freezer Refrigerator	冷凍冷蔵庫
HC	High Case	ハイケース
Hg	Hanger	ハンガー
M.WC	Men's Water Closet	男子便所
PS	Pipe Space	パイプスペース
PT	Package Table	包装台
R	Register	レジスター
RCT	Register Counter Table	レジカウンター
RF	Refrigerator	冷蔵庫
S	Sink	シンク
SC	Show Case	ショーケース
Sh	Shelf	陳列棚
St	Show Stage	ショーステージ
Sw	Show Window	ショーウインド
T	Table	テーブル
TEL	Telephone	電話
WC	Water Closet	便所
WT	Work Table	作業台
W.WC	Women's Water Closet	女子便所

PART 1 ファッション Fashion

ファサード　The facade.

ショールーム アッシュドゥ

東京都港区北青山3-10-2　Phone/03-486-6501

撮影／本木誠一

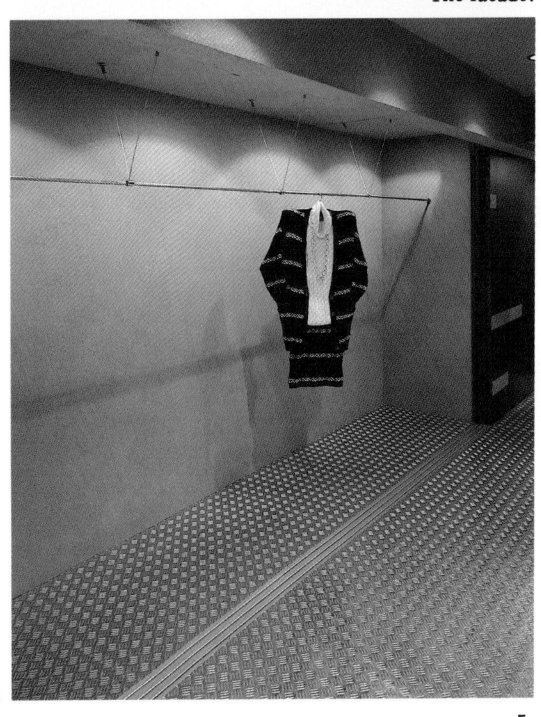

スライティングドアを開放し　ハンガースペースをみる
The hanger space viewed by opening the sliding door.

アルミ縞板　ステンレスワイヤーによるディスプレイスクリーン

材料仕様

床／コンパネ t ＝12下地　アルミ縞板 t ＝ 3 ×2000×1000　壁面及び天井／ＰＢ下地　樹脂モルタル金鏝仕上げ　テーブル／甲板・栓材板目練付け染色ＣＬ　脚・スチールパイプϕ=150
下地ステンレスワイヤーϕ ＝ 3 巻き　ディスプレイスクリーン／ステンレスワイヤーϕ ＝ 3　ピッチ30

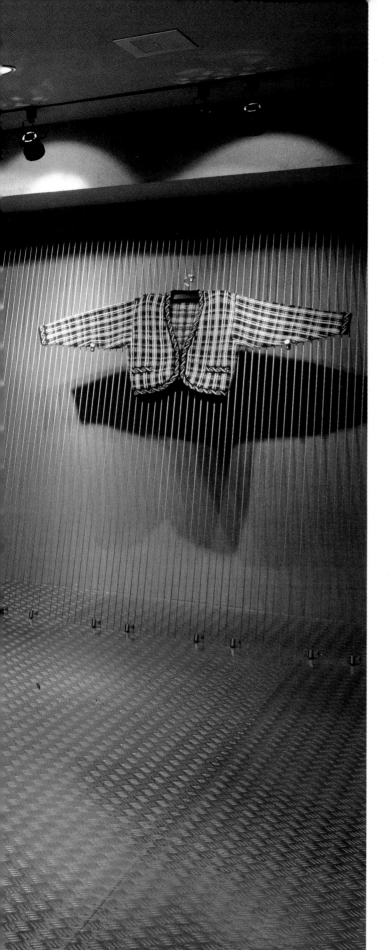

渾然さを整理し再構築する
ジャパンテキスタイル「アッシュドゥ」は東京・表参道の「モリハナエビル」の裏手にある。この計画は改装以前の姿　つまりオフィスとショールームとの渾然さを分割し　デザインにより目的の距離を最大に確保することにあった。
材質——アルミの縞板　ステンレス　ワイヤー　栓材　イタリアンテックス——の構成要素を幾何学の規制　分解のバリエーションのスタディを繰り返し構図(デザイン)を決めた。
現実の世界に息づいているリアリティーの欠如　人を惑わすような脈絡のなさの中で　人間の知性や　精神が構築するもっとも自由な環境を踏破して行きたいものだ。 〈滝内高志〉(86-8)
設計／滝内高志
施工／藤工芸
面積／54㎡
工期／1986年2月3日～3月1日

Showroom H. DEUX

Reorganizes the harmonious whole for reconstruction
Japan Textile "H. Deux" stands at the back of "Mori Hanae Building," Omote Sando, Tokyo. The current plan was intended to divide the harmonious whole of the office and showroom which existed before the reconstruction, and secure a maximum target distance through design.
By repeatedly subjecting the element materials – striped aluminum plate, stainless steel wire, stopper, Italian textile – to geometrical regulation and decomposition variation studies, the whole design was determined.
In the midst of the actual world where realities are lacking and the logical connection is illusorily absent, it is desired that the freest environment built up by the human intelligence and mind be explored.

3-10-2, Kita-aoyama, Minato-ku, Tokyo Phone: 03-486-6501

Design / Takashi Takiuchi
Area / 54 m²

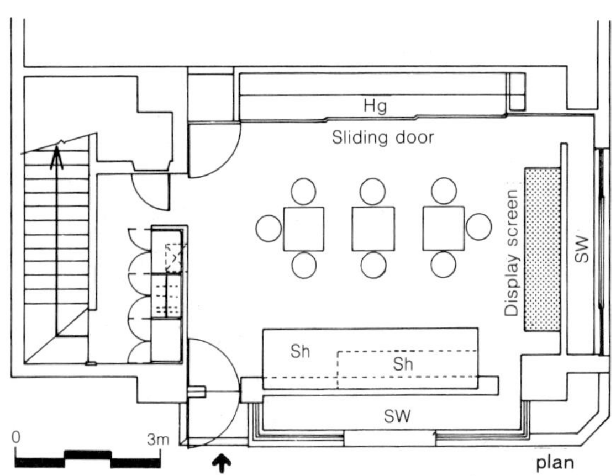

The display screen of striped aluminum plate and stainless steel wire.

営業内容
開店／1986年3月3日　営業時間／午前9時～午後6時　休日／毎週日曜日　経営者／ジャパンテキスタイル㈱

中央商談テーブルより入口方向をみる

The entrance area viewed from the business talk table in the center.

ショールーム
H.ツネマツ

東京都渋谷区猿楽町2-1 アベニューサイド代官山
Phone/03-464-9621

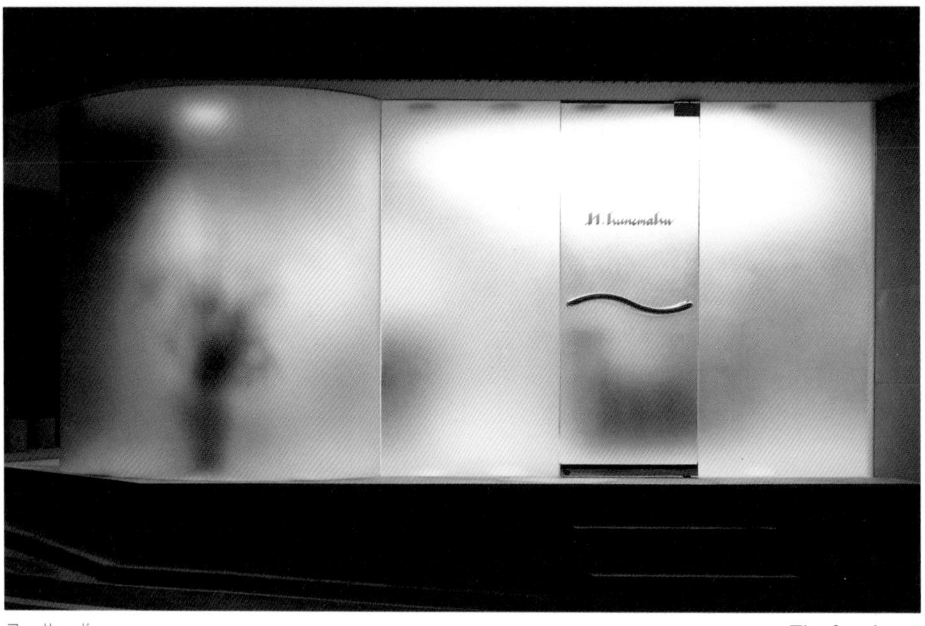
ファサード

The facade.

撮影／田中宏明

材料仕様

外壁／大谷石　ウレタン塗装　サイン／真鍮フェロネリ仕上げ　床／地下１階・大谷石貼り　１階・黒御影石貼り　壁面／地下１階・ＰＢｔ＝12下地　特殊吹付け塗装　一部ＰＢｔ＝12下地　寒冷紗パテしごきの上ＡＥＰ吹付け塗装　天井／既存天井にＡＥＰ吹付け塗装及びクリンプネット焼付け塗装　スクリーン／抗火石特殊吹付け塗装　什器／スチール紋様研磨の上ウレタン塗装　カウンター／黒御影石

営業内容

開店／1985年９月20日　営業時間／午前９時30分～午後６時　休日／毎週日曜日　祭日　経営者／㈱ブロードキャスティング　主な商品／ブロードキャスティング　ブランドのレディスウエア　靴　アクセサリー

中央商談テーブルと引き出しユニット棚をみる

The business talk table in the center and drawer unit shelves.

用途に即した表情をつくる

この「H.ツネマツ」の基本は　情報の器であること　つまり　どんな情報が入ってきても　それらをすんなり呑み込めること　しかも時代性　エンターテイメント性　可変性をいつまでも失わないこと　そして　あくまでもプレーンでニュートラルな器でなければならないことにある。
したがって　壁面展開における可変性　仕掛けにポイントを置いた。組み合せのできる引き出しユニット　収納（ハンガー）扉を格納することによって　フラットな壁面からディスプレイ壁面への可変システムがそれである。
このスペースは　ショールームであり　商談スペースであり　かつプレスルームでもあるわけで　可変システムによって　それぞれの用途にあった表情を創り出せるものとした。

〈渡部　隆／ヨコタデザインワークスタジオ〉(86-12)

設計／ヨコタデザインワークスタジオ　名取和彦　富澤　実
施工／白水社　面積／64.86m²　工期／1986年4月28日～5月20日　工費／1750万円

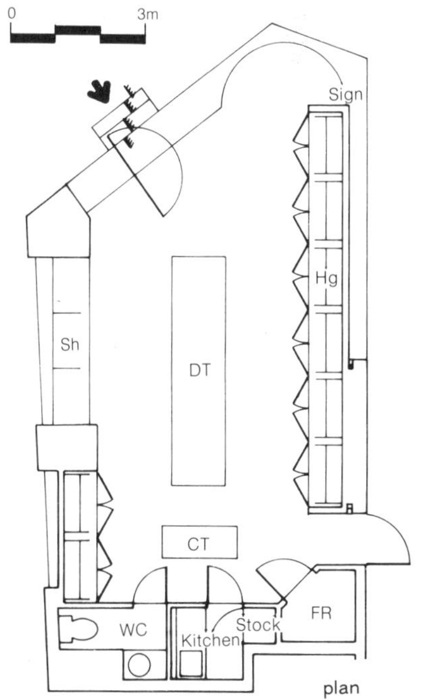

Showroom H. TSUNEMATSU

Makes an expression according to use

The basic purpose of "H. Tsunematsu" lies in serving as a container of information. That is, it must be able to contain any type of information smoothly whenever it enters, and must always keep pace with the times, maintain the element of entertainment and changeability. And, it must fundamentally be a plain and neutral container.
Accordingly, design emphasis was placed on the changeability and setting of wall surface layout. By means of drawer units that can be combined and accommodation hanger doors, the flat wall surface can be changed to a display wall surface.
This space can thus serve as a show room, a business talk space and also as a press room. By the changeable system, it can make an expression according to each use.

2-1, Sarugaku-cho, Shibuya-ku, Tokyo　Phone: 03-464-9621

Design / Kazuhiko Natori
Area / 64.86 m^2

ディスプレイテーブルを通してみる

A scene viewed across the display table.

ファサード

The facade.

ショールーム
ブロード キャスティング

東京都港区赤坂8-10-22 ニュー赤坂ビル
Phone/03-475-6052

撮影/瀬口哲夫

スクリーン方向をみる

The screen area.

階段よりみる

A scene viewed from the staircase.

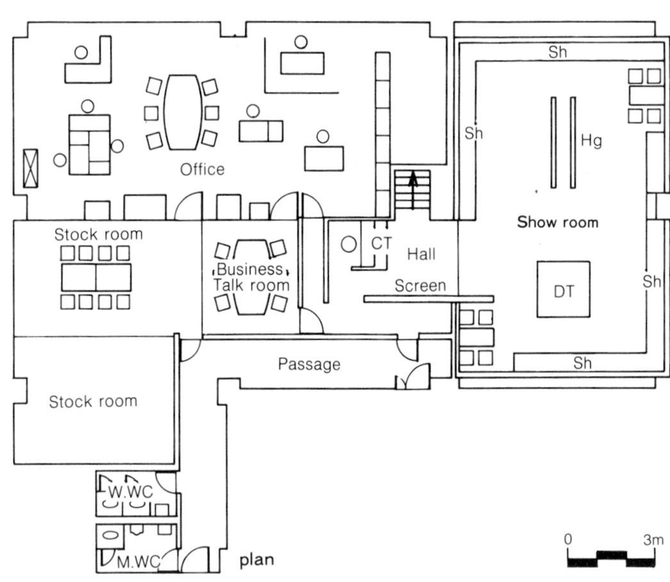

plan

中央ディスプレイハンガーをみる

The display hangers in the center.

イメージを表現　展開するメッセージの場

新しいブランド「ブロードキャスティング」がこれから展開されるショップ群の拠点　発進基地として　赤坂にショールームを誕生させた。
スペースは　ショールームとしての機能と展示会その他の企画　イベントやギャラリーとしての使われ方など「ブロードキャスティング」の発進基地としての対応と多様性を持たせることを最重点とした。
この服のデザイナーである大西せつこさんは「ブロードキャスティング」の服は　アンビバレンツ（両面価値）にあるという。つまり　異なる2つの価値感を1つのオブジェ＝服に昇華させることにあると語る。

- 尖鋭的であるが　一過性の流行ではない。
- 奇を衒わないが　新奇性に富む。
- 硬質な鉱物イメージであるが　温かい。
- リラックスするが　ドレスアップできる。
- アバンギャルドな毒があるが　可愛い。

………など。
ショールームの空間構成は　上記のアンビバレンツのイメージそのものをベースにおき　素材には石　スチールを多用した。　〈本江謙治〉(86-1)

企画／イング
設計／本江保坂建築研究所　本江謙治　保坂　高
施工／地下1階110.80㎡　1階15.12㎡　ショールーム88.8㎡
工期／1985年8月20日～9月18日

Showroom BROADCASTING

A place for message to express and develop images

The new brand "Broadcasting" brought into being a showroom in Akasaka, as a base-launching station for a group of shops which will be developed from now on.
In designing the space, heaviest emphasis was placed on providing it not merely with functions as a showroom, but also versatility as a launching station for the "Broadcasting" brand serving as a place for exhibition and other events or as a gallery.
Setsuko Onishi, designer of this brand of apparel, says that the apparel of "Broadcasting" features an ambivalence, i.e. sublimation of two different senses of value into an object (= apparel).

- It is ahead of the times, but does not remain as a temporary fashion.
- It does not make a display of its originality.
- It gives a hard image of ore, but is warm.
- When wearing it, you can relax, but dress up.
- It contains an avant-garde poison, but is charming.

The space composition of the showroom bases itself on the very ambivalent image mentioned above, using stone and steel as materials.

8-10-22, Akasaka, Minato-ku, Tokyo　Phone: 03-475-6052

Design: Kenji Hogo + Takashi Hosaka
Area / Basement 110.80 m^2; 1st floor 15.12 m^2; Showroom 88.8 m^2

材料仕様
床／インド白砂岩貼り600角　壁面／楢柾目練付け合板染色ＣＬ　一部インド白砂岩貼り　天井／ＰＢｔ＝12目地　寒冷紗パテしごきＡＥＰ　家具／引き出しユニット・楢練付け合板染色ＣＬ　テーブル／トラバーチンｔ＝20　樹脂加工

営業内容
開店／1986年5月26日　営業時間／午前10時～午後6時　休日／毎月第2土曜　日曜及び祭日　経営者／㈱マスヤ　主な商品／H.ツネマツ　ブランドのオールアイテム

ファサード

The facade.

シューズショップ＆ショールーム
アンデックス

東京都港区南青山5-11-14 グレイセス ツチヤマ 1階
Phone/03-400-4791

店内左奥の照明を内蔵したレジカウンターをみる　ベンチ椅子は左右に回転する

The register counter with built-in lighting at the inner left corner. The bench chairs turn sideways.

撮影／T.ナカサ＆パートナーズ

入口に面した売場コーナーをみる

The selling corner facing the entrance.

展示会にも使えるフレキシブルな空間構成

東京の表参道界隈　通称"骨董通り"が青山通りにぶつかるT字路近くの路地を入ったところにできた　靴のショールーム兼ショップ。
小売よりも　どちらかといえば卸がメインのため　バイヤーのための展示会にも使えるように　展示機能は極力おさえ　商品も日本の靴店にしては少ない。中央の展示のためのテーブルも甲板が着脱でき　多目的な広いスペースが確保できるようになっている。
床のガラスブロックは　素材の使い方のおもしろさというよりも　設計者の頭の中に"なまず""水と砂がせめぎあう南太平洋あたりの波打ち際"のイメージが　浮び上ったという。そこは　また足下が最も美しく見えるシーンでもあり　そんな場所で靴を　自分の足に合わせてみるといった情景が　この砂をつめ込んだガラスブロックの床へ結びついていったのであろう。
照明を反射させたガラスブロックの面は　実際　水面のキラメキのように見える。　〈文責・編集部〉(85-6)

設計／デザイン・エム　森田正樹&マリア
施工／アール・アイ・ディー
面積／157m²
工期／1985年1月26日～3月7日
工費／2300万円

Shoes Shop & Showroom ÉDEX

Flexible composition of space that can also be used for exhibition

Shoes shop & showroom opened along a lane near T-shape lane where the so-called "Antique Street" crosses Aoyama Street in the vicinity of Omote Sando, Tokyo.
Since this combined shop is mainly intended for wholesaling, rather than for retailing, its display function is minimized so that it may be used for an exhibition for buyers. The number of items is also small for a Japanese shop. The table deck for the central display is detachable, so that a multi-purpose, wide space can be secured.
As for glass blocks on the floor, the designer seems to have hit on an image of "catfish" and an image of "beach of the South Pacific where water and sand mix with each other." This was more interesting to him than the use of materials. In this scene, your feet look most beautiful, where you can make your feet suit your shoes. This scene seems to have been connected to the floor of glass blocks into which sand is filled.
The surface of glass blocks on which illumination is reflected, in fact, looks like sparkling on the water surface.

5-11-14, Minami-aoyama, Minato-ku, Tokyo　Phone: 03-400-4791

Design / Masaki Morita
Area / 157 m²

材料仕様
外壁／漆喰仕上げ　扉／強化ガラス　ドア／テンパーライト　外部床／磁器タイル貼り　サイン／スチール焼付け塗装　床／ガラスブロック砂詰め　壁面及び天井／漆喰仕上げ　照明器具／ダウンライト及びスポットライト　椅子及びソファ／スチールフレーム皮張り　カウンター／ガラス製照明組込み

壁面にモニターＴＶを埋め込んだエキジビションルームをみる

The exhibition room where a monitor TV set is buried in the wall.

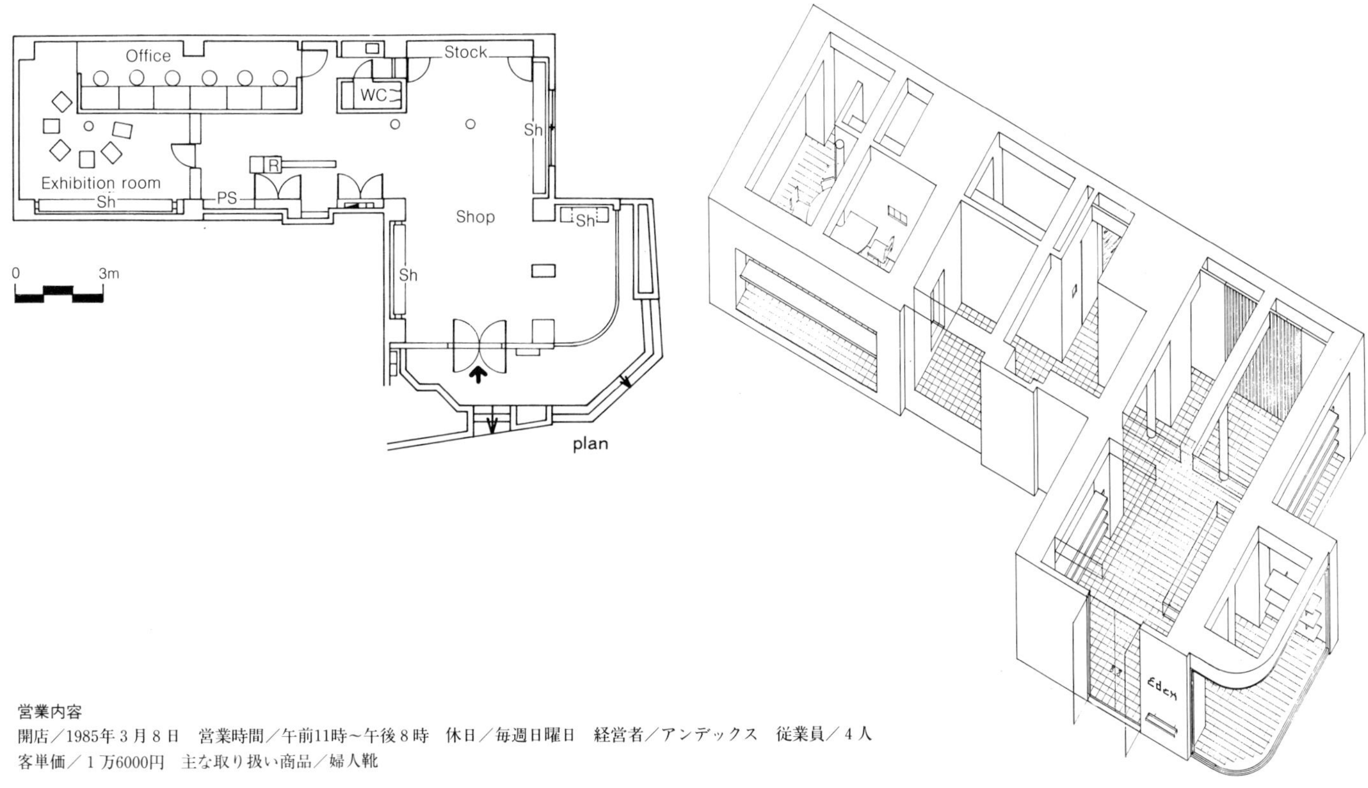

営業内容

開店／1985年３月８日　営業時間／午前11時～午後８時　休日／毎週日曜日　経営者／アンデックス　従業員／４人

客単価／１万6000円　主な取り扱い商品／婦人靴

プレスルームの奥より中央部デスク方向をみる

The desk area in the center viewed from the inner part of the press room.

プレスルームのファサード

The facade of the press room.

ヒト　モノ　コトを都市感覚で組み合せる

ファッションのブランド化が進み　徐々にポピュラー化していながらも　一方で　生活者にとっては　まだ特別なコトとして意識されている感じがある。

アパレルメーカーでは　インフォメーションを兼ね備えるプレスというアクションと機能は　各メーカーとも必ず持ち備えているものの　その"箱"自体の機能が欠落し　本来の基本的なセールスプロモーションの機能に欠けていたのではないかと考えている。

この店は　以前はショールームであったが　今回のリニューアルによって　これらをクリアすることができたと思う。アパレルメーカーが　デザインから制作　販売に至るまでおし進めようとする上で　プレスルーム　ショールーム　ショップ　この3つが一体となった時　初めて機能しはじめるのだと考えている。しかし　その"箱"は"箱"だけで存在し得ないものであり　そこに必ず　ヒト　モノ　コトが介入してくるのである。都市の感受性　即ち　ヒューマニックな感覚　ヒト　モノ　コトらのノーワードを組み合わせることを意識しながらできあがったのが　この空間である。　〈渡部　隆〉(85-10)

設計／横田良一　グッドスピン　スタジオ　山本有子

施工／スタット

面積／プレス・66.1m²　ブティック・72.8m²　合計138.9m²

工期／1985年2月3日～23日

工費／1900万円

プレスルーム＆ブティック
ヒロミチ ナカノ＆ビバ ユー

東京都渋谷区神宮前2-13-4　Phone/03-405-6249(プレスルーム)　03-405-6193(ブティック)

撮影／T.ナカサ＆パートナーズ

ブティックのショーウインドより店内をみる

The inside viewed from the show window of the boutique.

Press Room & Boutique
HIROMICHI NAKANO & VIVA-YOU

Combines man, matter and thing with an urban sense

While the brand development of fashion is going on, and the fashion is gradually becoming popular, it seems that ordinary people are conscious of it as a special "thing."

As for apparel makers, while each maker always comes with action and functions of a "press" which offers information, it seems that the very functions of the "box" were absent, and it was therefore lacking in the basic sales promotional functions.

Previously, this shop was a showroom, but by the current renewal, it is believed that those drawbacks could be overcome. When each apparel maker wishes to treat design, production and sales totally, it may be realized only when the press room, showroom and shop are integrated harmoniously. The "box," however, cannot exist alone, and there always come in man, matther and thing. This space was created by combining 'no words' – man, matter and thing – with an urban sensitivity, i.e. human sense.

2-13-4, Jingu-mae Shibuya-ku, Tokyo
Phone: 03-405-6249 (Press room), 03-405-6193 (Boutique)

Design / Ryoichi Yokota
Area / Press room 66.1 m², Boutique 72.8 m²; Totalling 138.9 m²

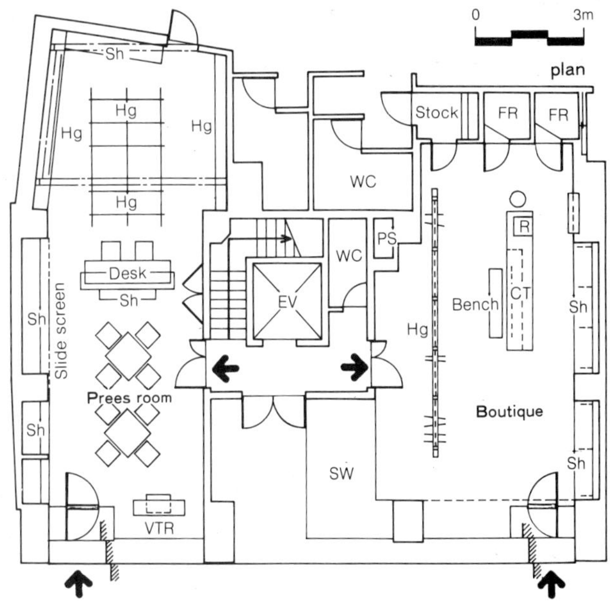

材料仕様

〈プレス〉 床／ラワン積材フローリングＣＬ 壁面／ＰＢ貼り 寒冷紗パテしごきＡＥＰ 天井／コンクリートスラブ直天井塗装仕上げ 棚板／メラミン化粧板フラッシュ仕上げ スライドパネル／大平フラッシュパネルＣＬ 〈ブティック〉 床／平板コンクリート貼り ウレタンクリア仕上げ及び楢フロリング染色仕上げ 壁面及び天井／ＰＢ貼り 寒冷紗パテしごきＡＥＰ 棚／ラワン積層材ｔ＝50フラッシュ染色仕上げ ハンガー／フレーム・軽鉄下地 ラワン積層材ｔ＝50染色仕上げ パイプ・スチール丸パイプφ＝30クロームメッキ仕上げ

営業内容

開店／1985年２月23日 営業時間／プレス・午前９時30分～午後６時30分 ブティック・午前11時～午後８時 休日／プレス・毎週日曜日 祭日 ブティック・なし

エントランスホールより奥のオフィススペースをみる

The inner office space viewed from the entrance hall.

ショールーム
美濃屋 別館

岐阜市橋本町2-22　Phone/0582-53-4599

撮影／加斗タカオ

ファサード

The facade.

展示室全景　The entire view of the showroom.

運送会社の旧倉庫をファッションメーカーのショールームにリニューアル

この建物は　運送会社の倉庫として使用されていたものを　地元のファッションメーカーが　ショールームとしてリニューアルしたものである。ＪＲ岐阜駅より数百メートルの線路際　どこにでもある単純な切妻屋根を持つ２棟の倉庫が　幅8.6ｍの通路を挟んで並び建っている。各棟は２つの室に等分され　通路より出入口が設けられている。

倉庫全体は　屋根に日本瓦をのせ　外壁は　かつての倉庫会社のシンボルカラーである黄色が色あせ　汚れたままで　それがおもしろいとも言えなくもない。

内部は矩形の部屋にトラスが架けられただけであるが　高いところで10ｍを越す天井は　サイドライトの光に　にぶく光る。これだけの空間はめったに得られるものではなく　さまざまなショールームの展開を彷彿とさせた。〈柳瀬真澄〉(84-10)

設計／長田雅弘＋環境計画　柳瀬真澄

施工／イズミ建設　石田義美

構造／ＲＣ造り　一部Ｓ造り　面積／敷地・1463㎡　床・1345㎡

工期／1984年４月１日～５月31日　工費／3500万円

展示室のステージよりエントランス方向をみる

The entrance area viewed from the stage of the showroom.

Showroom MINOYA Annex

Renewed two old warehouses of a forwarding agent into a fashion maker's showrooms

Formerly, these buildings were used as warehouses of a forwarding agent, and they were renewed by a local fahsion maker into its show-rooms.

Along the rail several hundred meters away from JR Gifu Station stand two warehouses having an ordinary gable roof, across a passage 8.6 m wide. Each building is divided into two chambers to which exits are provided from the passage.

The warehouses are roofed with Japanese tiles, and the outer walls come with a faded yellow color – a symbol color of the old forwarding agent – that remains stained, and strangely interesting.

Inside are provided rectangular chambers using trass. The ceiling, 10 m at highest, glistens dimly with the side light. In this rarely available space, various types of showroom were arranged.

2-22, Hashimoto-cho, Gifu City, Gifu Prefecture
Phone: 0582-53-4599

Design / Masahiro Osada
Area / Site 1,463 m^2,　Floor 1,345 m^2

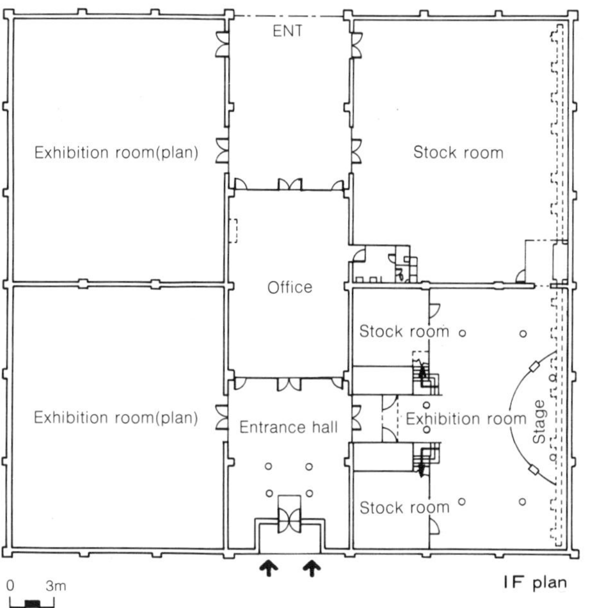

1F plan

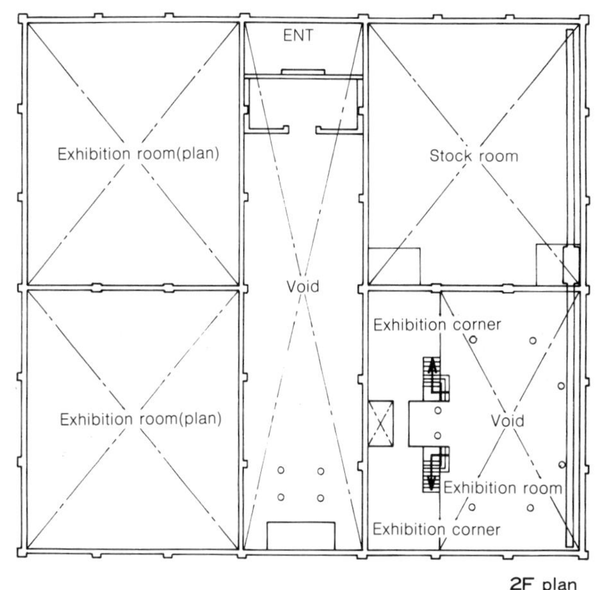

2F plan

材料仕様

屋根／既存　一部補修　外壁／既存　中央部のみフレキシブルボード下地　銀ペイント　メタリック仕上げ　開口部／スチールサッシ　外部床／エントランスのみタイル貼り　サイン／ステンレス板ヘアーライン　エッチング　床／Ｐタイル貼り　幅木／マンガシロ材ＯＰ塗装　壁面／ＰＢ下地　ＡＥＰ吹付仕上げ　天井／既存　オフィスのみジプトーン貼り　照明器具／ＨＩＤランプ

ファ

The facade.

フ　　メーカー
シ　ム
ア　エ恵
ショールーム

東京都渋谷区神宮前4-26-28　Phone/03-404-7053

撮影／本木誠一

サッシ廻り　外部と店内に玉石が敷き込まれている

Around the sash. Outside and inside the shop are placed pebbles.

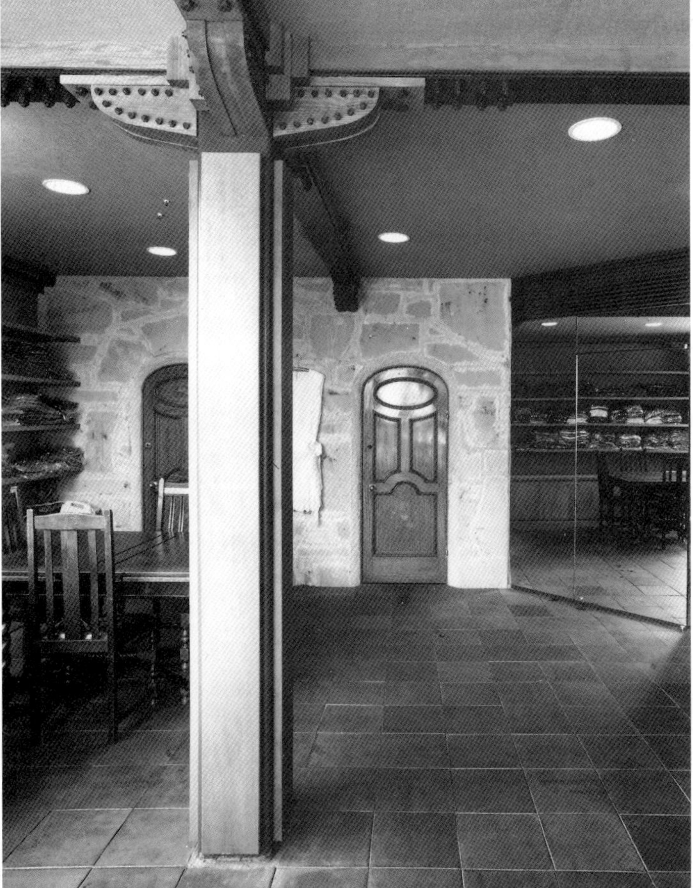

入口より奥をみる　　The inner area viewed from the entrance.

ショールーム　　The showroom.

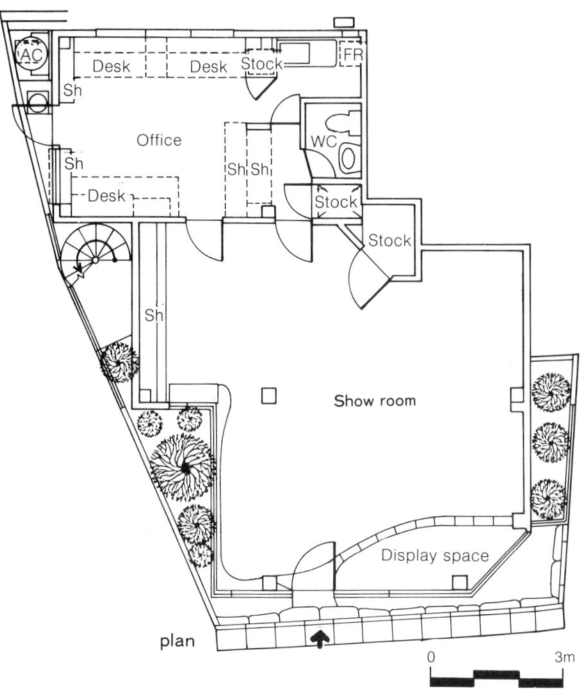

制約の多いなか如何に表現方法を工夫するか

原宿のファッションメーカー「アトリエ恵」のショールームである。明治通りを挟んだ竹下通りの延長上に位置している。

「アトリエ 恵」というファッションメーカーは　綿　麻　シルクといった自然素材を　手染めで表現している。　流行とは無縁の服づくりをしている特異なメーカーであり　その面で　私の仕事と意気統合するものがあり　3年ほど前から展示会の構成を引き受けている。

展示会の構成では　毎回単一要素をダイナミックに使用した表現方法で　大いに遊んでいたのだが　日常の営業活動の場となると　展示会場と異なって　必然的にスペース効率　フレキシビリティなどの制約を受けることになる。よって表現方法が薄らぐこともやむを得ず　遊びきれなかったことも確かである。

しかしながら　立地条件が三方を通りに囲まれているという好条件があって　坪数のわりには　アピール性の強い建物になったと満足している。

〈今井　正〉(85-4)

設計／今井正建築研究所
施工／城南佐藤工務店
面積／73.9㎡
工期／1985年９月13日～10月13日

Showroom **ATELIER KEI SHOWROOM**

How to express under many restrictions

This is a showroom of the fashion maker "Atelier Kei" in Harajuku. This is situated along an extension of Takeshita Street across Meiji Street.

The fashion maker "Atelier Kei" expresses natural materials, such as cotton, hemp and silk, with hand dyeing. It is a unique maker engaged in apparel making unrelated to fashion. In this sense, I found myself kindred in spirit, and has undertaken its exhibition composition since 3 years ago.

In the exhibition composition, I made it a rule to amuse myself greatly with an expression in which single element is dynamically used. However, different from the exhibition place, daily operations are inevitably limited in space efficiency, flexibility, etc. Therefore, the expression method was inevitably limited and I could not amuse myself fully.

However, since it favorably faces the street on three sides, this building, I believe with satisfaction, has become very appealing for its floor space.

4-26-28, Jingu-mae Shibuya-ku, Tokyo　　Phone: 03-404-7053

Design / Tadashi Imai
Area / 73.9 m^2

材料仕様

外壁／米松枠ガラスｔ＝10　一部センチュリーボード貼り　外部床／玉石敷込み　床／燻しタイル貼り300角 一部玉石敷込み　㯃フローリング貼り　幅木／米松h=30 壁面／インド砂岩貼り　一部合板下地ヘンプクロス貼り　天井／合板下地ヘンプクロス貼り　鉄骨部分ＶＰ　棚／米松練付け

営業内容

開店／1984年10月16日　営業時間／午前９時30分～午後６時　休日／日曜日　祭日
経営者／㈱アトリエ恵　従業員／６人

ファサード

ショールーム ベルピアス

名古屋市中区大須1-4-7　Phone/052-211-1151

撮影／加斗タカオ

The facade.

スタンドハンガーをみる

ディスプレイテーブルを通して原反棚をみる

(Photo captions)
Top / The stand hanger.
Bottom / The piece goods shelves viewed across the display table.

材料仕様
外壁／開口部・透明ガラスｔ＝10　サイン／ネオン　床／モルタル下地　玉砂利洗い出し　色分け　壁面／ＶＰ(既存型)及びＰＢ.ＶＰ　天井／ＶＰ(既存)及びＰＢ.ＶＰ　家具／色ラッカー吹付メタリック塗装　什器／スチール　メラミン焼付け

営業内容
開店／1984年２月１日　営業時間／午前９時〜午後６時　休日／毎週日曜日　祭日　経営者／中京三洋住宅機器販売㈱　従業員／サービス２人　主な取り扱い商品／テキスタイルデザイン用品及びそれを用いた加工用品

倉庫的要素をドッキングさせる

全体構成を考える場合　まず平面から入らなければならないのですが　その時　どうしても無視できないものに対して　どう対処するかです。「ベルピアス」の場合　無視できないものとして階段がありました。しかも中央付近にあり　これをどうとらえるかが　大きなポイントでした。

私は　階段横に壁面を設け　そこまではエントランスのアプローチとして“物理的に”外部としてとらえたいと考えたのです。どうして“物理的に”と断りを入れたかというと　実は精神的に内部として　とらえてあるからです。つまり　階段下のショーウインドに挟まれた　このエントランススペースは　外部空間であって　同時に内部空間でもあるということです。

内部は天井の高い空間であり　その利点を活かし　ショールーム的要素と倉庫的要素のドッキングの場として空間をとらえ　前部をショールーム的に　後部を倉庫的に考えています。

色彩的には　鮮やかなテキスタイル商品をサポートする役割としての配色にとどめています。つまり無彩色のトーンの違いを天井　壁面　梁の　それぞれの面にペイントすることにとどめています。　〈岡本輝男〉(84-5)

設計／岡本輝男　施工／六合建設

面積／87㎡　工期／1984年1月5日～29日　工費／988万円

ディスプレイテーブルを通して入口方向をみる

The entrance area viewed across the display table.

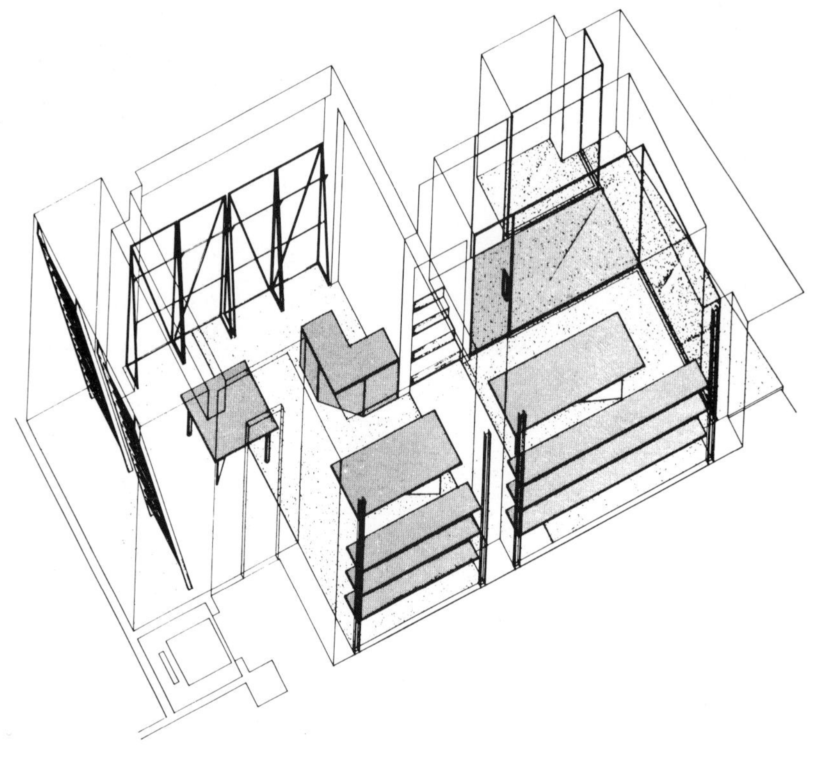

Textile Showroom BELEPIECE

Docking the elements of a warehouse

When considering the overall composition, we must primarily treat the plane. At this time, we must take care of those which cannot be neglected. As far as "Belepiece" is concerned, we could not neglect the staircase. Additionally, since it lay in the center, its treatment was the major point.

By providing a wall surface beside the staircase, I would like to position that area as an approach of the entrance, "physically" regarding it as the outside. I used the word "physically," because I grasped the inside "mentally." That is, this entrance space sandwiched by the show windows under the staircase constitutes both an external space and an internal space.

The inside is a space having a high ceiling, and by utilizing its advantages, the space is regarded as a place for docking the elements of a showroom and a warehouse, with the front part to be regarded as a showroom and the rear part as a warehouse.

As for colors, we limited the role of coloring to the supporting of vivid textile goods. That is, we limited it to painting the differences in non-color tone on the ceiling, wall and beam surfaces.

1-4-7, Ohsu Naka-ku, Nagoya City
Phone: 052-211-1151

Design / Teruo Okamoto
Area / 87 m²

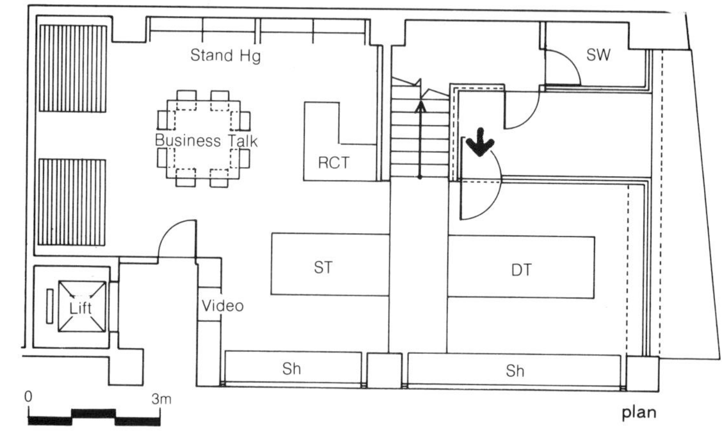

plan

収納を兼ねたディスプレイテーブル

The display table that can also accommodate goods.

ショールーム＆ブティック

エゴイズム コレクションズ

大阪市西区北堀江町1-23-3 殖産ビル地下1階　Phone/06-535-5497

撮影／川元　斉

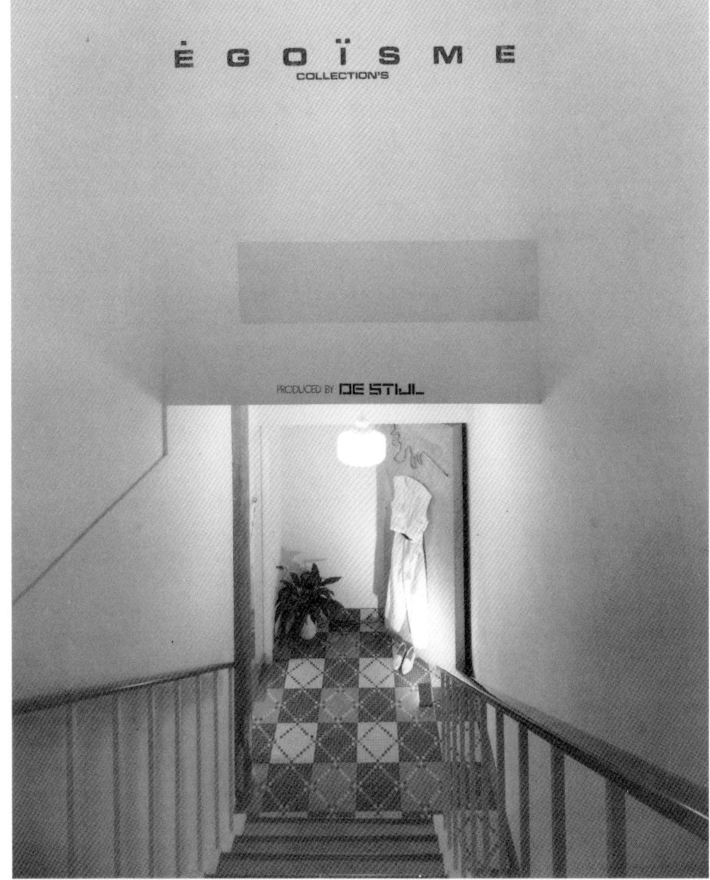

階段よりエントランス廻りをみる

The entrance area viewed from the staircase.

古いと感じるか　新しいと感じるか　客の感性を問うのが設計者の意図
Guests can freely feel old or new, depending on their sensitivity. In this freedom lies the designer's intention.

すべてがエゴを主張しながら共鳴している居心地よいエゴの世界

「エゴイズム」は　オリジナルファッションをコミュニケートするショップと　アトリエを持つスペース。そこにはファッション　人　カウンター　ミラー　ライト　キャビネット等。フォルムのあるもの　ないものすべてが　エゴを主張しながら共鳴している　居心地の良い世界。

80m²のスペース内に　適度な高さを持つ１枚のモルタルスクリーンはショップとアトリエを分割し　６枚のモルタルスクリーンは　６カ所のエリアを有効に配分している。

モルタルスクリーンの隙間から見え隠れするアトリエでの進行している感性をのぞく期待感。ルージュに塗られたパイプとキャビネットの扉の１枚は　モノトーンの中でワンポイントメークのように映えるリップスティック感覚。モノトーンとルージュは　ホワイトのライティングで忠実な色を主張している。ハンガー上部のミニランプは　ホワイトの基本照明と交差し　あらゆるファッションカラーをソフトに包み込んでいる。新しいものと感じるか　古いものと感じるか。新鮮なショックを感じるか　感じないか。それは感性の問題。　〈西谷憲彦〉(85-8)

設計／デ・スティル　西谷憲彦
施工／ウエムラ工芸社
面積／80m²
工期／1985年１月５日～２月７日
工費／716万円

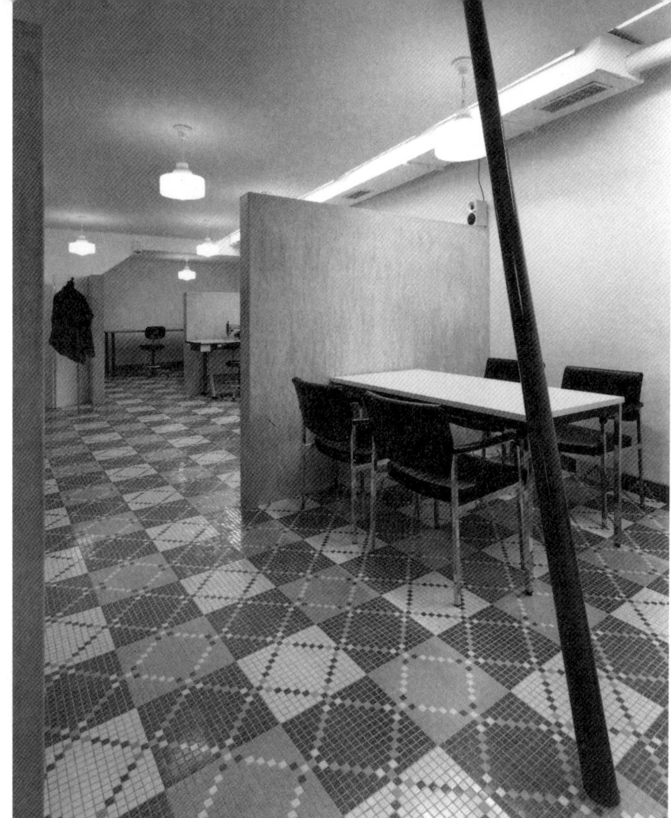

ミーティングルームよりソーイングルームとデザインルームをみる
The sewing room and design room viewed from the meeting room.

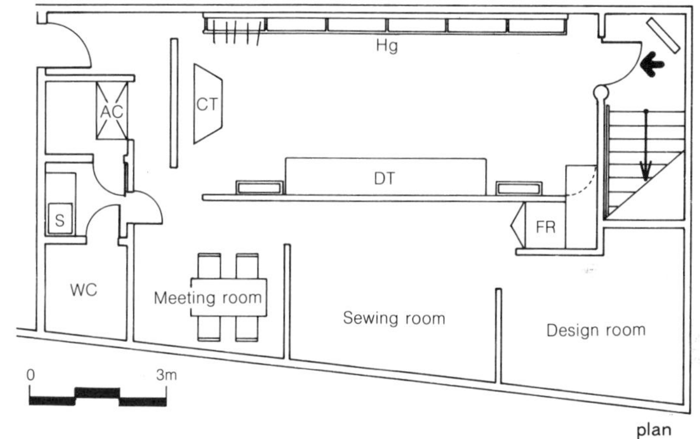

材料仕様
サイン／亜鉛鉄板　床及び幅木／モザイクタイル貼り　壁面／モルタルＶＰ　天井／ＰＢ下地ＶＰ　一部モルタルＶＰ　照明器具／コードペンＬ　キャビネット／木製ポリウレタン仕上げ　カウンター／マーブル　真鍮　ステンレス木部ラッカー仕上げ　ミラー／真鍮及びステンレス埋込みラッカー仕上げ　スクリーン／ブロック積み（ＣＢ100）モルタル仕上げ

営業内容
開店／1985年３月８日　営業時間／午前11時～午後７時30分　休日／毎週日曜日　経営者／西谷順子　従業員／２人　客単価／４万円　主な商品／エゴイズムのオリジナルファッション　ジャケット　ジャンプスーツ　ワンピース

Showroom & Boutique ÉGOÏSME COLLECTION'S

The comfortable world of ego where everything is asserting its ego resonantly

"Egoism" is a space that comprises a shop where the original fashion is communicated and an atelier. There, everything that has a form or is formless, exists resonantly while asserting its own ego.

A sheet of mortar screen having an adequate height within 80 m² of space, divides the shop and atelier, while six sheets of mortar screen effectively divide the space into six partitions. We expectantly peep into the atelier that comes in and out of sight from the opening of mortar screens, in order to see what kind of sensitivity is being created. The red-colored pipe and cabinet door look like a lipstick shining like a one-point makeup in the monotone. The monotone and red assert themselves faithfully against the white lighting. The mini lamps at the upper part of hangers intersect the basic white lighting, and softly cover all fashion colors. Whether you feel it new or old, or feel as a fresh shock or not, depends on your sensitivity.

1-23-3, Kita-horie, Hishi-ku, Osaka　Phone: 06-535-5497

Design / Norihiko Nishitani
Area / 80 m²

ロビー右側の展示　商談室Aをみる

The display and business talk room A to the right of the lobby.

ショールーム

チクマ レディス ショールーム

神戸市中央区浜辺通り2-1-30　Phone/078-231-7700

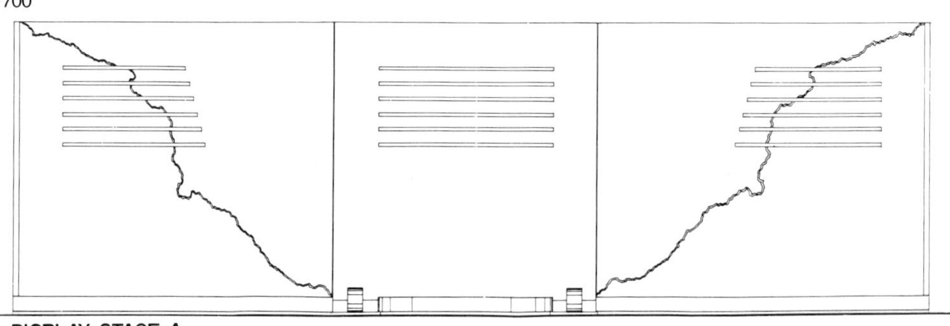

DISPLAY STAGE-A

撮影／畑　義温

入口ロビーよりアプローチ正面の展示　商談室Bをみる
The display and business talk room B in the front side of the approach, as viewed from the entrance lobby.

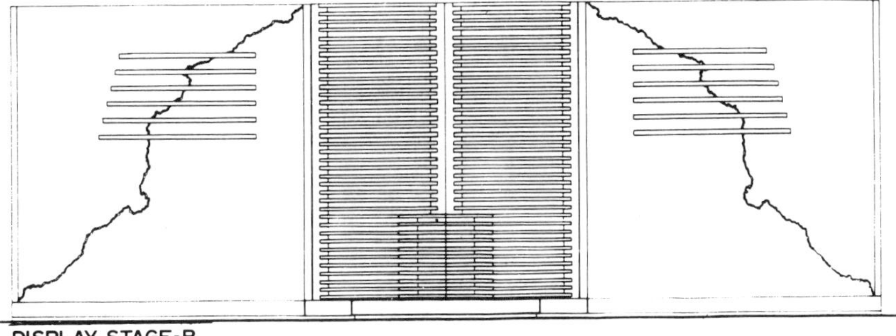
DISPLAY STAGE-B

材料仕様
床／タイルカーペット500角貼り　一部不整形貼り　柱及び梁／既在ＲＣ造　ＶＰ塗装　ステージ／榀合板メラミン化粧板貼り　受付カウンター／榀合板フラッシュメラミン化粧板貼り　一部ラッカー塗装　ミーティングルーム／榀合板ラッカー塗装　フィッティングルーム／榀合板ラッカー塗装　一部クリアミラー貼り　上部・真鍮ϕ=27.2クロームメッキ　ライティングポール／スチールパイプϕ =165 クロームメッキ　ハンガー凡立／榀合板フラッシュラッカー塗装

営業内容
開店／1984年４月23日　営業時間／午前９時30分～午後５時30分
休日／毎週日曜日　祭日　経営者／竹馬産業㈱婦人部

単純な平面に距離と時間を与える鏡

このショールームは　エントランスホールと３つのブランドのため独立した展示室　予備室で構成されている。

オフィスビルの性格上　床　壁面　天井は　あらかじめ仕上げられているため　床をパターン化し　規定していくこと。家具に位置を与え方向を与えること。これらによって空間構成を図った。

構成のベースは　初等幾何学立体の整合性に置かれカタストロフィーを暗示する不整合な"線"の挿入によって　空間の増幅を図った。

また　展示室に設けられた整形な鏡の壁面は小壁の連続性を通じて　部屋の奥行きを不連続に示している。

今回　鏡面を多用したのは　単純な平面展開に距離と時間を与えることにあった。とりわけフィッティングルームの通路側の鏡面は　風景の錯綜を通じてタイムトリップのような効果を狙った。　〈池上俊郎〉(84-9)

設計／池上俊郎建築事務所　池上俊郎　池上明　松尾しのぶ

施工／大丸装工事業部　藤原卓也

面積／223.72m²(ショールーム)

工期／1984年３月21日～４月19日

ロビーより奥をみる

The inner area viewed from the lobby.

CHIKUMA LADIES' Showroom

The mirror giving distance and time to a simple plane

This showroom consists of an entrance hall, three independent display rooms for three brands and a reserve space.

Since the building, in which this showroom is accommodated, is an office building, the floor, wall and ceiling are finished as such. Thus, our design emphasis was placed on the patterning/ruling of the floor, positioning/directing the furniture, and thereby achieving the space composition.

The space composition is based on the cubic conformity of elementary geometry, and the space was amplified by introducing disconformable "lines" that suggest a catastrophy. The disconformable mirrored wall provided in the display hall discontinuously shows the room depth through the continuity of small walls.

The reason why the mirrored surfaces were heavily used this time, lay in giving distance and time to the simple plane development. The mirrored surface in the aisle side of the fitting room was designed so that you feel as if you are making a time trip through the complicated scenes.

2-1-30, Hamabedori, Chuo-ku, Kobe City
Phone: 078-231-7700

Design / Toshiro Ikegami
Area / 223.72 m² (Showroom)

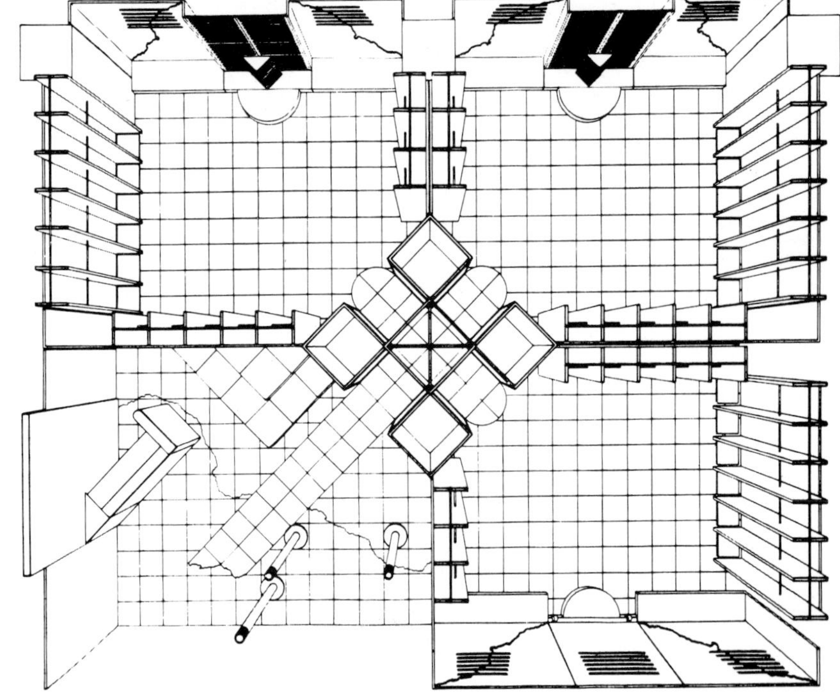

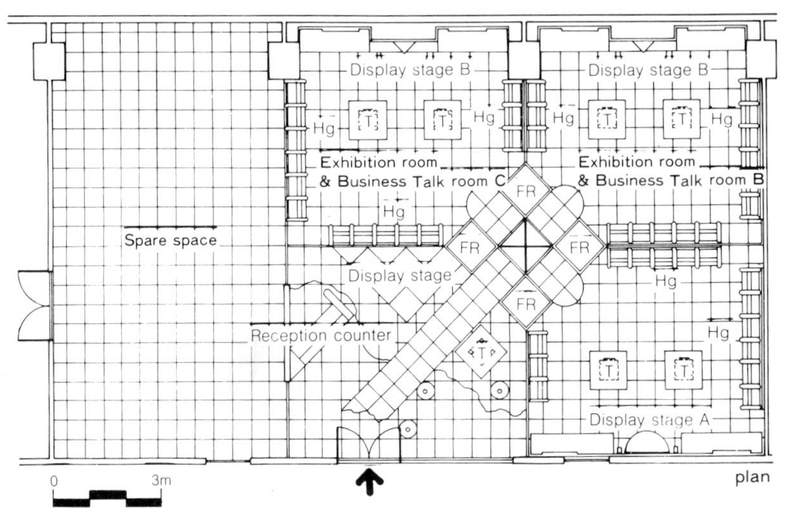

plan

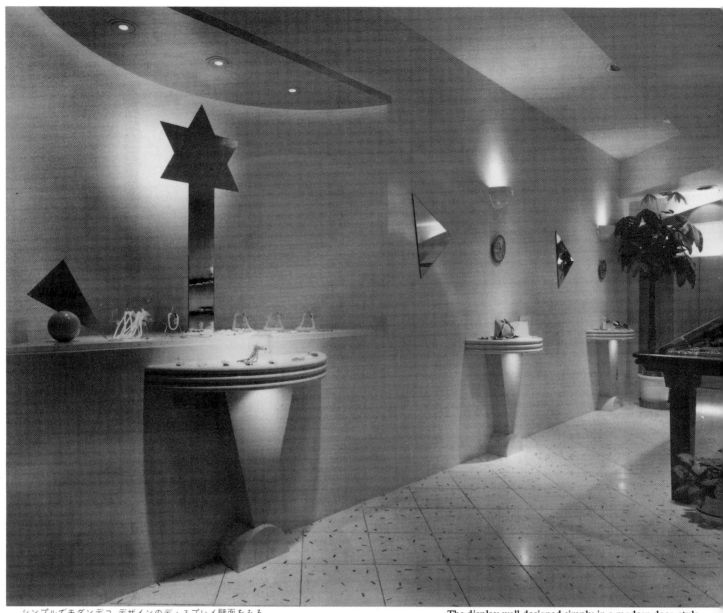

シンプルでモダンデコ デザインのディスプレイ壁面をみる

The display wall designed simply in a modern deco style.

アクセサリー ジンジン

福岡市中央区天神4-3-8　松屋レディス７階
Phone/092-713-1600

撮影／寺沢雅典

外観全景

The entire view of the appearance.

シンプル＆モダンデコ

松屋　レディス7階フロア「サボディーノ」全体が　新鮮さが欠け　もっとフレッシュなイメージづけをするために　フロアリフレッシュ計画が行われた。「ジンジン」も　この新しい構想にそって　改装することになった。

改装のポイントは　もっと商品価値を高めた演出と　フロアの客層をあまり意識せず「ジンジン」の顧客に対する感性のグレードアップを図た。また販売員1人ひとりが　もっと大切に商品を提案できるように　従来より在庫を減らし常に新しい情報(商品)がまわる売り方ができる店舗という点があげられる。

〈ライフスタイルの提案〉といった　ショップコンセプトに沿って　シンプルナイズされた　都市空間における人間らしさ　遊び感覚のある生活　フュージョン感性といった点から　新しい「ジンジン」のヴィジュアルデザインをつくった。従来のアクセサリー店に多かったモノトーンからパステルカラーへ　直線から異形交差のシルエットへ　シンプルデザインからモダンデコデザインへ　ハードライティンドからソフトライティングへと180度違った空間づくりをした。

〈松本晃尚〉(84-1)

設計／リックデザイン
施工／オオモリ
面積／24.94㎡　工期／1983年4月18日～28日
工費／680万円

Accessory Shop JIN-JIN

Simple & modern deco

Since "Savodino" (at the 7th ladies' floor of Matsuya Department Store) as a whole lacked freshness, a floor refreshing plan was implemented to give a more fresh image. It was also decided to redecorate "Jin-Jin" according to the plan.

The points of redecoration lay in presentation of goods for an enhanced value, and an upgraded sensitivity to "Jin-Jin" customers, without becoming conscious of the floor guests much. Additionally, in order to allow each salesman to make more attentive presentation of goods, the inventories were decreased compared to the conventional level, so that goods may be sold always with new information.

Along with the shop concept of "proposal of life style," a new-type visual design was attempted to create a humane space in a simplified urban space, a life with a play spirit, and a fusion sense, thereby giving a new image of "Jin-Jin." From monotone that has been often employed in the conventional accessory shops, to pastel colors, from straight lines to silhouetting of various shapes intersecting with each other, from simple to modern deco design, and from hard lighting to soft lighting – the space was changed radically.

4-3-8, Tenjin Chuo-ku, Fukuoka City
Phone: 092-713-1600

Design / Teruhisa Matsumoto
Area / 24.94 m²

中央のショーケースをみる　The showcases in the center.

小物棚をみる　The fancy goods shelves.

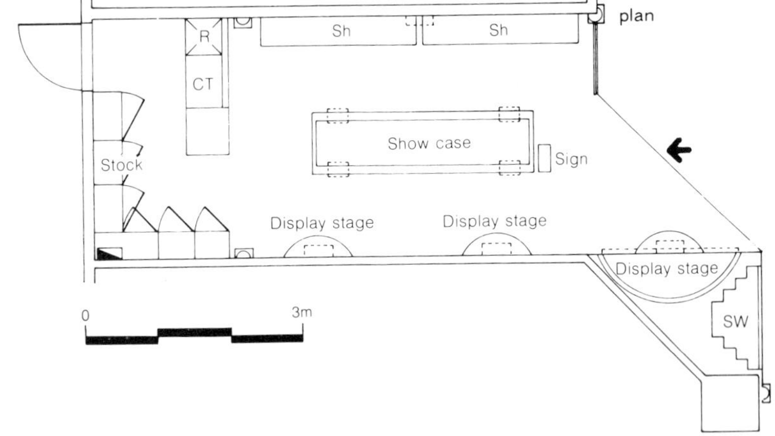

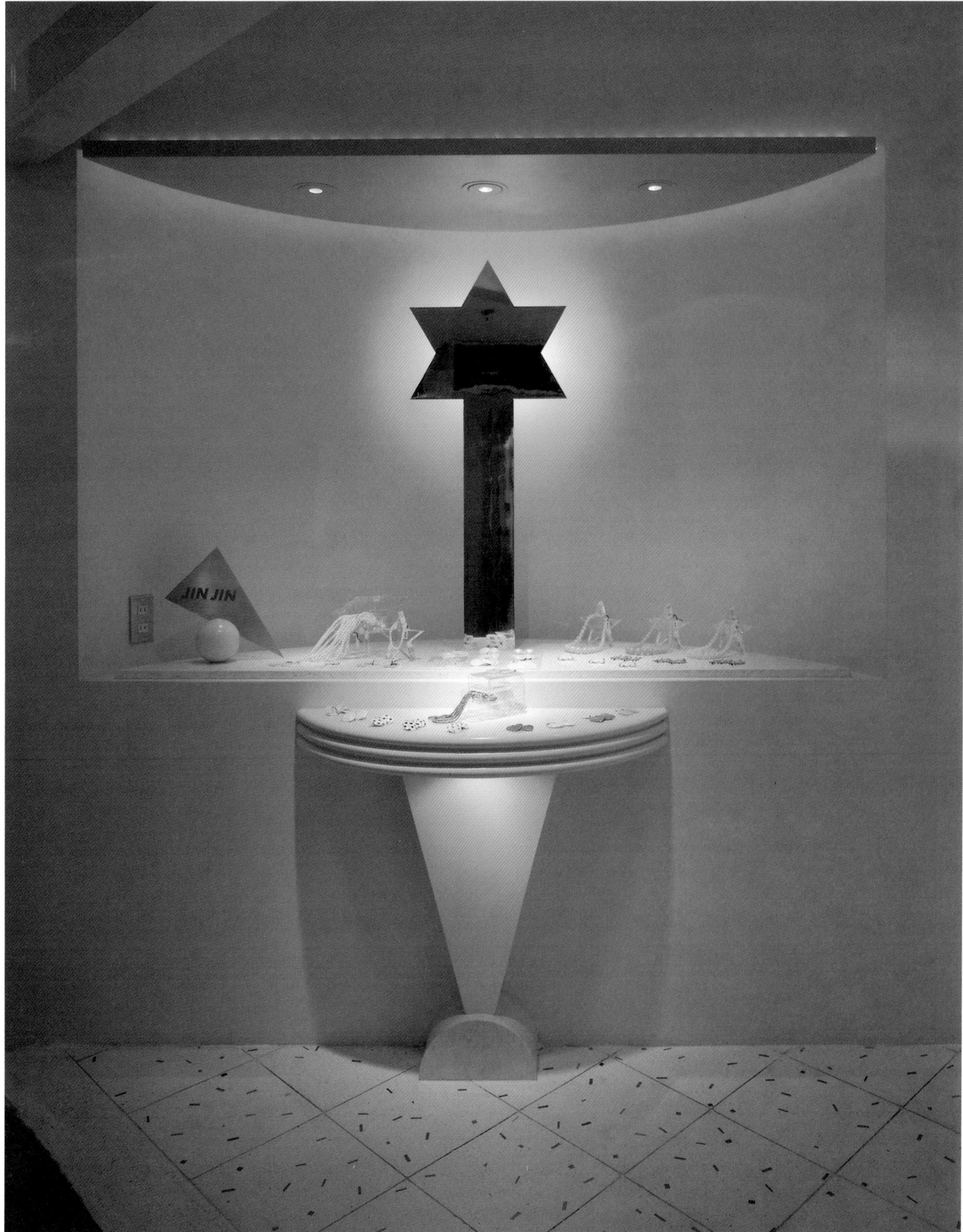

壁面ディスプレイ棚をみる

The wall surface display shelves.

材料仕様

床／特注テラゾーブロック　飾台／大理石　型面／ＰＢｔ＝12　ＶＰ　家具／榀合板ウレタン塗装　一部楢材ＯＳＣＬ

営業内容

営業時間／1983年４月29日　営業時間／午前10時～午後８時　休日／月に２日間　経営者／㈱リック・後藤宣人　従業員／３人　客単価／4000円　主な取り扱い商品／シルバーアクセサリー　ゴールド　素材ものアクセサリー　皮小物　バッグ　傘　ライフグッグ(ランプ　時計など)

1階の左側カウンターケース横より壁面ショーケースをみる

The wall surface showcase viewed from beside the left counter at the 1st floor.

ファサード

The facade.

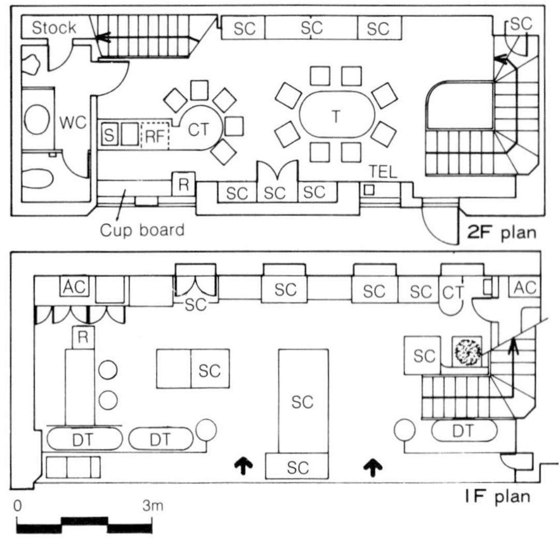

宝石 タカノ 四条店

京都市下京区四条河原町西入ル北側　Phone/075-321-1166

撮影／藤原　弘

2階のサービステーブル席より店内をみる

The inside viewed from the service table area at the 2nd floor.

ショーケースのデザインにポイントを置く

「宝石　タカノ」の出店は　今回が５店目である。京都の中心街にあり　立地としては申し分がないが　それだけ他店との競合も激しく　的確なコンセプトが要求された。

①ヤングミセスにターゲットを絞り　高感度な商品構成と　楽しく　明るい店づくり。

②気軽にショッピングができるように　入口の店舗構成を十分にする。

③手で触れることにより　宝石のもつ豊かさや　ハイクオリティーな生活の想像ができる話題性のある店づくり。

④顧客と店側のコミュニティーサロン的な空間。

⑤ショー的催しもできるような空間があり　季節や時間帯にも　きめの細かい対応ができる店づくり。

以上のような内容で設計が始まり　１階を白とピンク２階は白とブルーにした。

また　気楽に商品に触れられるように　ケースのデザインや製作には十分な注意をはらいつつ　軽く安価なイメージにならないように　素材やディテールには気を付けた。

とくに　ケース類は　ほとんどがスチール製で　細く　丸く　軽快にというイメージで製作した。　〈高野　昭〉(85-5)

設計／木嵜デザイン研究所　木嵜盛次

施工／建築・萬木工務店

　　内装・木嵜デザイン研究所工務部　織田優次

構造・規模／W造　地上３階建

面積／敷地・50m²　建築・42m²　床・１階42m²　２階37m²　３階37m²　合計116m²

工期／1984年10月１日～11月12日　工費／6900万円

営業内容

開店／1984年11月18日　営業時間／午前10時～午後７時　休日／毎週水曜日　経営者／高野　昭　従業員／サービス５人　主な取り扱い商品／宝石　アクセサリー小物

Jewelry TAKANO Shijo

Characteristic design of showcases

This is the 5th shop of "Jewelry Takano." Ideally located in the central street of Kyoto, but this means a severe competition with the other shops, and therefore an accurate concept was required for the current design.

(1) Focusing on young married ladies as the target, pursue a high sensitivity composition of articles, and accomplish bright, pleasant shop making.

(2) In order to make guests to enjoy shopping at ease, give due considerations to the entrance layout.

(3) By allowing guests to touch jewelry, make them feel the richness of jewelry, and imagine a high quality life, thus helping topical shop making.

(4) Create a space like a community salon between the customers and the shop.

(5) Also provide a space where a show, etc. can be held, and attentive responses are possible to different seasons and time zones.

We set about design to achieve the objectives listed above, and employed white and pink for the 1st floor and white and blue for the 2nd floor. Also, in order to allow guests to touch articles at ease, due considerations have been given to materials and details not to give a light, cheap image, while conducting the case design and production very carefully. Almost all cases, among others, are of stainless steel make, but were designed to give a narrow, round and light image.

Shijo-kawaramachi Nishi, Shimogyo-ku, Kyoto City
Phone: 075-231-1166

Design / Masuji Kizaki
Area / Site 50 m², Building 42 m²,
Floor: 1st floor 42 m², 2nd floor 37 m², 3rd floor 37 m²;
Totalling 116 m²

入口右手より店内をみる

The inside viewed from the right side of the entrance.

材料仕様

外壁／結晶化ガラス　サイン／スチールボンデｔ＝1.6 メラミン焼付け　床／１階・人造大理石貼り300角　２階・カーペット貼り　幅木／ステンレスHL　壁面／結晶ガラス　３階・クロス貼り　天井／ＰＢｔ＝12ラフトン吹付け　家具／ステンレス鏡面仕上げ　一部メラミン焼付け　什器／ステンレス鏡面仕上げ　一部メラミン焼付け　結晶化ガラス貼り

店内中央の階段を取りまくショーケース群をみる

A group of showcases surrounding the staircase in the center.

宝石　時計

銀座 天賞堂

東京都中央区銀座4-3-9　Phone/03-562-0021

撮影／本木誠一

ファサード

The facade.

材料仕様

外壁／丹銅板t＝1.5　パーマネントＨＬ仕上げ　透明フロート板ガラスｔ＝10　一部曲げ加工　両端半円柱／24金サンドイッチモザイクタイル貼り　床／タイルカーペット敷き　幅木／丹銅板　メタリック化粧シート　人造突板　壁面／１階・ＰＢｔ＝12下地 ビニールクロス貼り　地階・ビニールクロス貼り　一部ＯＰ　天井／１階・ＰＢt＝12下地曲げ加工　ビニールクロス貼り　地階・ロックウール天井板貼り　照明器具／黄銅板ｔ＝0.8　ｔ＝1.6パーマネントHL仕上げ　什器／１階・メタリック化粧シート　黄銅ＨＬフレーム　透明ガラスＦｉｘ　地階・ウレタン塗装水研き　ショーケース／人造突板　黄銅ＨＬフレーム　透明ガラスFix（パワーウインド電動開閉方式）

営業内容

開店／1985年９月１日　営業時間／午前11時30分～午後７時　休日／毎月第２　４木曜日　経営者／㈱天賞堂・新本秀雄　従業員／14人（１階８人　地階６人）　主な取り扱い商品／宝石　貴金属　時計

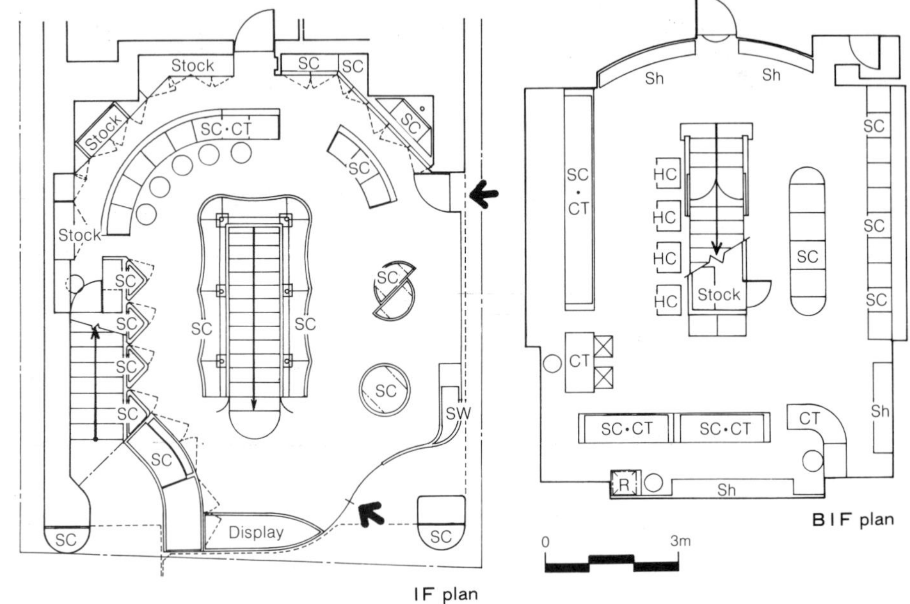

街路にインパクトを与え　仕掛けをデザインする

天賞堂ビルは　建築後12年の補修時期を迎えるにあたり　①有楽町周辺の変化による若い女性客の増加　②銀座通りと晴海通りを中心とした人の流れが脇道へも波及し　線から面への発展へと変貌したことから　街路に面したビルの足下を　リフレッシュすることになった。

貴重な角地であり　自社使用のビルにおける店舗のイメージチェンジは近頃ファッションの流行が　過去への回帰を強める傾向にあるが　今回のリフレッシュにあたっては　むしろ改装効果を最大限に発揮するため12年間の蓄積から多くを学びとり　これを設計与条件とした。新しいプロジェクトとして　最適なコンセプトを目指した。

正面中央にあった出入口を　曲面ガラスの奥へ引き入れたり　脇道側へも店内が見通せる開放的な表情とした。長大なビルのマッスを与えるにふさわしい独立柱状の両端部を　店頭ショーケースとして活用した。宝石　時計同様　メルヘンと精密さを売りものとする模型売り場の入口も独立させ　上階への階段をみせている。　〈藤井栄一〉(86-4)

設計／建築・日建設計

　　内装・日建設計（１階）　桂建築綜合研究所（地階）

施工／建築・戸田建設

　　内装・戸田建設　船場（１階）桂工務店（地階）

面積／１階・70.1m²　地階・67.9m²　合計138m²

工期／1985年８月６日～29日

Jewelry & Clock Shop TENSHODO

Gives an impact on the street and designs the setting

On the occasion of repairing Tenshodo Building after 12 years from its construction, it was decided to refresh the foot of the building facing the street, in view of the fact that (1) the number of young ladies as guests has increased along with the changes in the vicinity of Yurakucho, and (2) the stream of people mainly along Ginza Street and Harumi Street has extended to branch roads, thus developing from line to plane.

Standing at a precious corner site, this building is owned by Tenshodo. Recently, there is a growing tendency for the fashion to recur to the past. In the current refreshing, however, in order to derive a maximum effect from the redecoration, we have learned much from 12 years' experiences and regarded them as our design conditions when changing the image of the shop in the company's own building. As a new project, we pursued an optimum concept.

The exit, which existed in the front center, was relocated behind the curved glass, and the shop was given an open expression by making it to be seen through from the branch road side. Both ends of independent pillars worthy of supporting the massive building were utilized as a shop-front showcase. The entrance to the model selling corner, which features Märchen (fairy tale) and precision as with jewelry and clock, was made independent, with the staircase to the upper floor made visible.

4-3-9, Ginza Chuo-ku, Tokyo　Phone: 03-562-0021

Design / Ejichi Fujii

Area / 1st floor 70.1 m², Basement 67.9 m²; Totalling 138 m²

1階中央階段左手より店内奥をみる
The inner area of the shop viewed from the left side of the staircase in the center of the 1st floor.

地階の時計フロアをみる
The clocks floor at the basement.

ＲＣ打放しの入口スクリーンをみる

The entrance screen of RC as placed.

眼鏡 メガネの宝月堂

岐阜県本巣郡北方町大字高屋字大河間554 Phone/0583-24-4116

撮影／加斗タカオ

店内右奥コーナーの接客カウンターをみる

The guest service counter at the inner right corner.

RC打放しの“自立した建築的形態”をもつ郊外型眼鏡店

この店は　コンクリート打放しのフレームと壁で成り立っている。ここで表現された可視的な形態は　かなり強いものであるが　形態自身が問題なのではなくそこに生みだされた空間の形式の　関わる人に対するありようを問いたかったのである。強い形態で明確に限定され　囲い取られて現出する空間が醸し出す“ニオイ”や“触感”を問いたかったのである。したがって　支配的で明視性の高い色彩は　この建物には不必要であった。自立した形式は　身体化されることによって　初めてその存在を主張するであろうし　曖昧な表現では時間の経過に伴い　当初の意味を次第に失うか　日常の生活に押し流されてしまう。

設計行為を推し進める形成過程のイメージは　選び取られた素材に　的確な表現と使命を与えることによって具体化され　機能と意味とが限定されなければならない。

ファサード正面にアールを用いたのは　2つの理由からなっている。1つめは　光と時間と影のかかわりを持ちたかったこと。2つめは　軸としての建築の構成に　結合　分離　転位　そして開放という運動の軸を与えるためであった。

〈二宮昭二郎〉(85-6)

設計／建築・バウハウス丸栄一級建築士事務所　二宮昭二郎
　　　内装・赤木デザイン＋二宮昭二郎

施工／建築・上村建設
　　　内装・赤木デザイン

構造・規模／RC造・地上3階建

面積／敷地・696.15m² 建築・210.81m² 床・1階(店舗) 202.72m² 2階(貸事務所)169.61m² 3階(貸事務所)136.51m² 合計508.84m²

工期／1984年4月9日～10月4日

工費／8600万円

Optician HOGETSUDO

Suburban free-standing optician shop having an "independent architectural style" with RC as placed

This shop consists of frames and walls of reinforced concrete (RC) as placed. The visible style expressed here is very impressive, but our interest did not lie in the style itself, but in how the space style relates to those concerned. It was our intention to appeal "smell" or "touch" created in the space which is definitely limited and confined by the strong style. Thus, dominant, vivid colors were unnecessary for this building. The independent style with assert its existence only when embodied. When expressed vaguely, the original meaning will be gradually lost or swept along in the daily life, along with the lapse of time.

The image being formed along with the design must be materialized and limited in function and meaning by giving accurate expression and mission to selected materials.

The facade front was radiused due to two reasons: (1) It was intended to have relations with light, time and shadow, and (2) to give the axis of movement – coupling, separation, transfer and release – to the architectural composition as an axis.

Kitakata-cho, Motosu-gun, Gifu Prefecture　　Phone: 0583-24-4116

Design / Shojiro Ninomiya
Area / Site 696.15 m²; Building 210.81 m²
Floor: 1st floor (Shop) 202.72 m²,
2nd floor (Lental office) 169.61 m²,
3rd floor (Lental office) 136.51 m²;
Totalling 508.84 m²

入口左側より中央円形メインディスプレイをみる　裏側は待合コーナー

The main round display in the center viewed from the left side of the entrance. At the back lies the waiting corner.

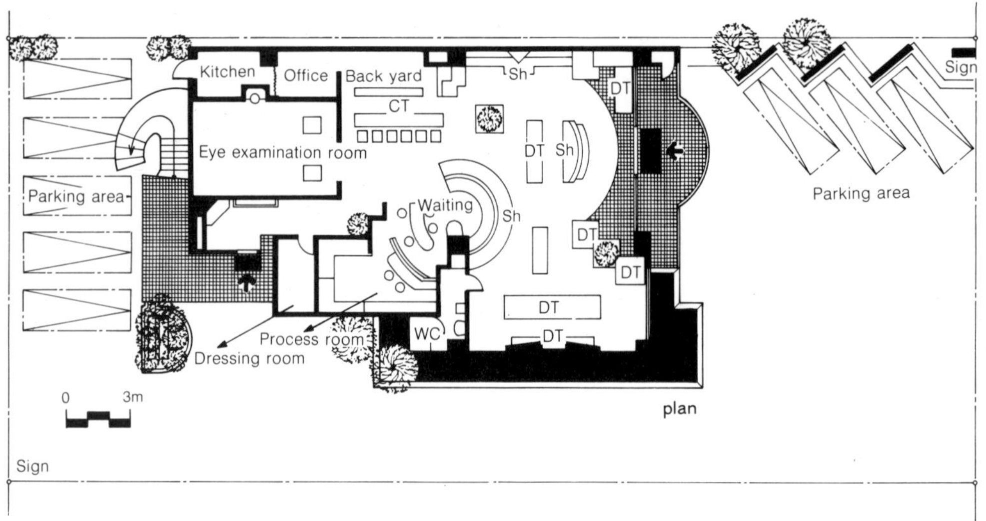

材料仕様

屋根／アスファルト露出防水　外壁／コンクリート打放し合成樹脂系塗膜防水材塗布　サッシ／ジュラクロン焼付塗装　ステンレス鏡面加工　外部床／磁器質タイル貼り　サイン／フレーム・スチール焼付け　乳半白アクリルネオン　床／長尺塩ビシート　幅木／ソフト幅木　壁面／コンクリート打放し合成樹脂系防水材塗布　楢合板　ウレタン塗装及びクロス貼り　天井／ＰＢ下地ＥＰ　照明器具／ＤＬ　間接照明・ＦＬ　家具／楢合板ウレタン塗装　什器／スチール焼付け　ステンレス　コーラ　楢合板

営業内容

開店／1984年10月５日　営業時間／午前10時～午後８時　休日／毎週水曜日　経営者／メガネの宝月堂　従業員／４人　客単価／メガネ一式４万～４万5000円　レンズ及びフレーム各１万5000円～２万5000円　サングラス5000円

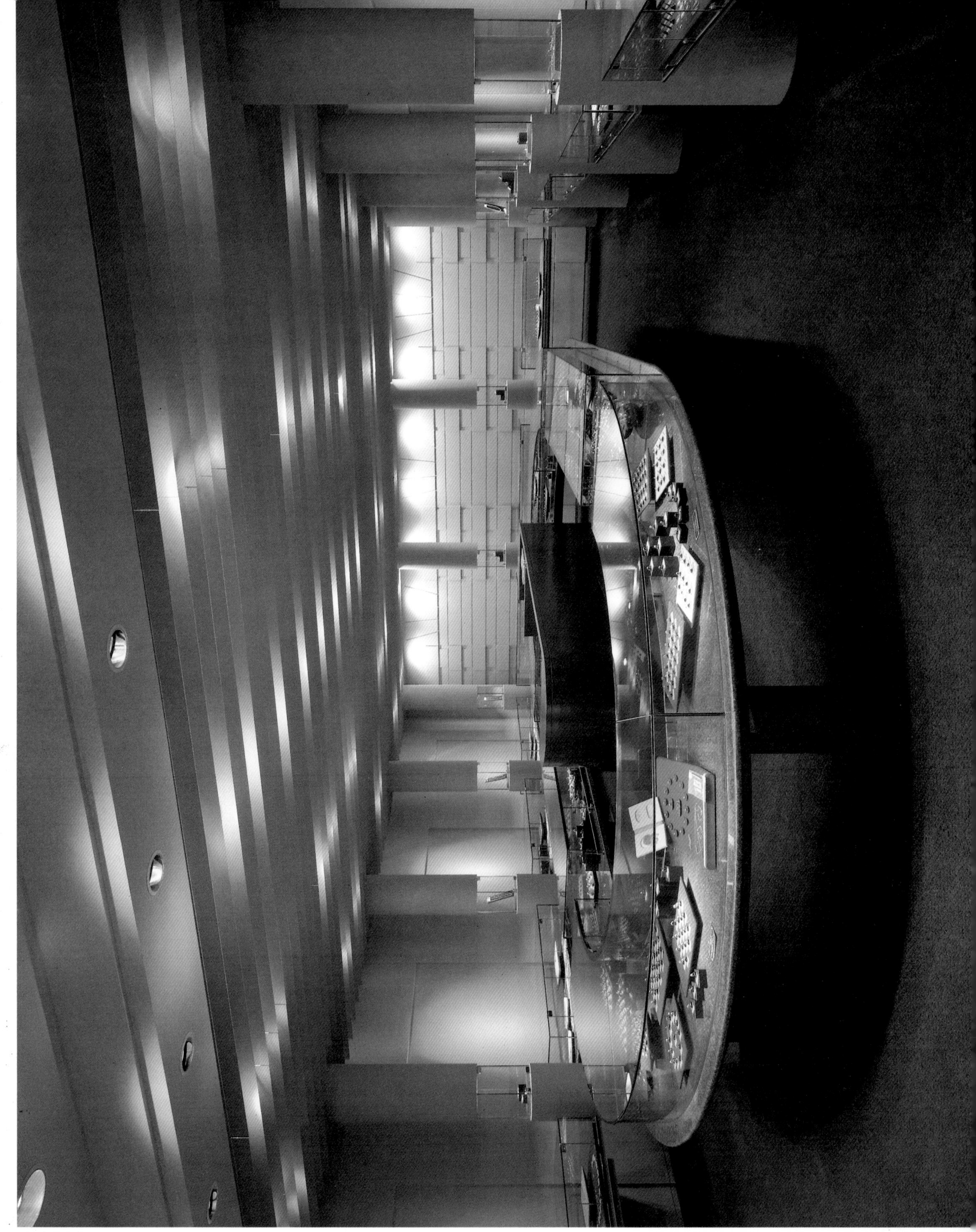

店内全景をみる

The entire inside view.

ジュエリー
ビジュ イルエル

神奈川県海老名市河原口1441 ダイエー海老名ショッパーズプラザ2階Phone/0462-31-3386

撮影／平井広行

ヨーロッパ建築の伝統的列柱をモテーフとした柱型ショーケースをみる
The column-type showcases employing, as their motif, traditional European columns in a row that constitute the European architecture.

パブリック通路よりエントランス廻りをみる
The entrance area viewed from the public passage.

システマティック＆ドラマティックな構成

「ビジュ イルエル」はナショナルチェーン化計画に基づいた１号店である。それゆえヨーロピアン トラディショナルというコンセプトが 明快に表現されなければならず また各エレメントの構成がシステマティックに展開されなければならない。
平面計画では 客動線を最大化するとともに 販売オペレーションの効率化のため 長円形のショーケースと壁面ケースをレイアウトし 空間構成においては ヨーロッパ建築における 伝統的列柱をモチーフとしたショーケースを配した。
また 素材計画にあたっては 石 または石をイメージできる素材（塗装)を 色彩計画では 柔らかさ(ベージュ)を意図した。照明はローボルト照明によるスポット効果と 間接効果を狙うなど 各エレメントを単純化するとともに システマティックかつドラマティックな ジュエリーショップの実験であった。 <We＋F>(85-3)

企画／Ｊハウス
設計／We＋F
施工／スタット
面積／90.6㎡
工期／1984年７月25日～８月10日 工費／2000万円

材料仕様
床／じゅうたん貼り 壁面／シグマルト吹付け 天井／ルーバー・シグマルト吹付け 什器／トラック型ショーケース・赤御影石ｔ＝30磨き仕上げ 柱型丸ケース・スチール曲加工 シグマルト吹付け

営業内容
開店／1984年９月２日 営業時間／午前10時～午後７時 休日／毎週水曜日 経営者／㈱三貴 従業員／５人 主な取り扱い商品／宝石 貴金属 アクセサリー

店内中央のトラック状ショーケースをみる

The truck-like showcase in the center.

Jewelry BIJOUX IL-ELLE

Systematic & dramatic composition

"Bijoux Il-Elle" is the 1st shop opened according to the national chain development plan. As such, the concept, "European tradition," must be clearly expressed, and each element must be systematically developed to complete the overall composition.

As for the plan layout, in order to maximize the guests' moving line and improve the efficiency of selling operations, oval showcases and wall surface cases were set, and as a space composition, showcases using the traditional European columns in a row were arranged.

As for the material plan, stone or material (paint) by which stone can be imaged, were selected, and as for the coloring, softness (beige) was aimed at. As for lighting, the spot effect by low vault lighting and indirect lighting were employed. Thus, while simplifying each element, a systematic & dramatic jewelry shop was designed experimentally.

1441, Kawaharaguchi, Ebina City, Kanagawa Prefecture
Phone: 0462-31-3386

Design / We + F
Area / 90.6 m^2

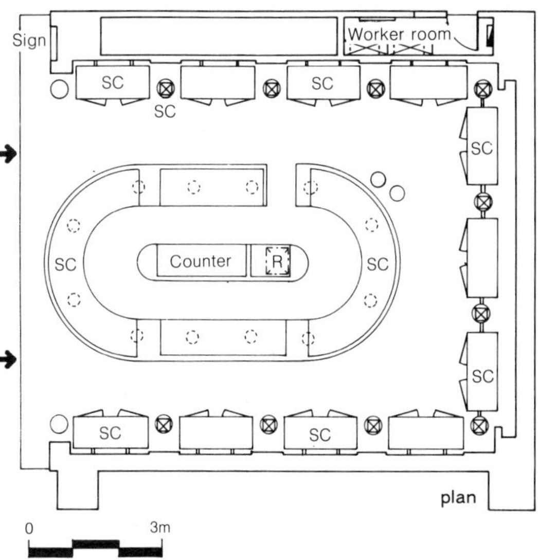

入口よりディスプレイテーブルをみる

The display table viewed from the entrance.

眼鏡 オーグリー

京都市中京区御池御幸町上ル西側　Phone/075-231-0901

撮影／藤原　弘

ファサード　The facade.

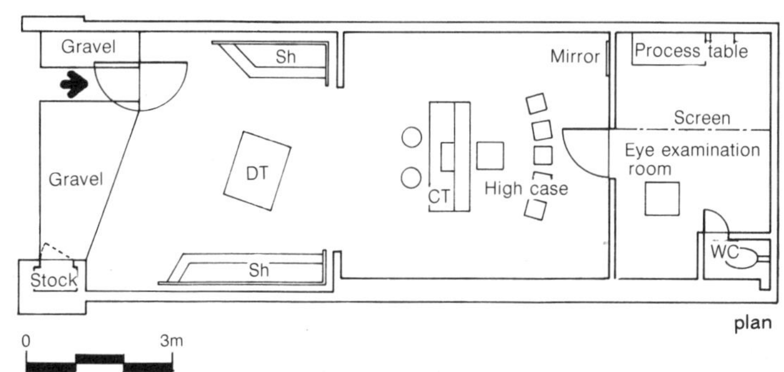

材料仕様
屋根／日本瓦葺き　外壁／モルタル下地ＶＰローラー引き　外部床／磁器タイル貼り100角　サイン／スチールプレートメラミン焼付け仕上げ　カッティングシート　ネオン管　床／楢フローリング貼り　テラゾ風長尺シート貼り　幅木／木製ＯＳ　ＣＬ　壁面及び天井／ＰＢｔ＝９下地クロス貼り　家具及び什器／シオジ材ＯＳ拭き取りの上ＣＬ

営業内容
開店／1986年４月19日　営業時間／午前11時～午後９時　休日／毎週火曜日　経営者／森　仁　従業員／２人　客単価／２～３万円　主な取り扱い商品／オーダーメードの眼鏡（フレーム）と現代ファッションに合った眼鏡用品

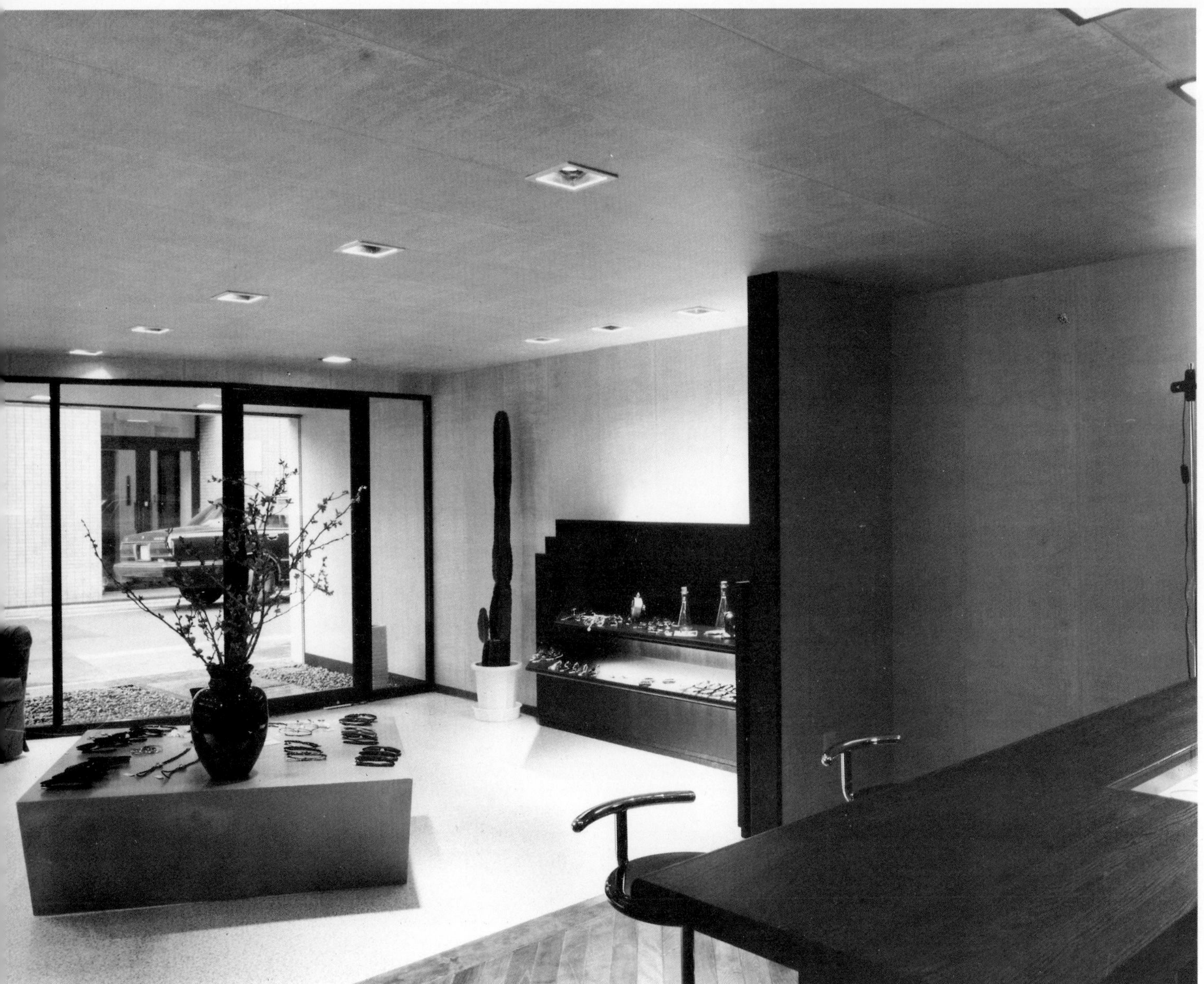

中央カウンターテーブル脇より入口方向をみる

The entrance area viewed from beside the counter table in the center.

接客のスペースがメインのモノトーン空間

“自分のファッションに合った眼鏡がほしい”
“自分の顔に合った眼鏡がほしい”
“オリジナルな眼鏡がほしい”
“眼鏡とファッションについて相談にのってほしい”等々という　ヤング層に的を絞った眼鏡店である。
上記のニーズを満足させられるような店づくりが基本とされ　接客スペースを十分に　ゆとりのあるものとし　顧客との対話を重要視した。
検眼に要するスペースは　コンピューター検眼を使用することと　検眼や加工場を　客に見せないことで　奥に押し込めてしまった。商品ディスプレイも　量のディスプレイではなく　オリジナル商品のワンポイントディスプレイとした。
全体のデザインは　モノトーンとし　接客スペースは　温かい空間とするため　床をフローリングとし　照明には　とくに注意をはらったつもりである。　〈木嵜盛次〉(86-11)

設計／木嵜デザイン研究所　木嵜盛次
施工／木嵜デザイン研究所工務部　インテリア錦越
構造・規模／W造・地上２階建
面積／敷地•91.3㎡　建築•77.5㎡　床•１階77.5㎡
工期／1986年４月４日～17日
工費／620万円

Optician OUGLEY

A monotone space mainly intended for guest service
“I would like to have glasses matching my fashion.”
“I would like to have glasses suiting my face.”
“I would like to have original glasses.”
“I would like to be advised about my glasses and fashion.”
“Ougley” intends to capture young guests who have such needs as mentioned above.
The shop making was primarily intended to satisfy the above-mentioned needs, so that the guest service space was secured enough and made leisurely, giving importance to dialogues with customers.
The space needed for eye examination was pushed behind the service space, since computer-aided eye examination is employed, and it was intended to put out of sight eye examination scenes and the processing factory. As the product display manner, one-point display of original goods – not display of quantity – was employed.
The overall design was made in monotone, and in order to set the guest service space in a warm atmosphere, the flooring was selectively provided, and special considerations were given to lighting.

Oikemiyuki-cho, Nakagyo-ku, Kyoto City
Phone: 075-231-0901

Design / Seiji Kizaki
Area / Site 91.3 m², Building 77.5 m², Floor: 1st floor 77.5 m²

透明アクリル板で人形を挟み込み　ポップアート的に演出したディスプライ人形をみる
The display dolls presented in a pop artistic manner by sandwiching them with transparent acrylic boards.

眼鏡 アイリスメガネ

撮影／鳴瀬　亨

東京都新宿区歌舞伎町1　新宿サブナード地下1階　Phone/03-354-6554

ファサード

The facade.

趣味的な発想で個性を演出した各種アクセサリーの眼鏡を提案

この店は ホームベーカリーの店舗システムを導入してみた。ホームベーカリーはトレーの上に欲しいパンだけを自分で選んでいく。こういう形式は すでにコンビニエンスストアーなどでお馴染みであり 間口の広さ スペース 価格等の点ではふさわしく パーソナブル時代にマッチした方法である。

商品は“見る”ための必需品ではなく 個性を演出するアクセサリー 趣味的な発想をもとに“ダテメガネ”“モドキ”といった とんでもない眼鏡から 特殊眼鏡(パソコン用 スポーツ用 偏光レンズ付き眼鏡)パーツ販売 オリジナル眼鏡などと 他店にみられない商品を置くことにより 眼鏡を必要としない人(目の良い人)にも 一層 眼鏡が親密になる。また カラーリングよりスタイル別に ファッション性のあるコース(4～5コース)を設けることにより 各種のアクセサリーとしての新しい眼鏡を提案してみた。 〈中石俊文〉(84-1)

企画・設計／アイリスメガネ企画室 明日香治彦
施工／マスコデザイルルーム＋船場
面積／21m²
工期／1983年10月3日～8日

Optician IRISMEGANE

Proposes various kinds of accessory glasses according to taste-oriented ideas to accentuate your personality

In this shop was introduced a home bakery shop system in which you can choose only those pieces of bread that you prefer and put them on the tray. This type of purchase is already popular at convenience stores, etc., and suitable for the age of personality-oriented shopping, in respect of frontage, space, price, etc.

At this shop, glasses as goods are not necessarily necessities to "see," but are accessories for accentuating your personality based on taste-oriented ideas. Thus, glasses displayed here range from quite extraordinary ones, such as those "for show" and "glasses-like," to special glasses (with polarizing lens for personal computers and sports). Thus, not only original glasses but also parts are sold here, making even those, who do not need glasses (having a good sight), feel familiar with glasses. Additionally, by providing 4 to 5 fashionable courses by style rather than coloring, glasses as various types of accessory were proposed.

1, Kabuki-cho, Shinjuku-ku, Tokyo Phone: 03-354-6554

Design / Toshifumi Nakaishi
Area / 21 m²

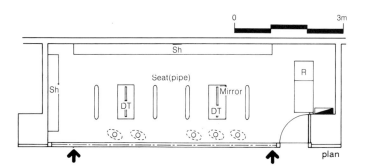

0 3m
Sh
Seat(pipe)
Sh
DT
Mirror
DT
R
plan

店内のディスプレイテーブルをみる

The inside display table.

材料仕様

床／モルタル金鏝仕上げ　一部桧板貼りｔ＝30　壁面／モルタル打放しＶＰ塗装　天井／ＬＧＳ　ＰＢｔ＝12貼り　ＶＰ塗装　照明器具／吊り型パイプ照明　一部ダクトスポット　家具　榀ベニヤ色ラッカー塗装　ディスプレイテーブル／トップ・スチールパイプ焼付塗装　テント地貼り　脚・コンクリート透水管　棚／スチールパイプ焼付塗装　テント地貼り　鏡／リフェクスミラー　壁面サイン／ネオン管　人形／人形を透明アクリル板にて両面挟込み

営業内容

開店／1983年10月９日　営業時間／午前10時～午後９時　休日／なし　経営者／小島栄太郎　主な取り扱い商品／サングラス各種　パーツ各種

入口より店内全景をみる

The entire inside viewed from the entrance.

眼鏡 ノー キディング

東京都港区南麻布5-15-22 ブリック広尾３階

入口廻り

The entrance area.

撮影／鈴木光隆

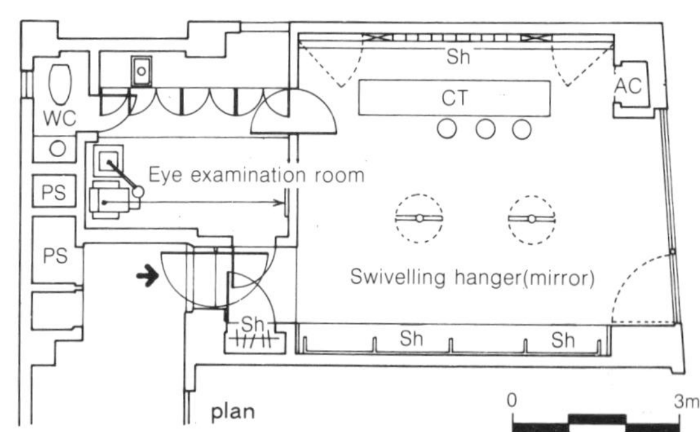

店内左側の接客カウンターをみる

The guest service counter in the left side.

全身が映る回転式大型ミラーがポイント

この「ノー キディング」は ニューヨークに本拠を置くH.L.パーディー社との提携により生まれた アバンギャルドなデザインの眼鏡サロンであり 特にこの広尾店ではリース等の新しい営業形態を試みている。

そこで デザイン コンセプトも 従来のように 陳列ケースやディスプレイ什器を並べ 対面販売形式を行うのではなく トータルファッションの一部としての眼鏡を“空間全体をフィッティングルームに見立てて”売るというスタイルの提案に主軸を置いた。

ポイントは 中央に吊り下げた全身が映る360度回転の大型ミラーで その脇には 御影石のハイカウンターを配し 気軽に相談に応じられるようにした。

また色彩も これまでのような単調な吹付け塗装とせず 壁面1800までを床と同色のグレーとし そこからホワイトを足した天井までを グラデーション仕上げにしてみた。 〈原 兆英／文責・編集部〉(85-6)

企画／谷内田デザインスタジオ

設計／ジョイントセンター 原 兆英 原 成光

施工／ノバ工芸

面積／42.75㎡

工期／1984年8月14日～9月4日

工費／1000万円

Optician NO KIDDING

Features large rotary mirrors in which your whole body is reflected

Born as a result of tieup with H.L. Pardy headquartered in New York, this “No Kidding” is an optician salon in avant-garde design. This Hiroo shop, among others, is experimenting with new-type operations, such as leasing.

Thus, in the design concept, different from the conventional man-to-man selling system in which display cases or utensils are located, “the space as a whole is likened to the fitting room” to sell glasses as part of total fashion.

The shop features large turning 360° suspended mirrors in the center which reflect your whole body. Beside it is arranged a high granite counter so that you can give advice at ease.

As for coloring, instead of the conventional monotonous spray painting, that part of wall up to 1,800 mm was grey-colored as with the floor, and the part above 1,800 mm up to the ceiling was graduated by adding white color.

5-15-22, Minami-azabu, Minato-ku, Tokyo

Design / Choei Hara
Area / 42.75 m^2

材料仕様

床／タイル貼り200角 幅木／榀合板ラッカー塗装仕上げ 壁面／ラッカー塗装仕上げ 上部ぼかし仕上げ 天井／ラッカー塗装仕上げ 家具／カウンタースツール・脚（スチールパイプ ϕ＝165.2 焼付け塗装仕上げ 座面(楢集成材ウレタン塗装仕上げ) カウンター／トップ・黒御影石磨き仕上げ 腰・黒御影石ジェット仕上げ

営業内容

開店／1984年9月5日 営業時間／午前11時～午後8時 休日／毎週水曜日 経営者／H.L.パーディー㈱・小島正敬 従業員／3人

5500Rの孤を描くショップフロント

コスメティック

バローニ 原宿店

東京都渋谷区神宮前5-10-1 ビブレ21原宿1階 Phone/03-409-9952

撮影／瀬口哲夫

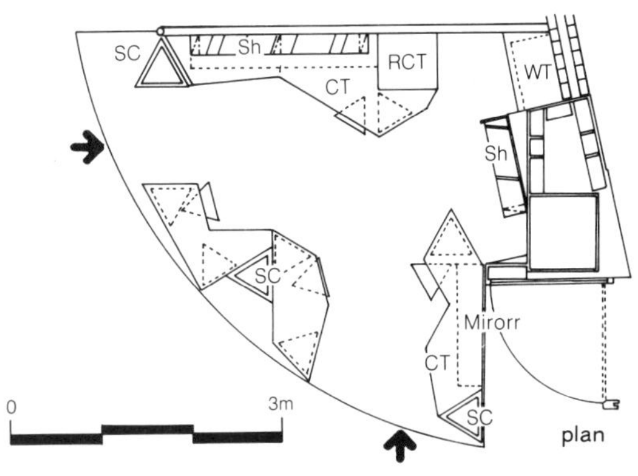

The shop front drawing an arc of 5500R.

材料仕様

床／テラゾタイル貼り　幅木／ステンレスH.L. 壁面／ＰＢｔ＝12 ＶＰ 天井／ＰＢｔ＝12 ＶＰ ボーダー・フレキシブルボードＶＰ　照明器具／ＤＬ(ハロゲン)　ディスプレイ什器／トップ・メラミン化粧板　腰・桐合板ラッカー吹付け

営業内容

開店／1984年11月16日　営業時間／午前10時～午後８時　休日／なし　経営者／インターナショナル コスメティック㈱　従業員／４人　客単価／５～6000円

アーティスティックなカラーリングとユニークなパッケージデザインに対応するディスプレイ什器と空間構成
The display utensils and space composition corresponding to the artistic coloring and unique package design.

アレンジメント & リ デザイン

「バローニ」はニューヨークのソーホーやブルーミングデールなどのデパートで展開しているコスメティック ショップです。

アーティストであるトニーバローニが　婦人と実験的にソーホーで始めたショップは　アーティスティックなカラーリング　バリエーションとユニークなパッケージ デザインでコスメティック業界に　一つのポジションを得　1984年から日本の㈱インターナショナル　コスメティック社が代理権を契約し　今後　日本　東南アジアで展開する予定になっています。

オリジナルデザインは　ショップ イメージとともにバローニ自身が行い　私の仕事は日本で初めてのショップのオープンということで　日本の事情に合わせてアレンジメントを行うことであり　いかにオリジナルのイメージをくずさずに　アレンジするかが目的でしたが　実際は　日本の狭いブースで展開するには　彼等のイメージがまとまらず　リ デザインすることになってしまった。　〈山森英夫／文責・編集部〉(85-11)

設計／トニー バロン
協力／エッチ・エスデザインファーム
面積／15.63㎡
工期／1984年11月1日～15日

Make-up Cosmetics BARONE

Arrangement & redesign

"Barone" is a cosmetic shop chain being developed at department stores in SoHo, Blumingdale, etc. in New York.

The shop started experimentally by Tony Barone, an artist, in SoHo, together with his wife, has secured a position in the cosmetic business for its artistic coloring variation and unique package design. In 1984, International Cosmetic Co., Japan, signed an agent agreement with Barone, and is going to develop the chain in Japan and Southeast Asia.

The original design, together with the shop image, is undertaken by Barone himself. So, my assignment was to make arrangements according to the Japanese situation, as "Barone," Harajuku, is the first shop opened in Japan. Thus, at first, I intended to arrange the design without destroying the original image. Actually, however, since Barone could not find an adequate image for the narrow space, I had to undertake the redesign.

5-10-1, Jingu-mae, Shibuya-ku, Tokyo　Phone: 03-409-9952

Design / Tony Barone & Hidenori Seguchi
Area / 15.6 m^2

1日22万人の通行客に訴求するファサード

The facade appealing to 220,000 passers-by a day.

コスメティック
タシロ 新宿ルミネ店

東京都新宿区新宿1-1-5 新宿ルミネ2階 Phone/03-348-5178

撮影／平沢 敞

Mirror
Sh
Facial & goods
Mirror
Presentation table
Sh
DT
Make-up
Facial
DT
Sh
Make-up
DT
DT
Mirror
0
3m
plan

二極化と統一をデザインする

この店のデザインイメージの展開は まずファサードの黒のフレームから始まり 床はホワイトオークのフローリングとし 足下の感触をソフトに 天井は拡がりのある空間を強調するために 中央天井を逆に下げ壁面天井の高さを十分にとった。壁面は 約12坪という狭い売り場スペースにとらわれずイメージ的には二極化させている。右壁面はフェイシャルゾーンとしての落ち着きと清潔感 左壁面はメークアップゾーンとしての楽しさ ユーモア 変化 カラーボリュームがあり 新宿一番の量感を表現するために 天井まで無駄なく利用している。加えて 奥正面サイド及び一部天井に ミラーを使用することによるボリューム感の倍増ライティングによるカラーイリュージョンなどを強調しつつ 奥正面とファサードのデザイン統一を図っている。中央のビッグテーブルはh＝900のガラス(中間 ミラー両面貼)によって仕切り 美容実習テーブルとしての利用 メークアップの新色プレゼンテーションのテーブルとした。

〈神蔵和明〉(85-11)

設計／ダイワ 神蔵和明
施工／ダイワ
面積／35.4m²
工期／1985年8月24日～31日

左側メークアップゾーンのディスプレイ棚をみる

The display shelves at the left-side makeup zone.

中央のビッグテーブル

The big table in the center.

Cosmetics TASHIRO Shinjuku Lumine

Designs two-polarization and integration

The design image of this shop began with the black frame of facade, and the white oak flooring on the floor to make you feel soft when walking. In order to give a strong impression that the inside space is expansive, the central ceiling was lowered while securing an ample height for the ceiling above the wall. Despite the small selling space (about 39 m^2), the wall surface is polarized into two sets of images. The right side of the wall surface gives a composed atmosphere and a clean sense as a facial zone, while the left side gives a pleasant atmosphere as a makeup zone, featuring humor, variation and color volume. In order to express the massive sense, No. 1 in Shinjuku, the entire space, including the ceiling, is effectively utilized. Additionally, by using a mirror for the inner front side and part of the ceiling, the sense of volume is doubled and a color illusion is stressed by lighting, thereby integrating the design of the front side with that of the facade. The big table in the center is partitioned by h=900 mm glass (whose both sides are mirrored), and utilized as a beauty artistic training table and a new makeup color presentation table.

1-1-5, Shinjuku, Shinjuku-ku, Tokyo　Phone: 03-348-5178

Design / Kazuaki Kamikura
Area / 35.4 m^2

材料仕様
床／ホワイトオーク　フローリング　壁面／クロス貼り　一部ミラー貼り　天井／ＰＢ　ｔ＝12　寒冷紗パテＥＰ　照明器具／アジャスタブルダウンライト　スカイビームダウンライト　ハロゲンスポット及びプリズムライト　什器／タモ材着色　黒御影石及び無機質含有ポリマー

営業内容
開店／1985年９月３日　営業時間／午前10時30分～午後９時　休日／毎月第３水曜日　経営者／田代商事㈱・田代正文　従業員／サービス４人　美容部員４人　パート及びアルバイト１人　合計９人　客単価／2000円　主な取り扱い商品／資生堂　カネボウ　コーセー　花王ソフィーナ　ブルジョア(フランス)のメークアップ及びフェイシャル商品

プランタン通路より店内をみる　中央にはオベリスクを模したオブジェ
The inside viewed from the passage to Plantin. In the center lies an objet imaging an obelisk.

コスメティック シュウ ウエムラ

東京都中央区銀座3-2-1 プランタン銀座1階　Phone/03-564-4765

ファサード
The facade.

撮影／狩野正和

材料仕様
床／磁器タイル貼り300角　幅木／ステンレス　鏡面仕上げ　壁面／ＰＢｔ＝12下地　寒冷紗パテしごきＥＰ　天井／ＰＢｔ＝９下地　寒冷紗ＥＰ　カウンター／色ウレタン塗装　棚・フロートガラス　オベリスク／木下地ウレタン塗装　座・大理石　オブジェ／ＦＲＰ　肌目石膏調

営業内容
開店／1984年４月27日　営業時間／午前10時～午後６時　休日／毎週水曜日　経営者／植村　秀　従業員／６人　客単価／4000円　主な取り扱い商品／口紅2000～　アイシャドー(200種)1500～　頬紅2000～　筆800～１万6000

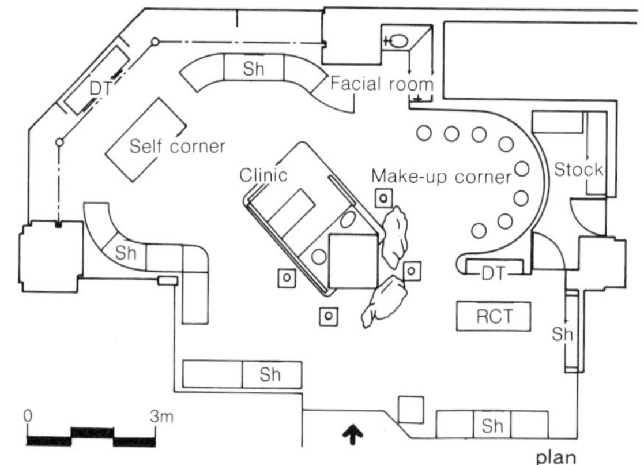

plan

白をベースとしたオアシス空間

「シュウ ウエムラ」は200余種のメークアップ商品をメインに　美顔に関した化粧品　小物類を扱うビューティー ブティックである。

この店は　①色モノを自分で選び　自由に楽しめるセルフメイクアップコーナー。②肌の診断を行うスキンケアコーナー。③自分の肌に合ったメイクを指導するスタジオコーナーの３つの機能を連動させた運営形態をとっている。

店舗設計にあたっては　店のオーナーであり著名なメイクアップ アーチストでもある　植村　秀氏が　自分のもっている美顔に対する理想　女性感を店舗の中で表現したいという要望があった。皮膚にとっては水分は必要不可欠なものであり　肌にとってはオアシスである……とのストーリーを受けて"都会の中のオアシス空間"をデザインコンセプトにした。このテーマに沿って　砂漠の中のオアシスシーンをＦＲＰ製肌目石膏調のラクダと椰子の木を　アイキャッチャーとして演出し　印象深いショップイメージを訴求した。〈岡田三千彦〉(85-3)

設計／ＪＴＦＡ 柳本　登　鈴木淑弘　柳田孝幸
施工／三好木工　船場
面積／100㎡
工期／1984年４月３日～23日

店内奥のメイクアップスタジオをみる

The makeup studio at the inner part.

メイクアップ商品棚をみる

The makeup commodity shelves.

Cosmetics SHU UEMURA

An oasis space with white as the basic tone

"Shu Uemura" is a new-type beauty boutique dealing with cosmetics and fancy goods for facial treatment.

This shop organically comprises (1) a self makeup corner where you can choose any desired color and enjoy freely, (2) a skin care corner where your skin is diagnosed, and (3) a studio corner where a makeup fitting your skin is instructed.

In the shop design, Mr. Shu Uemura, the owner and famous makeup artist, wished to express his ideal of beauty culture and his view of womanhood in the shop. To the skin moisture is indispensable and is an oasis for the skin. Thus, to materialize this "story," an "oasis space in a city" was adopted as the design concept. Along this theme, an oasis scene in the desert was presented by arranging FRP-made camels having plaster-like skin and coconut palms as eye-catchers, thus pursuing an impressive shop image.

3-2-1, Ginza, Chuo-ku, Tokyo
Phone: 03-564-4765

Design / JTFA
Area / 100 m²

入口側よりみる　中央ディスプレイ台には関連商品が陳列されている
A view from the entrance side. On the display table in the center are displayed related goods.

コスメティック ビサージ

東京都新宿区新宿1-31-1 寺田ビル1階　Phone/03-352-3911

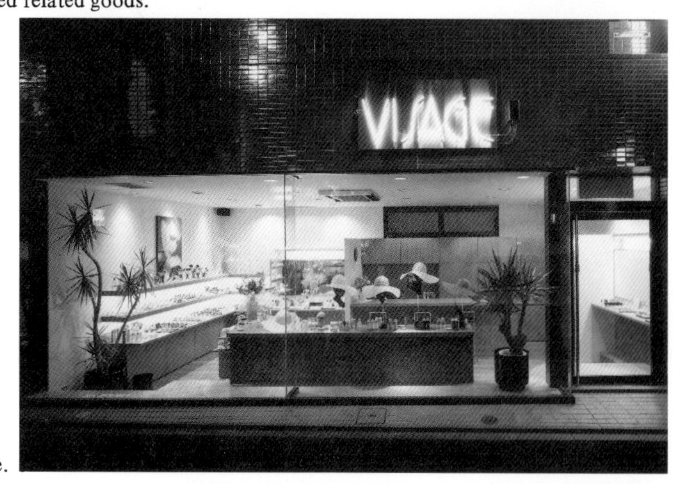

ファサード
The facade.

撮影／鳴瀬　亨

入口廻りをみる

The entrance area.

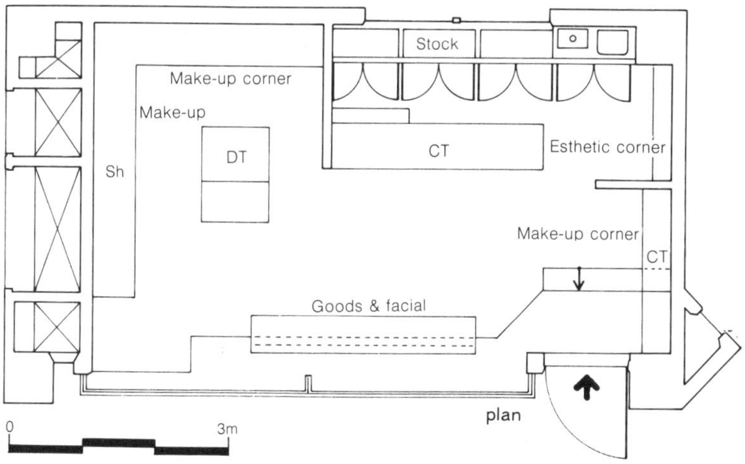

Stock
Make-up corner
Make-up
DT
CT
Esthetic corner
Sh
Make-up corner
CT
Goods & facial
plan
0
3m

材料仕様

床／楢フローリング貼りＯＳＷ　一部モルタル金鏝仕上げ　壁面／ＰＢｔ＝12ＡＥＰ　一部モルタル洗出し　天井／ＰＢｔ＝12ＡＥＰ　照明器具／ウシオスペックス

営業内容

開店／1985年４月５日　営業時間／午前11時～午後９時　休日／毎週日曜日祭日　経営者／渡辺兼道

ディスプレイ台とディスプレイ棚をみる　右側はメイクアップスペース

The display table and display shelves. In the right side lies the makeup space.

既成の概念を排したデザイン

オーナーは　新宿で永年化粧品店を営んでおられ　今回　場所も新たに出店することになった。

店内は　化粧品店としての既成の概念を排し　ランダムに各メーカーの制度品をディスプレイ要素の強い棚構成とし　センターには　アクセサリー　下着などの関連商品の陳列什器を配した。

カウンターは広く　客と店側の対話の場所として　落ち着きのある木の天板とし　店内に2ヶ所　各メーカーのテスターを置き　自由に試供できるスペースをつくった。ディスプレイスペースは　とくに重要なポイントであり　季節ごとに　店としてのセールス アピールができるようにレイアウトした。

〈和田　裕〉(85-11)

設計／ラップ　和田　裕

施工／藤工芸

面積／40m²

工期／1985年3月10日～4月3日

Cosmetics VISAGE

Presents a design clearing away the accepted concept

The owner has been engaged in operation of a cosmetic shop in Shinjuku. This time, he decided to open a new at a different location. In designing this shop, we have cleared away the accepted concept of a cosmetic shop. At random, each maker's products are displayed on the shelves, and in the center are arranged display utensils for accessories, underwear, etc.

The counter is wide, featuring a composed wooden surface so that it serves as a comfortable place for talks with guests. At two places are placed testers of different makers and their products can be tried freely. The display space is particularly important and its layout was made so that the sales appeal of the shop may be made in each season.

1-31-1, Shinjuku, Shinjuku-ku, Tokyo　Phone: 03-352-3911

Design / Yutaka Wada
Area / 40 m^2

PART 2 カルチュア & ホビー Culture & Hobby

レンガタイル貼りの外観をみる

The brick tiled appearance.

子供達のショッピング遊園地
自由ヶ丘 チルドレン ミュージアム

東京都目黒区自由ヶ丘1-25-17　Phone/03-718-8855

撮影／平沢　敞

シンボルのサンタクロース

The Santa Claus as a symbol.

1階「ドゥーブルペ」

Children's shoe shop at the 1st floor.

1階「ニューヨーク パパ」

地下1階「ポールナッシュ」

"Porl Nash" at the 1st basement.

1階「ミニK」

"New York Papa" at the 1st floor.

"Mini K" at the 1st floor.

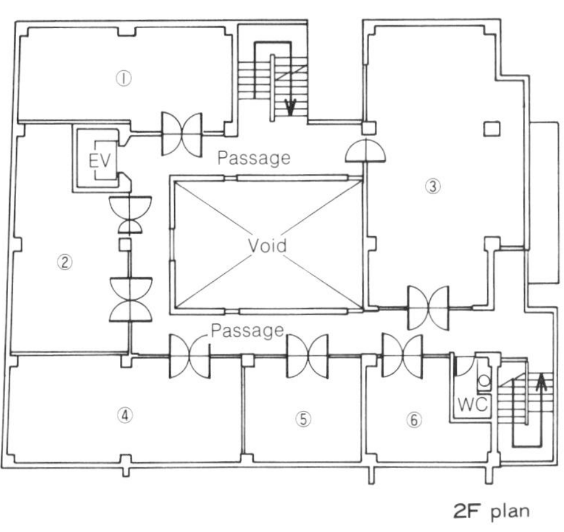

2F plan

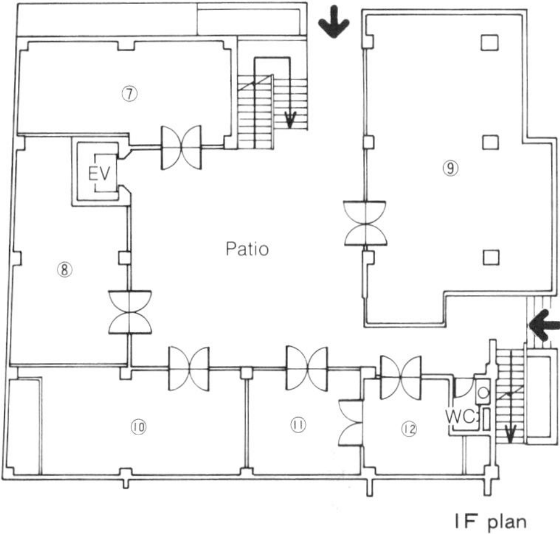

1F plan

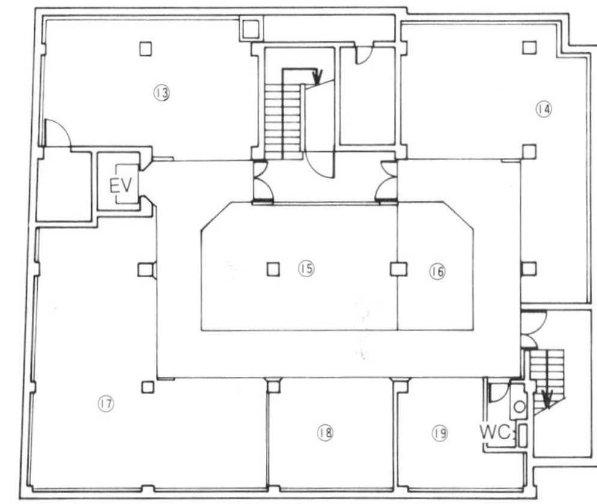

B1F plan

●各テナントの設計・施工

2階

①シャーリー テンプル：設計／ラップ　施工／白水社　②アプスアルソルバ：設計・施工／白水社 ③グランパパ ズー：設計／金丸建築　施工／港造形社　④ティンカーベル：設計／バルバス　施工／白水社　⑤フィユ コム サ デ モード：設計／ファイブフォックス　施工／ア ファクトリー ⑥ベネトン：設計／鬼工房　施工／白社

1階

⑦ミニK：設計／プラスチックスタジオ アソシエイツ ⑧ミニバツ：設計・施工／白水社　⑨ニューヨークパパ：設計・施工／港造形社　⑩ストリートオルガン：設計・施工／白水社　⑪ドゥーブルベ：設計／ジェトゥファ　施工／白水社 ⑫サイモン：設計ヌル ハウス　施工／白水社

地下1階

⑬パブ：設計／鬼工房　施工／白水社　鬼工房　⑭べべ：設計／イーブンハウス　施工／白水社　⑮ベビーディオール：設計／ＪＭＳ企画　施工／ニシモト　⑯こどもの森：設計／イタルマエダ デザイン オフィス 施工／白水社　⑰ミキハウス：ミキハウス：設計／ミキハウスＳＤ企画　施工／デザインスペース羂露　⑱ポールナッシュ：設計／ファイブ ワン 施工／白水社 ⑲プチ シャンブル：設計・施工／ヤマトマネキン

ヨーロッパ調アンティークショップをイメージ
子供の身になって考えた設計

建物は　ヨーロッパ調アンティークショップをイメージした煉瓦造りで　地下1階から地上2階が物販　3階はベンチを置いた憩の場と事務所。中庭は　陽の光が差し込む吹抜けになっており　1階～2階の各ショップはそれぞれの個性を発揮した独立店舗スタイル。地下1階は　ひとつの大きな店(フロア)の中に　各ショップの個性をうまく出し合い　ミックスさせたオープンスタイルとなっている。また、子供専用にと作られたトイレを1階に設置したり　吹抜け2階部分の手摺を子供の目線100cmに合わせ　大人用　子供用に2つ取り付けたり　ウインドーの腰を90cmから60cmに落とすなど　子供の身になって考えた設計。もちろんシンボルのサンタクロース(FRB)も設置。高さ3mの巨大なサンタクロースがビルによじ登っている姿は　なんともユーモラスで　あたたかい気持ちになれるでしょう。　〈中山純一〉(86-6)

企画・コンセプト／津川雅彦
　(チルドレンミュージアム館長)
デザインディレクション／下山好誼
　(チルドレンミュージアム　テナント会会長)
総合プロデュース／松本瑠樹
　(チルドレンミュージアム経営企画)
設計／建築・久米建築事務所　井上　博
　環境・AD　白水社　中山純一
施工／建築・佐藤秀工務店
　内装・白水社
構造・規模／RC造・地下1階　地上2階
面積／敷地360.12m²　建築268.22m²　延床720.22m²
工期／1985年3月20日～11月20日
工費／4億1000万円

Children Land of Dreams
CHILDREN MUSEUM

Imaging a European antique shop – really designed for the sake of children

The building is bricked imaging a European antique shop. The 1st basement, 1st floor and 2nd floor are used to sell goods, while the 3rd floor is used as a rest space with benches and for an office. The courtyard comprises a stairwell through which the sunlight comes in. The shops at the 1st and 2nd floors stand in an independent style, each coming with its own characteristic features.
The 1st basement, in one large shop (floor), comes in an open style with the characteristic features of different shops mixed harmoniously with each other. The toilets exclusive children are installed at the 1st floor, while the handrail of the 2nd floor portion of the stairwell is lowered to the eye-level of children (100 cm), side by side with the handrail for adults. Also, the window base is lowered from 90 cm to 60 cm. Thus, the shop is really designed for the sake of children. Santa Clauses (FRP) as the symbol are installed, of course. The appearance of huge (3 m high) Santa Claus climbing up the building is quite humorous, making us warm-hearted.

1-25-17, Jiyugaoka, Meguro-ku, Tokyo
Phone: 03-718-8855

Design / Hiroshi Inoue & Junichi Nakayama
Area / Site 360.12 m², Building 268.22 m², Floor 720.22 m²

2階「グランパパ ズー」　"Grandpapa Zoo" at the 2nd floor.

2階「ティンカーベル」　"Tinkerbell" at the 2nd floor.

材料仕様
屋根／磁器タイル貼り100角　外壁／煉瓦タイル貼り　一部吹付けタイル　外部床／磁器タイル貼り100角　床／地下1階・Pタイル貼り1～2階・煉瓦タイル貼り　壁面／煉瓦タイル貼り　天井／PB下地　ローラー塗装

営業内容
開店／1985年11月22日　営業時間／午前10時30分～午後4時　休日／月1回(不定期)　経営者／㈱チルドレンミュージアム　松本瑠樹　津川雅彦　下山好誼　館長／津川雅彦

入口より中央スロープをみる

The center slope viewed from the entrance.

子供のための知・遊・健・装・環・食空間
ワイワイワイ プラザ

名古屋市昭和区山手通り3-21 ワイワイワイビル1・2階
Phone/052-833-2254

撮影/加斗タカオ

南側外観をみる

The southern appearance.

2階通路より吹抜けスロープをみる

The stairwell and slope viewed from the aisle at the 2nd floor.

子供たちの遊び場〝プラザ〟

Children's playground "Plaza."

スロープ中央より入口方向をみる

The entrance area viewed from the center slope.

1階「クレージュ ペペ」 "Children's wear shop" at the 1st floor.

1階「フィユ コム サ デ モード "Fue commse ça du mode" at the 1st floor.

2階「書籍 Y. A.」 "Ehon Dowa Y. A." at the 2nd floor.

シンプル&アメニティ

この「ＹＹＹ」のある本山－八事間の山手・四谷通りは緑も多く　自然が残っている地域である。名古屋市の道路としては　変化しているところであり　大学も数校あり　環境的特性のあるところである。それを生かし　街づくりに時間をかけようという考えの芽生えているところでもある。オフィスが複合されたこの施設は　近隣に名古屋市立動物園　植物園　墓地等があり　立地には好条件である。
“大人から子供への思い入れ”を込めたライフサイクルはやがて巡り巡って　子供が大人になったとき　生きたものとなると考える。
オフィスの顔と商業施設の顔が隣接する建物に対応して白いガラス繊維入ブルー系複層ガラスのカーテンウォールで表情をかもし出している。カーテンウォールはシンプルなディテールになるように心掛け　アメニティとしての提案と１階から２階への内部スロープ（30ｍ鋼板吊り構造）は外から内へ　また内部での演出空間としてきわめて多様な利用が考えられている。　〈渋谷美宏／青島設計〉（86-6）

設計／建築・青島設計
　　内装　管理・青島設計　丹青社
施工／建築・鹿島建設名古屋支店
構造・規模／Ｓ造　一部ＳＲＣ造り・地下１階　地上４階　塔屋１階建
面積／敷地4521.27m²　建築2711.74m²　延床（ワイワイワイプラザのみ）１階2367.23m²　２階2315.98m²　合計4683.21m²
工期／1984年10月初旬～1985年11月３日
工費／17億3000万円

Children's Plaza YYY

Simple & amenity

Yamate-Yotsuya Street between Motoyama and Yagoto where this "YYY" stands, is rich with green and nature. Among the streets in Nagoya City, it is rather changing. There are several universities, forming one of the environmental features. Here, by utilizing it, the inhabitants are increasingly interested in making a desirable community. This center, where offices are also incorporated, is surrounded with Nagoya Municipal Zoological Garden, Botanical Garden, graveyard, etc., constituting a favorable location.
The life cycle, in which "adults' considerations of children" are incorporated, is believed to be enlivened eventually when children have grown up.
Responding to the building where the features of office and commercial facilities lie side by side, curtain walls of blue, multi-layer glass with white glass fibre serve as a symbolic expression. The curtain walls are simply designed, and to propose amenity the inside slope from the 1st to 2nd floor (30 m steel plate suspended structure) is presented from outside to inside, while utilizing the inside space in a wide variety of ways.

3-21, Yamatedori, Showa-ku, Nagoya-city
Phone: 052-833-2254

Design / Yoshihiro Shibutani
Area / Site 4521.27 m², Building 2711.74 m²,
Floor (YYY plaza only): 1st floor 2367.23 m²,
2nd floor 2315.98 m²; Totalling 4683.21 m²

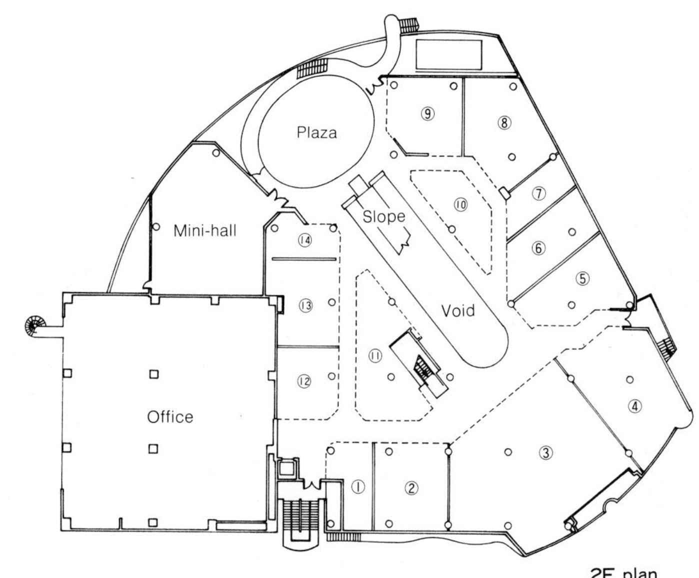

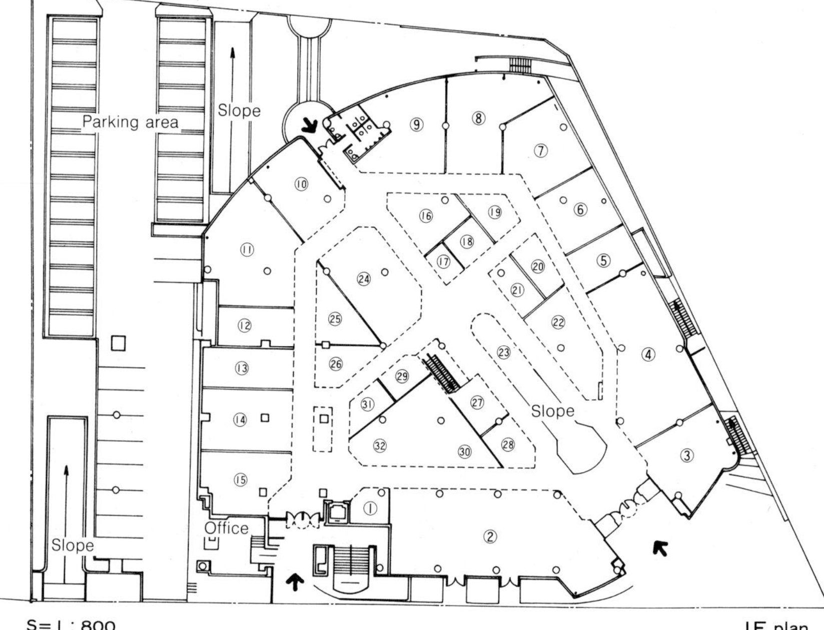

●各テナント
２階
①中国料理 点心　②お好み焼 大樹　③ベンガル　④パスタ カフェ カルロフェリーチェ ⑤和風甘味 ザカンミ　⑥スポーツショップ バンビーニＳＰ　⑦自転車 サンク　⑧書籍 Y.A. ⑨文具 雑貨 パピエ プリュス　⑩雑貨 B.B.ブラス　⑪生活雑貨 パディントン　⑫⑬家具　インテリア イン ハウス コア　⑭ホビーショップ833
１階
①クレープハウス ユニ　②カフェテリア シンフォニー ③雑貨 ユー&ミー　子供服　④ファミリア　⑤フィユ コム サ デ モード　⑥そばかすメリー　⑦サンタフェ　⑧シーズリ パブリック ⑨Ｉ+2　⑩プチエルショップ　⑪コンパス　⑫ベビー ディオール　⑬べべ　⑭クレージュ べべ　⑮ムゥ ジョンジョン　⑯リトルランド ディ&ディ　⑰サイモン ⑱シャーリー テンプル ⑲ラパリオ　⑳ミキハウン アンファン ㉑ティンクルベル　㉒アリス　㉓花 日比谷花壇 ㉔㉕玩具 ファミリーランド　㉖靴 銀座ワシントン　㉗雑貨　ずーじーずー ㉘ケーキ ガトーフランセ　㉙雑貨 キンダードルフ ヘロ　㉚雑貨 いーすたぁ ㉛靴シャイ　㉜雑貨 いーすたぁ ㉝宝石 彫金ショップ パートII

材料仕様
屋根／店舗部分・アスファルト防水押え　コンクリート　人工芝貼り　外壁／アルミカーテンウォール　ＡＬＣ版ｔ＝120の上ウレタン塗装　外部床／タイル貼り150角及びホモジニス系デザインタイル　壁面／モルタル金鏝押え　ＶＰ　天井／岩綿吸音板ｔ＝９ＥＰ

営業内容
開店／1985年11月３日　営業時間／午前10時～午後８時　休日／毎月第2・3火曜日　経営者／㈱ジョット

カウンターを通して造形教室をみる

The formative arts classroom viewed across the counter.

造形教室をもつ児童図書　絵本専門書店

桃太郎

東京都国立市東2-12-26　Phone/0425-76-2189

ファサード

The facade.

撮影／景山　亨

ディスプレイテーブルを通して書棚をみる

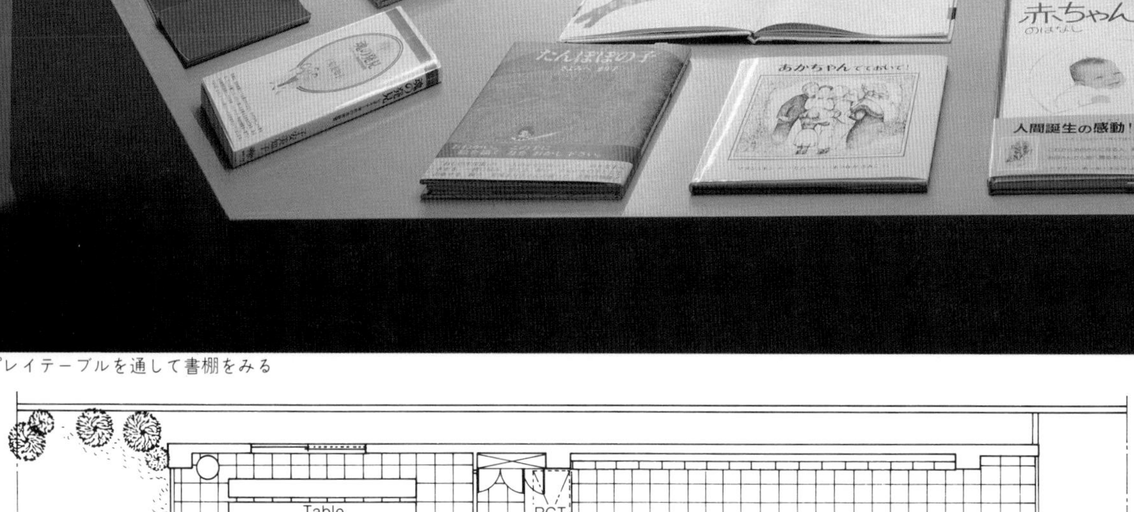

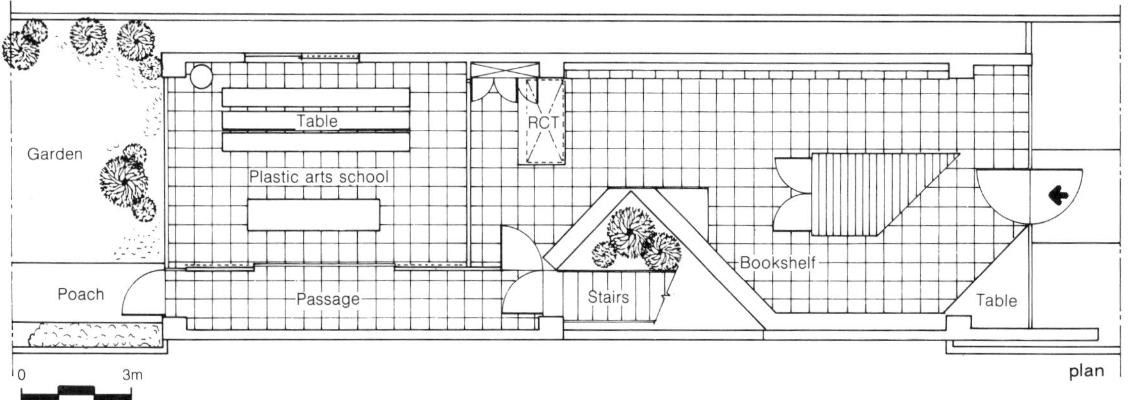

The bookshelves viewed across the display table.

カウンター前より入口方向をみる　The entrance area viewed from the counter.

時間をかけてじっくりと

この住宅ができ上がってから　もう7年半ほどになる。商店街の中の狭小敷地という性格から　1階部分はピロティによって完全に開放し　生活空間は2階に持ち上げて町のざわめきから縁を切った。その結果生まれたピロティ部分の空間は当初から用途は未定であった。
オーナーの田中和子さんは幼児教育の専門家で教育の現場にも立っていた人で　永年グループによる研究活動も続いている。
種々の職業の友人との接点の中から　良質の絵本の専門店が国立周辺になく不便を感じているということが出てきた。商売は未経験の田中さんにとって　時間をかけてじっくりと準備がはじまった。店舗の設計　施工も並行してゆっくりと進むこととなる。必要条件として考えたことは中庭の欅を残すこと　店舗プラス幼児の造形教室のスペース（各種研究会にも使用される）。
店のイメージはピロティの透明感を消さないように　壁はすべてガラスフィックスとし　枠　方立など単純で安価で済むディテールにしてある。建築は極力発言しないようにモノクロームで統一し　点在する書架の一部　テーブルなどにのみ赤と青の強い色が表現されている。
この店には　インテリアはじめ　設計の私もふくめ　家具制作　仕入れ　運営など多くの友人　知人が参加している。本体の住宅の生成と同様にゆっくりとしたペースで成長発展を始めている。何事にもテンポの速い商店建築の世界だが　"少量でも良質のもの"主義のユニークな店である。

〈石田信男〉(84-7)

設計／建築・石田設計事務所　石田信男　内装・飯島　誠
施工／建築・富田工務店　内装・ザ ウッド
面積／57.06m²(店舗のみ)　工期／1982年7月1日～1983年4月30日
工費／505万円

Children's Book Store MOMOTARO

Taking time – thoroughly

Nearly 7.5 years have passed since this house was built. In consideration of its characteristic narrowness in a shopping street, the 1st floor was completely opened by using pilotis, while the living space was moved to the 2nd floor, being shut away from the bustling street. From the beginning, the pilotis space has remained unfixed in its use. Ms. Kazuko Tanaka, owner, is a specialist in infant education, and was actually engaged in educational practice once. She has also continued group study activities for many years.
From her contacts with friends of various professions it was noticed that people often felt inconvenient as there is no specialty picture book store in the vicinity of Kunitachi. Since Ms. Tanaka was unexperienced in business, she began to take time in thorough preparation. The shop design and installation thus started slowly. In designing the shop, it was thought necessary to keep intact zelkova trees, and secure a space for shop plus formative arts class for infants (also used for various study meetings).
In order not to damage the transparency of pilotis, all the walls come with glass fixed, and simple, cheap framing, etc.
As for architecture, in order to make it as less talkative as possible, it is standardized with monochrome, using vivid red and blue colors for only part of dotted bookshelves, tables, etc.
In making this, many friends of mine have participated in interior/furniture layout, purchase, management, etc., apart from myself in design. As with formation of the main residential part, the shop is growing at a slow pace. Amidst the world of shop building where everything is changing rapidly, this shop is unique in that it adheres to the policy "small in quantity, but high in quality."

2-12-26, Higashi, Kunitachi City, Tokyo　Phone: 0425-76-2189

Design / Nobuo Ishida
Area / 57.06 m^2 (shop space only)

材料仕様

外壁／スチールサッシ(特注品)　一部石綿板t＝6ＶＰ塗装　外部床／ポーチ・チェッカープレート敷　床／ビニールタイル貼り　壁面　天井／既存RC　ＶＰ塗装　棚／ラワンＶＰ　ディスプレイテーブル／楢ベニヤＶＰ

営業内容

開店／1983年5月5日　営業時間／午前11時～午後6時　休日／毎週月・木曜日　経営者／田中和子　従業員／2人　主な取り扱い商品／児童図書　絵本　教育学図書（3500余点）

中央ディスプレイスペースをみる

子供服ブティック
1＋2（アン エ ドゥ）

名古屋市昭和区山手通り3-21 ワイワイワイプラザ 1階　Phone/052-834-6271

撮影／加斗タカオ

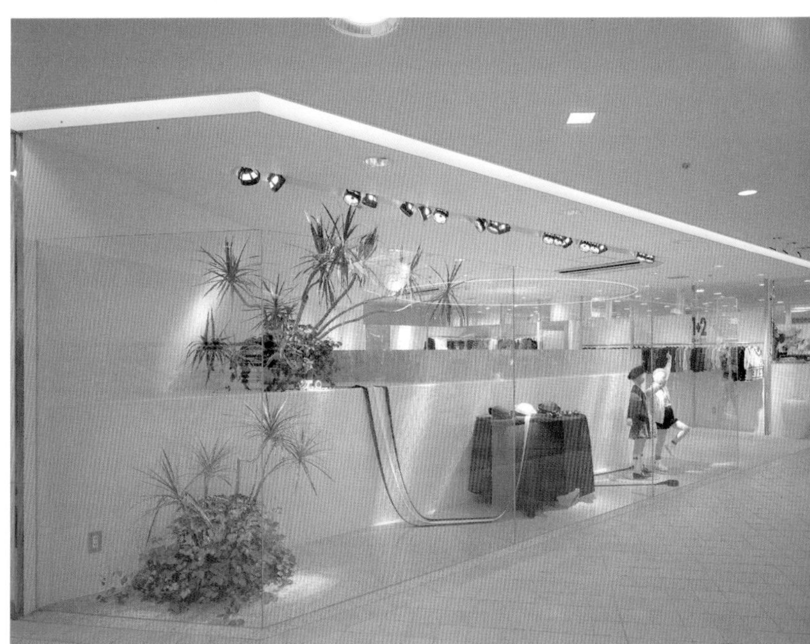

ファサード　The facade.

おとなのブティックのミニ版
昨今の子供服ショップは　子供に媚びている。たとえば　いたずらに色を多用したり　床は　ころんでも怪我のないように　やわらかい素材を用いたりしている。
その子供イコール○○○という方程式が　画一的な空間を増大させている。
子供服を大人の視点(目線)にもどすことが　多数の子供服ショップとの差別化を決める大切なキイである。
まして　今回の「１＋２」は大人のブティックのミニ版である。それであるならショップも　床は御影石　壁はタイル貼りにしても　良いのではないだろうか。
〈大塚孝博〉(86-6)

設計／プラスチックスタディオ　&　アソシエイツ　大塚孝博
施工／船場(名古屋)
面積／78㎡
工期／1985年10月11日～20日

Children's Boutique 1 + 2 (AN ET DEUX)

A mini version of adult boutique
Children's wear shops today are flattering children. For example, they heavily use colors, or employ a soft material for the floor so that children may not be hurt even when turned over.
This equation, children equal ○○○, is expanding the uniform space.
Returning children's wear to the sight (eye-level) of adults holds an important key for differentiating this shop from many other children's wear shops.
This "1 + 2" is a mini version of adult boutique. If so, wouldn't it be allowable to use granite for the floor and tile the walls?

3-21, Yamatedori, Showa-ku, Nagoya City　Phone: 052-834-6271

Design / Takahiro Otsuka
Area / 78 m²

材料仕様
床／白御影石サンド仕上&セン材フローリングＣＬ　壁面／タイル貼り10角　天井／ＰＢ下地APE·
家具　什器／セン材ＣＬ

営業内容
開店／1985年11月３日　営業時間／午前10時～午後８時　休日／毎月第2·3火曜日　経営者／㈱ルシックライカ　従業員／２人　主な取り扱い商品／１＋２ブランド(ルシックライカ)の子供服全般

The central display space.

中央ディスプレイスペースよりディスプレイ棚をみる

The display shelves viewed from the central display space.

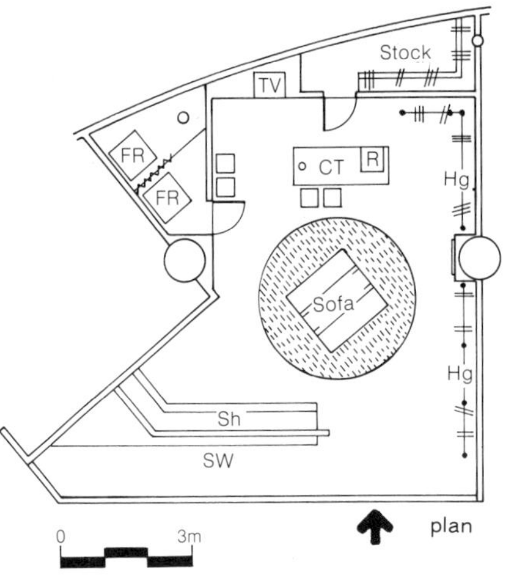

入口よりハンガースペースをみる

The hanger space viewed from the entrance.

ファサード

The facade.

側面入口より店内をみる

The inside viewed from the side entrance.

子供ブティック
ヤングエージ

東京都世田谷区玉川3-17-1 玉川高島屋ショッピングセンター南館 3階
Phone/03-709-2222

撮影／本木誠一

デザイナーズブランドショップのイメージ

銀座からスタートした「ヤングエージ」は 子供服の老舗ともいえます。従来の"子供服屋"というイメージが強かったようですが 玉川高島屋の改装にあたって まず 新玉川線 田園都市線沿線の新興住宅地の20代後半～30代後半のブランド指向型のヤングミセスにターゲットを絞りました。そして 今までの"子供服屋"のイメージを変えて デザイナーズブランドショップのようなイメージに対し そのような客層が納得できるショップ空間を提供しました。

これは いわゆる冒険でもありましたが 最近街でよく見かけるデザイナーズブランドや キャラクターズブランドできめている子供たちをコーディネートしている ヤングママたちを引きつける 魅力あるショップに生まれ変えることができました。 〈臼井洋治〉(86-6)

設計／スケルトン 臼井洋治
施工／綜合デザイン
面積／67.84㎡
工期／1985年5月19日～23日

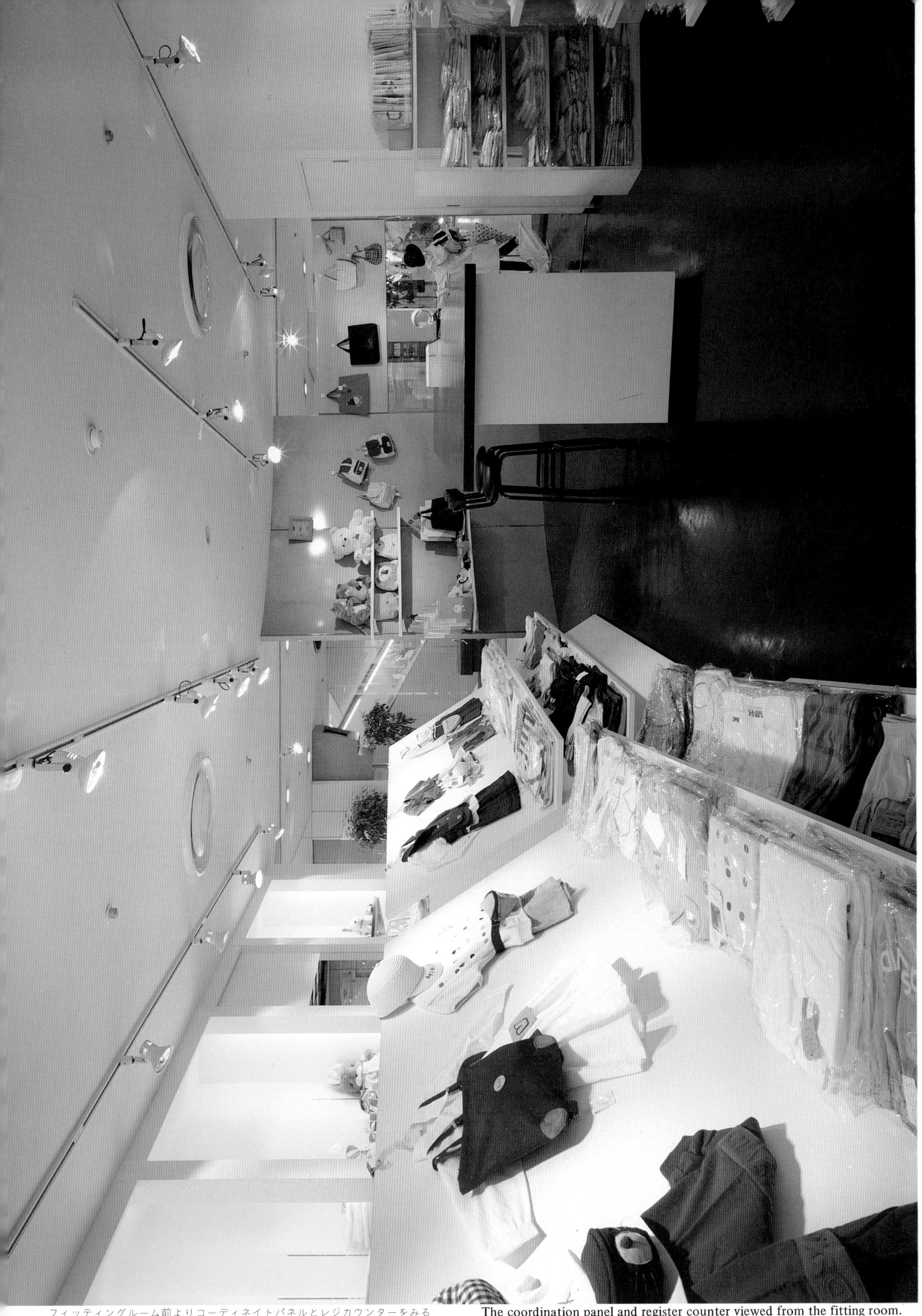

フィッティングルーム前よりコーディネイトパネルとレジカウンターをみる　The coordination panel and register counter viewed from the fitting room.

円形フォルムで形成された入口廻りとディスプレイステージをみる

The entrance area and display stage come in a circular form.

Children's Boutique YOUNG AGE

An image of designer's brand shop

"Young Age," which made its start from Ginza, may be said to be an old established children's wear shop. The former shop had a strong image of "children's wear shop." In redecorating Tamagawa Takashimaya Department Store in which this shop is open, they at first focused their target on brand-oriented young married women in their latter half of 20's to 30's, who live in newly born residential areas along Shin-Tamagawa Line and Denen-Toshi Line.

And, by changing the conventional image of "children's wear shop," we designed a space which will satisfy guests who prefer a shop giving an image of designer's brand shop.

This was quite adventurous. However, it is believed that we could change this shop into an attractive shop for young mothers coordinating their children with designer's brands or character's brands which we often come across in the town.

3-17-1, Tamagawa, Setagaya-ku, Tokyo Phone: 03-709-2222

Design / Yoji Usui
Area / 67.84 m²

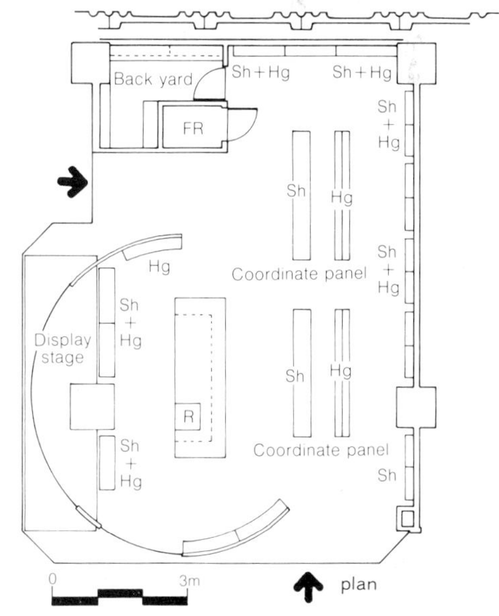

材料仕様

床／ビニールシート貼り　幅木／木製幅木　壁面　天井／ＰＢｔ＝12下地　ＥＰ仕上げ　ディスプレイステージ／柄合板染色仕上　スクリーン／スチールメラミン焼付け塗装

営業内容

開店／1985年５月24日　営業時間／午前10時～午後９時　休日／なし　経営者／㈱ヤングエージ　従業員／３人　パート　アルバイト２人　合計５人　主な取り扱い商品／ベビーから16歳までを対象とした　オリジナル・輸入・ブランド子供服

店内中央より奥をみる　アーチは店内へ誘導とともにコーナー分けの役割も果す
The inner area viewed from the center of the store. While leading you into the shop, the arch serves as a partition of corners.

ファサード

The facade.

ベビー＆子供ブティック
ペティランド　サカイヤ

兵庫県洲本市本町6-2-28　Phone/0792-2-0037

撮影／高橋　章

中央左より右方向をみる　２つのディスプレイステージは平面上の楔として斜めに配置されている
The right side viewed from the left side of the center. The two display stages are inclined as wedges on the plane.

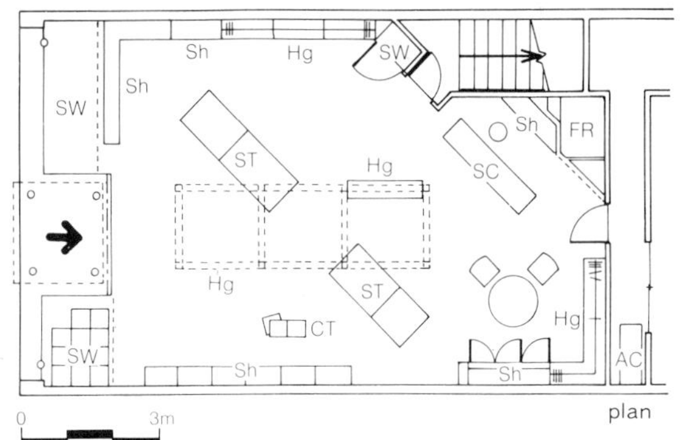

材料仕様
外壁／アルミ板塗装　入口ゲート／結晶化ガラス貼り　外部床／タイル貼り 200角　床／ビニルタイル貼り 300角　幅木／ソフト幅木　壁面／ＰＢ下地　クロス貼り　天井／ＰＢ下地クロス貼り　一部アルミ塗装ルーバー天井　照明器具／ＤＬ　テーブル／天板・ピーラ寄木　椅子／スチール焼付け仕上げ　座・布地張り　什器／木製ラッカー塗装　ステージ／結晶化ガラス貼り　アーチ／ピーラ材　ウレタンクリア仕上

営業内容
開店／1986年３月１日　営業時間／午前10時～午後７時　休日／毎週木曜日　経営者／左海雄次郎　従業員／２人　客単価／5000円　主な取り扱い商品／子供服　靴　ベビー服用品　マタニティ用品　入浴用品　化粧品　下着　新生児用品　肌着　アクセサリー　ぬいぐるみ

アーチによるセグメントとピンクの可愛らしさと高級感をねらう

この店はこれまで比較的若い婦人服の店だったが　オーナー夫妻の年も若く　ベビーと子供ファッションへの思い入れもあり　設計計画は出産準備品　マタニティ　ベビー用品　子供用品　アクセサリー玩具という似て非なるアイテムを　それぞれの壁面をバックに展開し　相互の連帯性と独立性を強調するために木組の連続アーチを設置した。このことにより各コーナーは知覚的・心理的にも独立したものとなった。また　来客の歓迎　店内への誘導の効果もこのアーチで意図した。そして全体の統一性を維持するため　ステージを店の中央斜めに　平面上の“くさび”として配置した。色彩計画は子供ベビー　ヤングママ対象という事もあり　また流行の白い店に対する反発もあり　思い切って壁面はピンクのクロス貼り一色とした。床はローズ色のPタイルである。このカラーリングによって可愛らしさと高級感が出せたと思う。

〈井手慎助〉(86-8)

設計／井手慎助
施工／美術工房工作部
面積／95.7m²
工期／1986年2月1日～25日

店内左隅をみる　ルーバーからの照明で明るさが一段と際立つ
The inside left corner. Lighting from the louver intensifies the brightness.

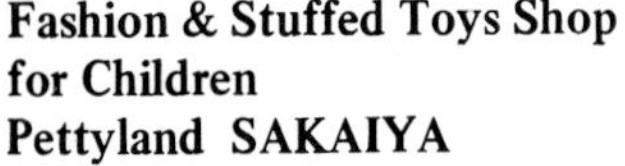

Fashion & Stuffed Toys Shop for Children
Pettyland SAKAIYA

Pretty, high-grade images pursued by arched segments and pink color

So far, this shop has been mainly intended for relatively young ladies' apparel. However, the owner and his wife are young, and they are deeply interested in babies' & children's fashion. Thus, our design was made to develop the display of items quite differing from each other (items necessary for childbirth, maternity ware, baby ware, children's ware and stuffed toys) against the respective wall surfaces. In order to stress the solidarity and independency of these corners, wooden arches were continuously installed. As a result, each corner has been made independent both visually and psychologically. These arches are also intended to effectively serve in welcoming and introducing guests into the shop. And, in order to maintain the unity as a whole, the stage was placed in the center inclinedly so that it may serve as a "wedge" on the plane. As for the coloring, since this shop is targeted at children, babies and young mothers, and in reaction to the white shops now in fashion, the shop boldly employed pink cloth alone on the entire wall, while the floor is covered with rose-colored P tiles. It is believed that by this coloring we could produce pretty, high-grade images.

6-2-28, Hon-cho, Sumoto City,
Hyogo Prefecture.　Phone: 0792-2-0037

Design / Shinsuke Ide
Area / 95.7 m²

入口前のディスプレイステージをみる　The display stage in front of the entrance.

オーディオ ショップ
ミュージック プラザ

東京都新宿区西新宿1-1-5 新宿ルミネ 5階
Phone／03-348-5241

パブリック通路より入口廻りをみる
The entrance area viewed from the public passage.

壁に向う道
どこからともなく聞こえる音楽に誘われ　旅人はいつしか店の前に立っていた。
その店は　少し変わった店で　中に〈道〉がある。それは氷河のごとく　時の流れとは無関係に存在しているようにみえた。店は〈道〉によって2つのエリアに分けられ　そのそれぞれに違う特色の“記憶の果実”のようなものが陳列されていた。また〈道〉の両端には並木のように立ちならぶ　上品に燈を持った列柱が立っていた。その燈に導かれ店の中に入ると　そこには氷のような〈壁〉が立ち塞がり　短すぎる旅の終りを告げていた。〈壁〉にはあらかじめ用意された仕掛けが施してあり“ある記憶”のメッセージを伝えていた。旅人はしばらく見入っていたが　やがてエリアの方へ歩いて行き　そこで“記憶の果実”のようなものを手にし　また新たな旅に旅立った。
〈高畠　直〉(84-8)

設計／アスクスペースコンサルタンツ　高畠 直
施工／アスクショップサービス　八谷直樹
面積／138.6㎡
工期／1984年2月15日～25日

Audio Visual Shop MUSIC PLAZA

A way towards the wall
Allured by music reaching his ear from nowhere, a traveller has stood in front of the shop before he was aware of it.
That shop is a little strange, having a "road" inside. It was white just like a glacier, and appeared to exist independently of the passage of time. By the "road," the shop is divided into two areas, and something like the "fruit of memory" differing in character was displayed. Along both sides of the road stood top-lighted pillars, just like a low of trees. When entering the shop guided by the lights, a "wall" like ice stood in his way, telling the end of too short a journey. The "wall" was provided with a device conveying the message of "a memory". The traveller stood for a while gazing at the "wall." Then, he walked towards the area, where he secured something like the "fruit of memory," and started on a journey again.

1-1-5, Nishi-shinjuku, Shinjuku-ku, Tokyo
Phone: 03-348-5241

Design / Naoru Takabatake
Area / 138.6 m^2

撮影／鳴瀬　亨

コンパクトディスク試聴カウンターよりプレイガイド方向をみる
The play guide area viewed from the compact dish test hearing counter.

レコード売場よりニューメディア関連商品売場方向をみる

The new media related goods selling corner viewed from the record corner.

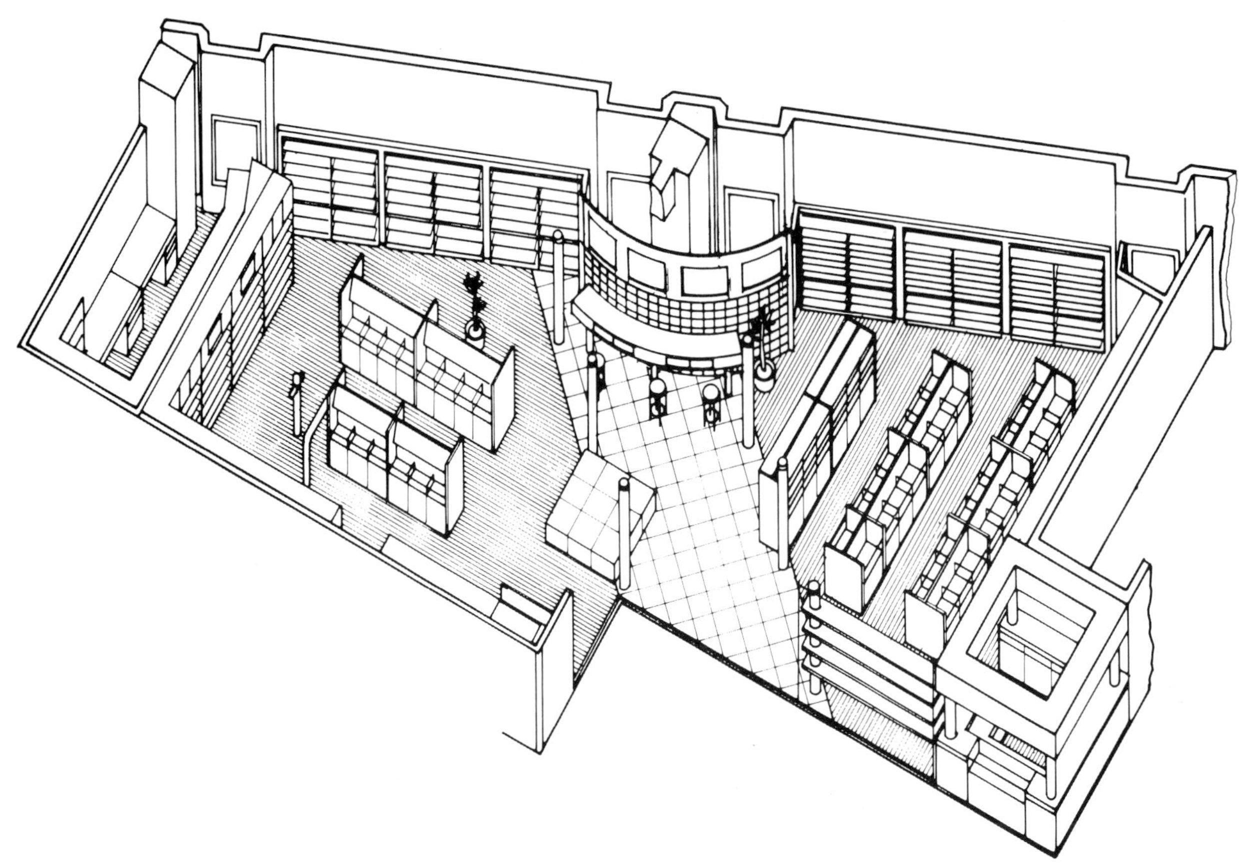

ＶＨＤ売場より中央のＡＶコーナーをみる

The AV corner in the center viewed from the VHD corner.

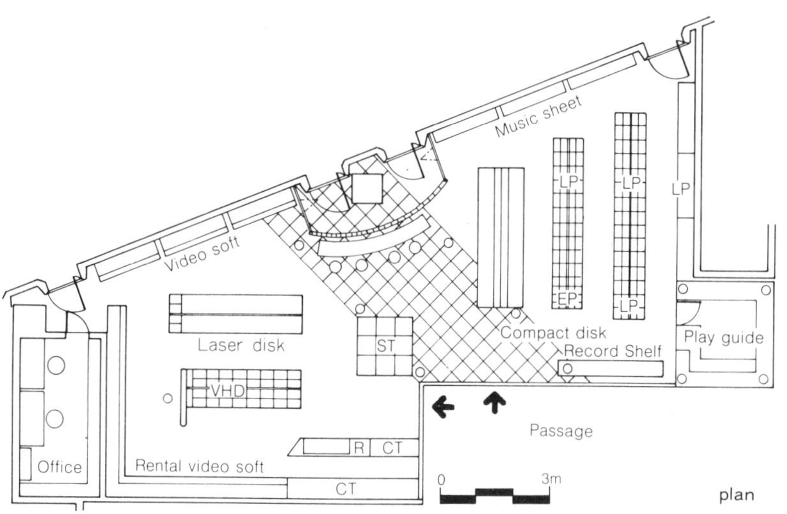

材料仕様
床／コンパネ下地　栖材フローリング貼りＯＳＣＬ　モルタル下地大理石貼り　壁面／ＲＣ軀体ＶＰ仕上　一部ガラスブロック　天井／ＰＢｔ＝９下地　寒冷紗貼りパテしごきＶＰ仕上　照明器具／直付シーリングライト　ＦＬ間接照明　家具／栖材練付ＯＳＣＬ仕上

営業内容
開店／1984年２月25日　営業時間／午前10時30分～午後９時　休日／毎月第３水曜日　経営者／㈱ミュージックプラザ　従業員／３人パート６人　合計９人　客単価／3500円　主な取り扱い商品／ＬＰ・ＥＰレコード　コンパクトディスクソフト　ビデオソフト(ＶＴＲ)ミュージックテープ　レーザーディスク　ＶＨＤソフト　プレイガイド(コンサートチケット)

試聴カウンターとレコード売場をみる

The test hearing counter and record corner.

スクランブルド マーチャンダイジング ショップ

フィオルッチ ショップ

東京都豊島区南池袋1-28-1 西武百貨店池袋店 2階
Phone／03-989-0111

ファッション売場をみる　ＡＶの音と映像による環境演出

The fashion corner; in an atmosphere presented by AV sound and images.

撮影／鳴瀬　亨

材料仕様

床／オリジナルＰタイル　一部楢材染色仕上　幅木／塗装仕上　壁面／塗装仕上　一部経師貼り　天井／露出天井ＶＰ塗装　照明器具／スタジオライト　家具／ユニクロメッキパイプ&塗装仕上　レジカウンター／ガラス天板&パイプの組合わせ　カフェカウンター／白御影石ミガキ仕上

営業内容

開店／1984年４月27日　営業時間／午前10時～午後６時　休日／毎週木曜日　経営者　西武百貨店池袋店　従業員／17人　客席数(カフェ)／50席　客単価(衣料)／7000円　主な取り扱い商品／ファッション衣料　化粧品　家庭雑貨　ポスター　ビデオソフト　レコード　ステーショナリー

くだりエスカレーター前よりレコード売場をみる
The record corner viewed from this side of the descending escalator.

「カフェ　デ　フィオルッチ」　"Café de Fiorucci."

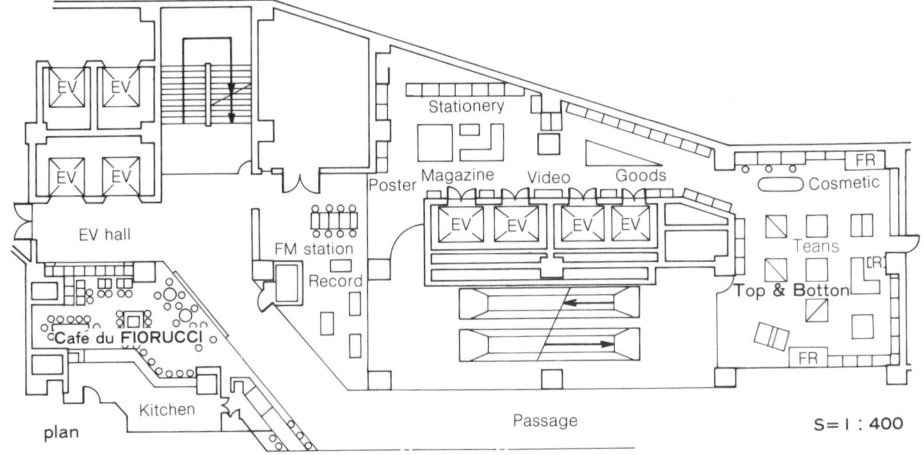

音と映像のメディアが意外性とドラマティックな環境をつくりだす

「フィオルッチ」の店舗環境は　それ自体　現代人に対する未来形をノンフィクションで物語っている。大量生産的な天井材や蛍光灯照明は取り除かれ　コンクリートはむき出しにされ　ダクトやスプリンクラーが無造作に入り乱れ　現代建築の真の姿をそこにさらけ出している。一方「フィオルッチ」の商品の持つホットマインドが無機質な空間を逆に包み　ねじ曲げ　そこに奇妙な調和を生み出している。
もう一つ　商品と環境の奇妙な関係に食い込むように　映像とFMステーションは「フィオルッチ」のライフスタイルにおける情報をビジュアルに発信する要素と「フィオルッチ」の環境イメージを発信するという２つの要素からなる重要なキャラクターである。映像機器自体は現代人にとって　存在してあたりまえのものであり　床の間にテレビ然として飾られる必要は何も無く　むしろ無造作に転がっていたり　思わぬ場所に存在した方が意外性があって楽しい。
また　定期的にＤＪするＦＭステーションと映像ソフトが一体となり　特に「カフェ　デ　フィオルッチ」のくつろぎ空間と　イベントスペースでホットな情報を提供している。

〈横井直道〉(84-8)

企画／西武百貨店　設計／横井直道　新妻　宏
施工／乃村工芸社　総合デザイン　面積／300m²
工期／1984年４月16日～４月26日

Composite Store FIORUCCI Shop

Sound and image media create an unexpected, dramatic environment

The very shop environment of "FIORUCCI Shop" tells in the form of nonfiction how moderns will become in the future. The ceiling material and fluorescent lighting, which are generally mass-produced, have been removed, concrete is exposed, and ducts, sprinklers, etc. are arranged carelessly. Thus, the modern architecture, as it really is, is exposed here. Meanwhile, the hot mind of "FIORUCCI" goods conversely wraps and twists the inorganic space, thereby creating a strange harmony.
Additionally, in order to cut into the strange relations between products and their environment, images and FM station serve as important character elements: (1) to visually transmit information in the life style of "FIORUCCI," and (2) to transmit the environmental images of "FIORUCCI." The presence of image display units is quite natural to moderns, and reed not be installed showily. Rather, it is amusing to see that they lie down carelessly or are present at an unexpected place. Additionally, the FM station where DJ is performed regularly, fuses with image soft, offering a restful space of "Café de Fiorucci," among others, while hot information is given at the event space.

1-28-1, Minami-ikebukuro, Toshima-ku, Tokyo　Phone: 03-989-0111

Design / Naomichi Yokoi
Area / 300 m²

入口廻りを通して店内をみる

The inside of the shop viewed through the entrance area.

トータル ステーショナリーショップ
アクセスアクト

横浜市西区南幸2-15-13 横浜ビブレ21 4階 Phone/045-314-2121

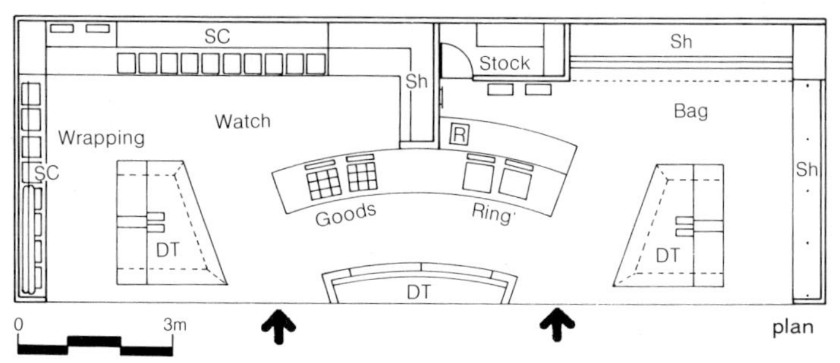

撮影／鈴木三男

材料仕様

外部床／ベース・楢材染色ＣＬ仕上　サイン／ステンレス鏡面ｔ＝５切文字貼り　床／コンパネ下地樹脂テラゾｔ＝４貼り　幅木／ラッカー仕上　壁面／ＬＧＳ下地ＰＢｔ＝12貼り　天然石配合樹脂系美装仕上　天井／ＰＢｔ＝12貼り　目地寒冷紗パテしごき　ＥＰつや消し　照明器具／改造器具(松下電工)　棚板／楢板目染色ＣＬ仕上　中央什器／支柱・天然石配合樹脂系美装仕上　上部・楢材板目染色ＣＬ仕上　ウレタンＣＬ仕上　カウンター／トップ・楢材板目染色ＣＬ仕上　腰・天然石配合樹脂系美装仕上　スクリーン／透明ガラスｔ＝８Ｆｉｘステンレスフレーム

営業内容

開店／1985年４月20日　営業時間／午前10時～午後７時　休日／隔週火曜日　経営者／㈱ビブレ　従業員／５人　客単価／3000～5000円　主な取り扱い商品／ステーショナリー　サック　革バッグ　革小物　アクセサリー　ラッピング

店内中央のアール状カウンターテーブルをみる

The radiused counter table in the center.

左側入口部より棚コーナーをみる

The shelf corner viewed from the entrance in the left side.

素材感　重厚感のある空間

私は　このショップを計画するにあたって　素材とその素材のもつカラーが空間を形成する上で　一番重要であったように思う。
レイアウトは　センターを基軸にシンメトリーで　空間を縦と横の軸　水平面と垂直面の構成で形成している。水平面を楢材板目染色(グレー)　垂直面をUMストーンで統一し　素材感があり　重厚感のある空間を造った。
中央のテーブルは　この空間の一つのオブジェとしてとらえ　床から立ち上がる2本の柱を基軸にレベル差の異なる2つの水平面が　いかにも床から浮いているかのように表現した。楢材染色(グレー)とウレタン(黒)のコントラスト　および45°のテーパーを取ることにより　シャープなフォルムを生んでいる。
アールのカウンターテーブルは　天板を楢材染色　腰をUMストーン仕上で　リング(指輪)什器が天板に埋め込まれている。レジ　サッカー機能をその後ろに配することで　管理面からも　ショップの顔としても受けとめている。
サイン計画は　ショップセンターにインパクトを強くするデザインとして∧∧∧型壁面を造りその中にベースとして楢材染色板にステンレス鏡面文字を取り付けた。ライティングに関しては　壁面をムラなく照射する器具を依頼して作ってもらった。 〈左鴻辰美〉(86-1)

設計／布谷ビブレスタッフ　左鴻辰美　施工／布谷ビブレスタッフ
面積／65.74m²　工期／1985年4月5日～15日　工費／1200万円

Sacks & Desk Accessories ACCESS ACT

A space rich with direct senses of materials in a massive atmosphere

In designing this shop I felt that materials and their colors were most important in space composition.
The layout is symmetrical in both sides of the center, and the space is composed of vertical and horizontal axes, and horizontal and vertical planes. The horizontal plane is evenly finished with the dyed (grey) grain of Japanese oak, while the vertical plan with UM stone, thus creating a space rich with direct senses of materials in a massive atmosphere.
The table in the center is regarded as an objet of this space, and based on the two pillars rising from the floor, two planes differing in level were expressed as if floating above the floor. By contrasting the dyed (grey) Japanese oak with urethane (black), and by securing 45° of taper, a sharp form was produced.
The radiused counter table is surfaced with the dyed Japanese oak, with its waist finished with UM stone, and ring utensils buried in the surface board. By arranging the register/sacker functions behind it, the table is accepted as the shop's face from the point of view of management, too.
As for the sign plan, in order to make the shop center give a strong impact, ∧∧∧∧∧ patterned wall was created to mount thereon the stainless steel mirror-finished, dyed Japanese oak bearing letters. As for lighting, order-made lighting apparatuses evenly throwing light on the wall are used.

2-15-13, Minami-saiwai, Nishi-ku, Yokohama City
Phone: 045-314-2121

Design / Tatsumi Sako
Area / 65.74 m²

"静"のティーサロンと"動"の生活雑貨フロアを意識的に分割したディスプレイステージをみる

The display stage consiously divided into the tea salon for "quietness" and the miscellaneous goods floor for "motion."

ミニホール内のミニバーをみる

The mini bar in the mini hall.

ステーショナリー＆生活雑貨 レシピ エフ

東京都新宿区新宿3-36-11 新宿高野5階 Phone/03-354-0222

撮影／本木誠一

生活雑貨コーナーをみる

The miscellaneous goods corner.

ティーサロンより生活雑貨コーナーをみる

The daily miscellaneous goods corner viewed from the tea salon.

多目的仕様に対応できる似合いの場

新宿高野100周年のイベントとともに５階の改装計画が進行した。

“もてなしの道具”であるテーブルウエア　カクテル用具　ステーショナリーなどとともに　プレゼンテーションの場としてのティーサロン　ミニホール　ミニバーという多種　多様で　多目的使用に対応できる似合いの場の演出である。

大きく空間を利用するため　什器類に動的意匠（スプリングやリフトの機能をイメージさせる）を加えた。

また　視覚的な高さ確保のために　天井を抜いたことから　動的空間の効果を狙った。

その結果が　“静”のティーサロンと　“動”の雑貨　ステーショナリーコーナーの意識的分割に役立った。

〈根本恵司〉(86-1)

企画／タカノフルーツギャラリープロジェクト　設計／タッチダウン　施工／丹青社　丹工社

面積／450㎡（うち厨房25㎡）　工期／1985年８月10日～９月１日

Stationery & Tablewear RECIPE. F

A place for suitability capable of meeting various uses

Along with the 100th anniversary event of Takano, Shinjuku, the 5th floor redecoration program has proceeded.

Together with tableware, cocktail ware, stationery, etc. which are "tools of hospitality," the tea salon, mini hall and mini bar present a place for suitability capable of meeting various uses.

In order to utilize the space widely, dynamic design considerations were given to the utensils (so that they may arouse images of spring or lift functions).

By making the ceiling naked, a visual height was secured so that a dynamic space effect may be produced. As a result, the tea salon for "quietness" and miscellaneous goods & stationery corner for "motion" could be consciously divided.

3-36-11, Shinjuku, Shinjuku-ku, Tokyo　Phone: 03-354-0222

Design / Keiji Nemoto
Area / 450 m^2 (kitchen 25 m^2)

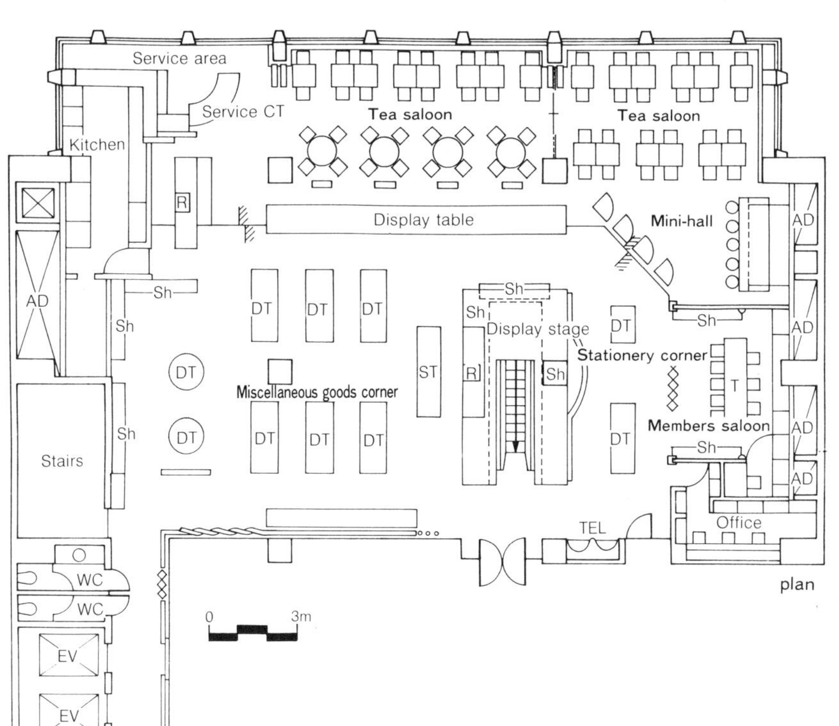

plan

材料仕様

床／モルタル金鏝　目地スチールｔ＝９一部唐松ｔ＝５ 500角ウレタン塗装　壁面／ＰＢ下地クロス貼り　パテしごきＣＬ　一部スチールｔ＝1.6黒皮仕上　ワックス仕上　柱巻／モルタル＋寒水石　ピシャン仕上　天井／ＰＢ下地ＡＰＥローラー　一部メタリック塗装　棚／合板下地メタリック塗装

営業内容

開店／1985年９月４日　営業時間／午前10時30分～午後８時　休日／不定期　経営者／㈱新宿高野　高野吉太郎　従業員／サービス８人　アルバイト７人　厨房３人　合計18人　客席数（ティーサロン）／61席　客単価／ステーショナリー・1500円　ティーサロン・650円　主な取り扱い商品／ラッピングペーパー　ペン　財布　スタンプ　スケジュールノート　和食器　ワイングラス　コーヒーカップ　エプロン　主なメニュー／サイドイッチ700 ケーキセット700 コーヒー450 ジュース600

ファサード

The facade.

ラッピング＆ギフトグッズ ゾナルト

東京都渋谷区神山町9-5 グリーンウエイビル Phone/03-467-4471

撮影／本木誠一

1階入口よりディスプレイテーブルをみる

The display table viewed from the 1st floor's entrance.

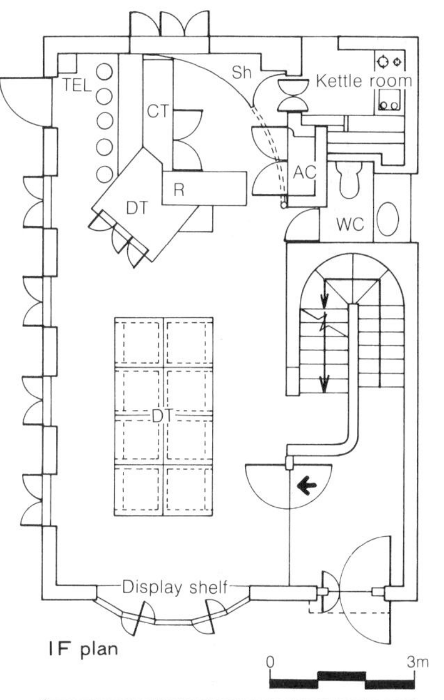

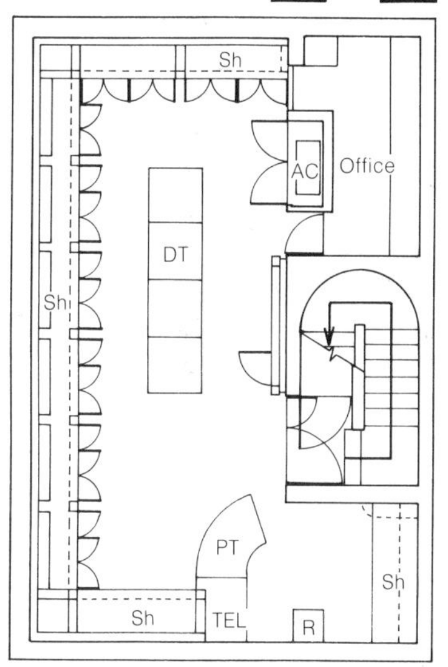

多品種多量な商品に対応した什器システム

常に斬新で　きめ細やかにデザインされた商品で知られる　ラッピング&ギフトグッズの店「ゾナルト」がオープンした。2階がオープンスペース　3階がオフィスという構成です。

設計にあたって　地下1階は　多品種多量な商品陳列と　その可変性　ストックスペースの確保という点で　システム内蔵の壁面構成とし　色はホワイト(2色)連続性を持った柱を配置し　全体を明るく均一な環境としました。

1階は中央に900角(高さ450×600)の収納つきローテーブルを集合させて大きなディスプレイ ステージを形成し　販売員1人でサービスできるように　高低差を持つ多機能カウンターを設置しました。アールの壁と　角度をつけたディスプレイ ステージ(1450角 高さ1050)により　空間に変化を与えました。

〈小野亮二〉(84-7)

設計／建築・AMO設計事務所
内装・オノデザインオフィス　小野亮二　アートディレクション

アートディレクション／木村　勝

施工／建築・三楽建設　内装・プランズマリオ

面積／地下1階・50.52㎡　1階・44.91㎡　合計95.43㎡　工期(内装)／1984年4月12日～27日

Wrapping & Gift Goods ZONART

A utensils system responding to quantitative goods of various kinds

The wrapping & gift goods shop "Zonart," known for its ever brand-new, elaborately designed goods, opened. The 2nd floor comes as an open space, while the 3rd floor is used an office.

In designing the shop, the 1st basement was provided with walls with a built-in system to secure a space for displaying quantitative goods of various kinds, and make them variable in image, while securing a stock space, finished in white (two colors). The pillars having a continuity are arranged, creating a bright, uniform environment as a whole.

In the center of the 1st floor are gathered 900 x 900 mm low tables (450 or 600 mm high) with goods accommodating boxes, making them form a large display stage. In order to make it possible for a salesman to serve guests, a multi-function counter having different heights was installed. By arranging the radiused wall and angled display stage (1,450 x 1,450 x 1,050 mm high), we provided the space with a variation.

9-5, Kamiyama-cho, Shibuya-ku, Tokyo　Phone: 03-467-4471

Design / Ryoji Ono

Area / Basement 50.52 m², 1st floor 44.91 m²; Totalling 95.43 m²

1階奥より中央ディスプレイテーブルを通して入口方向をみる The entrance area viewed across the central display table from the inner part of the 1st floor.

地下1階売場をみる
The selling area at the 1st basement.

材料仕様

屋根／銅板t＝3新硫化仕上　外壁／コンクリート化粧打放しAPカラークリアー　床・幅木／地階・塩ビ系床材　1階・テラゾ　一部幅木　ウレタン　チャコールグレイ塗装　壁面／地階・ＰＢ下地　シグマルト吹付　1階・ＰＢ下地　寒冷紗パテしごきＶＰ塗装　一部シグマルト吹付＆集成材　白染色ウレタンクリアー艶消し　天井／ＰＢt＝9下地　寒冷紗パテしごきＶＰ塗装　什器／1階カウンター＆ディスプレイ　ステージ・集成材　白染色ウレタンクリアー艶消し　腰・ウレタン　チャコールグレイ塗装

営業内容

開店／1984年5月1日　営業時間／午前11時～午後7時　休日／毎週水曜日　経営者／ゾナルト＆カンパニー　神谷誠一　従業員／3人　客単価／900～1000円　主な取り扱い商品／木村勝のアートディレクションによる：ギフトパッケージ　ラッピングペーパー　コースター　ランチョンマット　オリジナルギフト商品

上　右下／ファサード

Top, bottom / The facade.

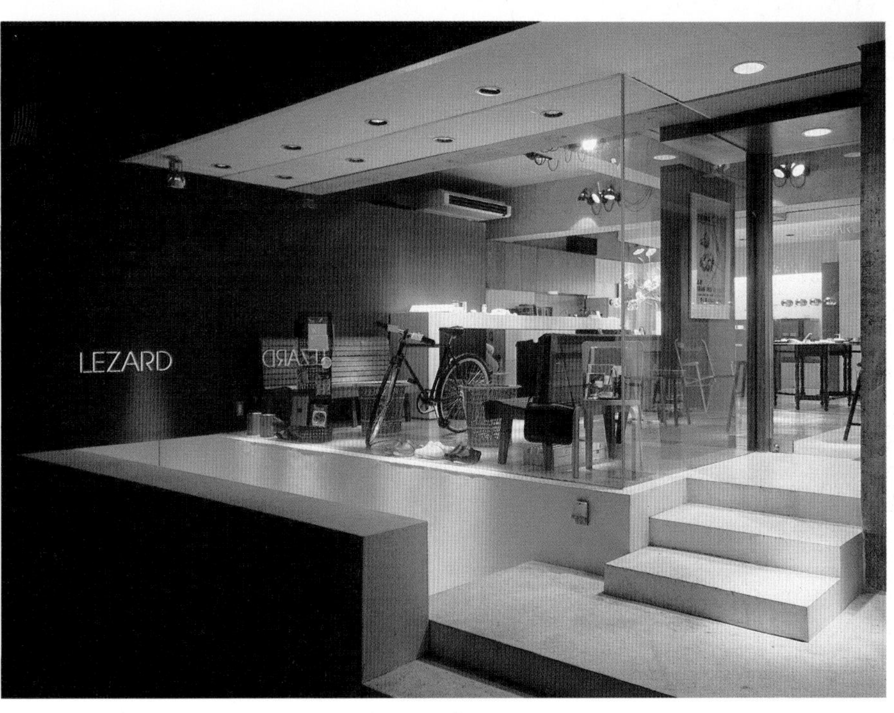

ステーショナリー レザール

東京都渋谷区渋谷1-6-3 高島ビル 1階・地下1階　Phone/03-406-8251

撮影／平沢　敞

1階のカウンターをみる

The counter at the 1st floor.

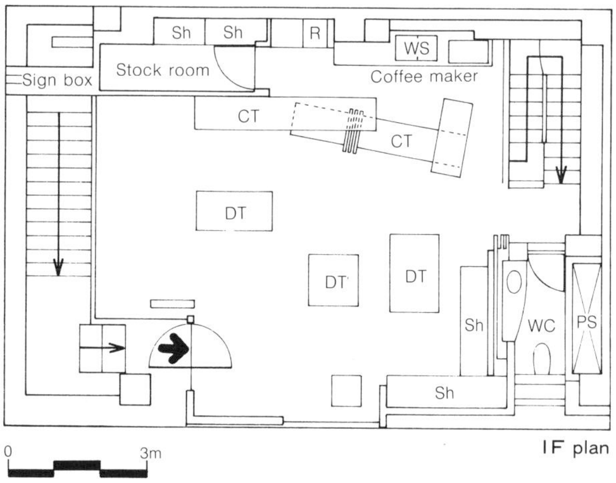

Sh Sh R WS
Sign box Stock room Coffee maker
CT CT
DT DT DT
Sh WC PS
Sh

0 3m

1F plan

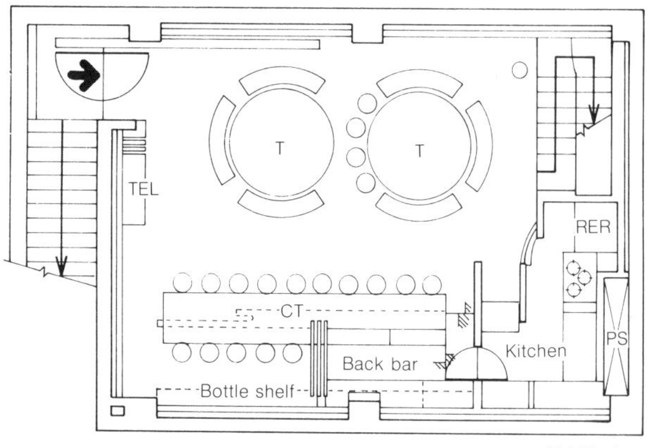

TEL
T T
RER
CT
Back bar Kitchen PS
Bottle shelf

B1F plan

1階奥の地階への階段廻りをみる

The staircase area at the inner part of 1st floor, leading down to the basement.

地階のカウンターをみる

The counter at the basement.

店自体を生活提案の商品と考える

1984年(昭和59年)の末に企画の話があり　当初はケンウッドがステーショナリーの世界を変える　プロトタイプの店づくりとしてスタートした。場所の選定に２転３転し　今回の所に落ち着いたが　青山でも立地としては　かなり難しい要素を含んでいるので　生活提案の場として　店自体を商品と考えることで　来店動機を増強させることを考えた。

内部に　フォルムとして１階と地階の意識を結びつける階段を作り　ステーショナリーとバーをフィックスしてみた。また　１階の床材である唐松積層材を　地階のカウンター　ビッグテーブルの素材として用いることで　視覚要素での統一も図ってみた。

地階のバーを全体として無機的な構造とし　唐松の自然素材としての美しさを強調し　バーでありながら　ステーショナリーの感覚を持たせてみた。一部に使った玉石モザイクの積層積みは　京都の土壁の瓦積みを見てヒントを得た。

〈高橋敬三〉(86-1)

設計／タッチダウン　施工／大成建設

面積／１階72.5m²　地下１階72.5m²(内厨房10m²)　合計145m²(うち厨房10m²)

工期／1985年７月１日～７月10日　工費／3000万円

Stationery & Bar LEZARD

Regards the shop itself as goods helpful for your living

At the end of 1984 we were inquired about the plan. At first, Kenwood set about it by making a prototype shop. After two or three rounds of location selection, we have finally chosen the current location. Although it is located in Aoyama – one of the most trendy areas – the location involves somewhat difficult elements. So, by regarding the shop itself as a kind of goods helpful for your living, we have tried to strongly motivate people to drop in this shop.

Inside was provided a staircase to link the consciousness of the 1st floor with that of the basement, thus fixing the stationery and bar. Also, by using laminated larch (flooring material for the 1st floor) as the material for the counter big table at the basement, we tried to give a unified image with the visual element.

By making the bar at the basement into an inorganic structure as a whole, the beauty of larch as a natural material was emphasized, thus equipping the bar with a contrasting sense of stationery. Laminated pebble mosaic used at some parts flashed across my mind when I saw bricks piled up to form an earthen wall in Kyoto.

1-6-3, Shibuya, Shibuya-ku, Tokyo　Phone: 03-406-8251

Design / Keizo Takahashi

Area / 1st floor 72.5 m^2, Basement 72.5 m^2 (kitchen 10 m^2); Totalling 145 m^2 (kitchen 10 m^2)

材料仕様

外部床／テラゾ現場研ぎ出し　床／１階・唐松積層材　地階・スウェーデン産石英岩　壁面／１階・ヘッシャンクロス　パテしごき　一部ＡＥＰローラー　地階・ヘッシャンクロス　パテしごき　玉石モザイク積層積み　天井／ＰＢ下地ＶＰローラー　カウンター／１階・ヘッシャンクロス　パテしごき＋榀フラッシュ材ラッカー塗装　地階・唐松積層材

営業内容

開店／1985年７月15日　営業時間／１階・午前11時～午後７時　地下１階・午後６時～11時30分　休日／毎週日曜日　祭日　経営者／㈱レザール　従業員／６人　客席数(地下１階)／28席　客単価／3500円　主な取り扱い商品(１階)／ノート　手帳　バッグ　洗面道具　陶器　グラス　時計　オリジナル自転車　主なメニュー(地下１階)／ウイスキー(ボトル)4500　オムレツ1000　和風スパゲッティ800

店内中央のディスプレイ什器をみる

The display utensils in the center of the store.

トラベルショップ
ピオ 八重洲店

東京都中央区八重洲2-1 東京駅八重洲地下街
Phone/03-274-6805

撮影/白鳥美雄

ファサード

The facade.

入口廻りに散らばせた波打った４種類メタリックタイル床をみる
Four kinds of corrugated metallic tiles scattered near the entrance area.

メタリックタイルの床の表情がポイント
トラベルショップ「ピオ」は　業務的には２つの要素から成立しています。１つは旅行取扱業務　もう１つはさまざまな小物を販売するステーショナリーショップです。
機能的には２つの要素の構成が大前提でプランニングを進めて行くのですが　これらの異なる機能を同時に取り込む空間の場合　棚のあり方や素材　色彩やバランス　納まり部分のこだわり等々が空間を表現するのだと思います。したがって　統一的考えからトラベル業務としてのゾーンにも　構成要素として計画した棚の機能を用いました。
プランニングの邪魔と思われる角の防火扉と柱が　むしろ四角い空間を考えていく時に　入口ゾーンとしてはっきりさせるきっかけとなりました。ガラスの設置は　視野の広がりを保ちながら　役割を明確にする必要を感じたわけで　もし　それがなければ　曖昧な空間になってしまうと感じたからです。つまり無意味と思われるガラスは規律を保つ役割をしているのです。
新しい感覚のショップとして　入口付近に散らばせた波打った４種類のメタリックタイルの床の表情を　この店の象徴的効果となるようにスクリーンにも使用しました。

〈岡本輝男／デザインスタジオ　オカモト〉(86-11)

企画／スタジオ29　今井輝光
設計／デザインスタジオ　オカモト　岡本輝男
施工／デザイン　コア　塩谷　宏　面積／66.6㎡
工期／1986年３月17日～４月２日　工費／1350万円

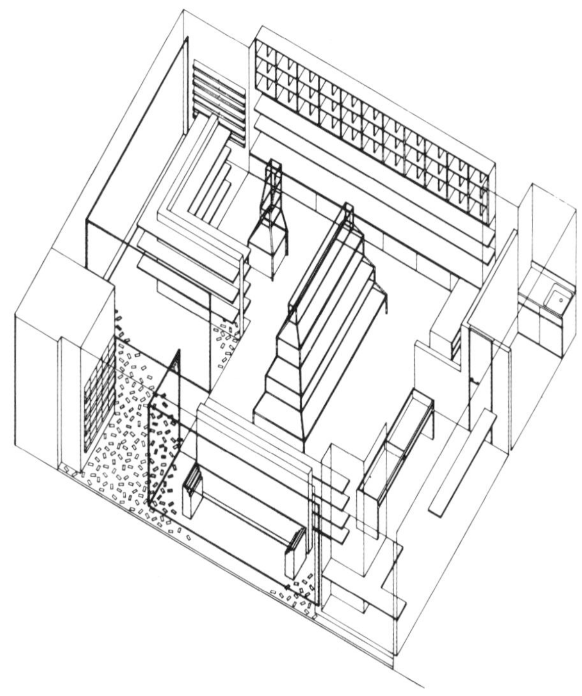

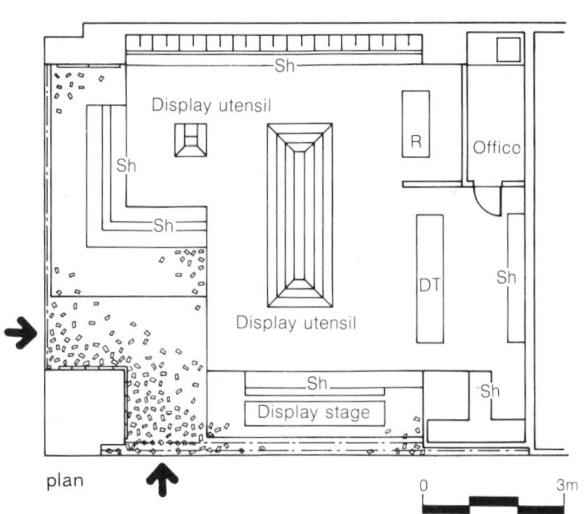

Travel Shop PIO Yaesu

Primarily features metallic tiled floor

In terms of operation, the travel shop "Pio" consists of two elements. The one is a travel agency service, and the other is a stationery shop selling various fancy goods.
From the functional point of view, we have proceeded with planning based on the composition of the two elements as the major premise. In designing the space incorporating these two different functions, it was thought that such space may be expressed by the layout of shelves, materials, balance, adherence to the accommodating parts, etc. Thus, from a unified point of view, the zone assigned to the travel agency service was also provided with the shelf functions.
The fireproof doors and pillars at a corner, which seemed to disturb the planning, rather made themselves felt clearly as an entrance zone when considering a square space. Glass was installed to define the role while keeping the spacious viewfield. It was felt that, if glass did not exist, the space would become vague in nature. That is, the glass, that appears to be meaningless, is helping maintain the order.
In order to stress the new sense of this shop, the feature of the floor – covered with four kinds of corrugated metallic tiles which are scattered near the entrance – was also used for the screen so that it may produce a symbolic effect on this shop.

2-1, Yaesu, Chuo-ku, Tokyo　Phone: 03-274-6805

Design / Teruo Okamoto
Area / 66.6 m²

材料仕様
床／タイル貼り(入口部)モルタル金鏝塗り床仕上　壁面／リシン吹付け　天井／ＰＢ下地ＥＰ　棚／楊合板色ラッカー吹付け　ディスプレイ什器／スチールメラミン焼付け

営業内容
開店／1986年４月３日　営業時間／午前10時～午後８時　休日／なし　経営者／㈱オーレ　従業員／３人　パート　アルバイト４人　合計７人　客単価（ステーショナリー）／1100円　主な取り扱い商品／文具　生活雑貨　コスメティック(輸入品)

レイ ステージをみる

The window display stage.

入口付近よりガラスで仕切られたAVルームをみる

AV room partitioned from the entrance area by glass.

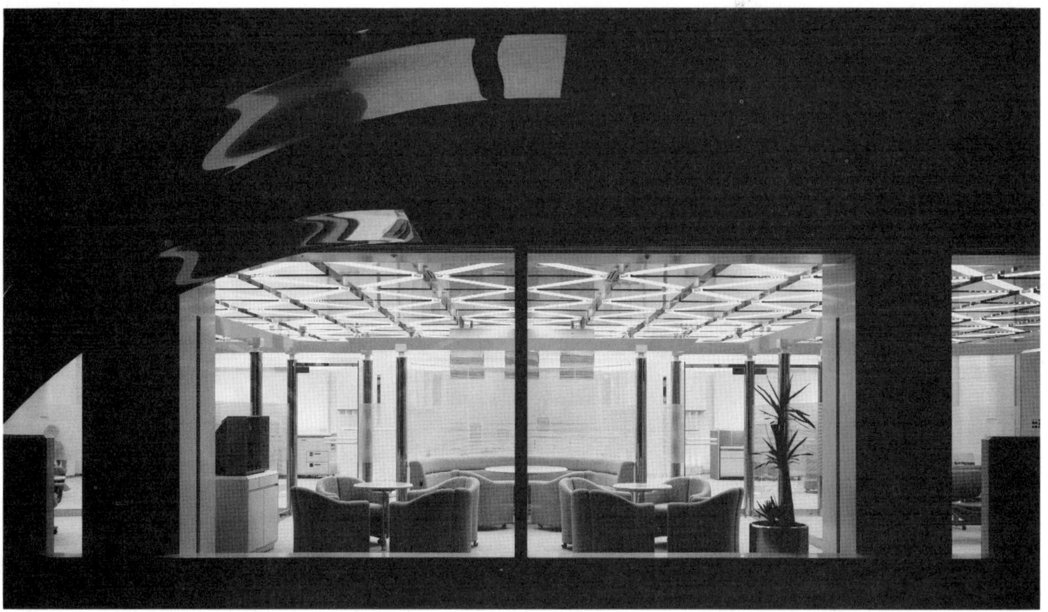

ファサード　中央がサロン

The facade. The salon in the center.

OA機器ショールーム リコーOAポート

東京都千代田区内幸町1-1-7 大和生命ビルアネックス1階　Phone/03-580-4171

撮影／狩野正和

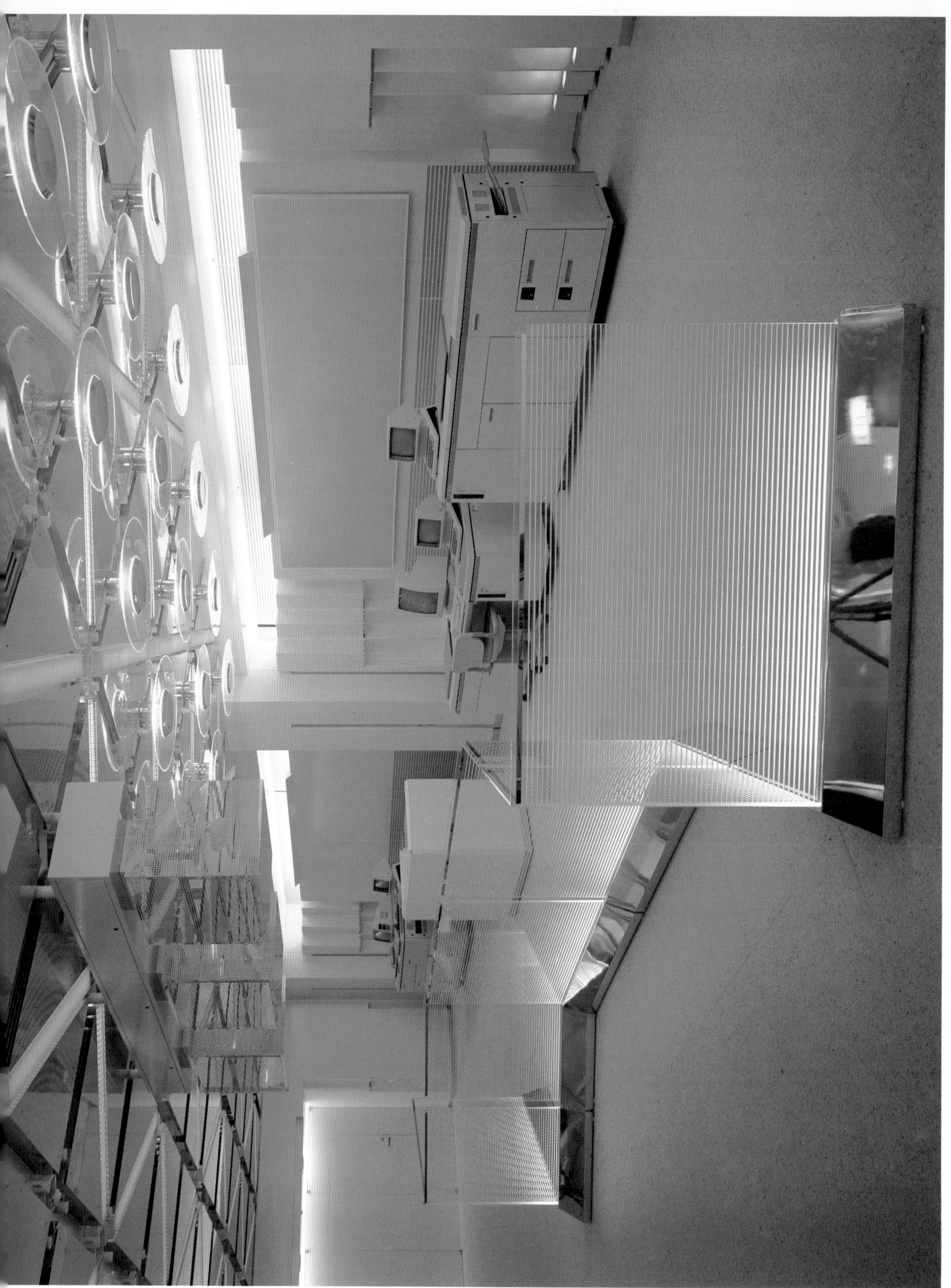

光スクリーンを通してＯＡ機器展示スペースをみる

The OA equipment display space viewed through the light screen.

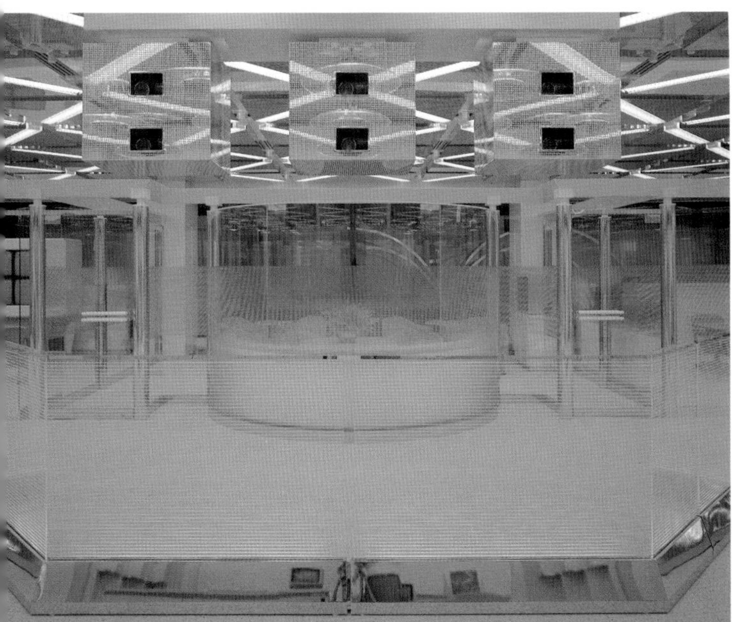

アクリルスクリーンを通してサロンをみる
The salon viewed through the acrylic screen.

オフィスオートメーションの環境づくりのためのデモンストレーションルーム

この「リコーＯＡポート」は　日比谷公園前　帝国ホテル隣の大和生命ビルのアネックス１階(約530m²)にある。またこのサポートセンターになる事務所が本館２階(990m²)にあり　この上下がワンセットして機能するように計画されている。この界隈には　近くの丸の内周辺のオフィス群を意識して他社のＯＡショールームも軒をつらねている。

このショールームは　文書作成　複写　転送　保管検索の４つの単一機能のＯＡ機器を統合し　それを有機的に結びつけて連動させるリンネットという画期的なＯＡステーションの開発を契機にして　ダイナミックなネットワークを作ろうとする第２世代に入ったＯＡ環境作りのためのデモンストレーションルームとして作られた。　〈北原　進〉(84-9)

設計／ＫＩＤアソシエイツ　北原　進　青戸　修　藤田政志
協力／鹿島建設建築設計本部(設備)
施工／内装・西武百貨店建装事業部
　　　設備・鹿島　大林　大成共同企業体
家具　什器　サイン／そごう
面積／530m²　工期／1984年４月１日～６月30日

OA Equipment Showroom RICOH OA PORT

A demonstration room for creation of an environment for office automation

This "Ricoh OA Port" is open at the 1st floor (about 530 m²) of the annex to Daiwa Seimei Building which stands next to Teikoku (Imperial) Hotel in front of Hibiya Park. The office serving as its support center is situated at the 2nd floor (990 m²) of the main building. These two – above and below – are designed to function as a set. Taking account of many offices in the vicinity of Marunouchi, the other competitive OA showrooms stand side by side.

This showroom was made as a demonstration room for creating an environment for OA that has entered into the 2nd generation which is intended to make a dynamic network. This was triggered by development of an epoch-making OA station called the Linnet that integrates OA units with four single functions – document preparation, copying, transfer and storage/retrieval, and links and interlocks them organically.

1-1-7, Uchisaiwai-cho, Chiyoda-ku, Tokyo　Phone: 03-580-4171

Design / KID Associates
Area / 530 m²

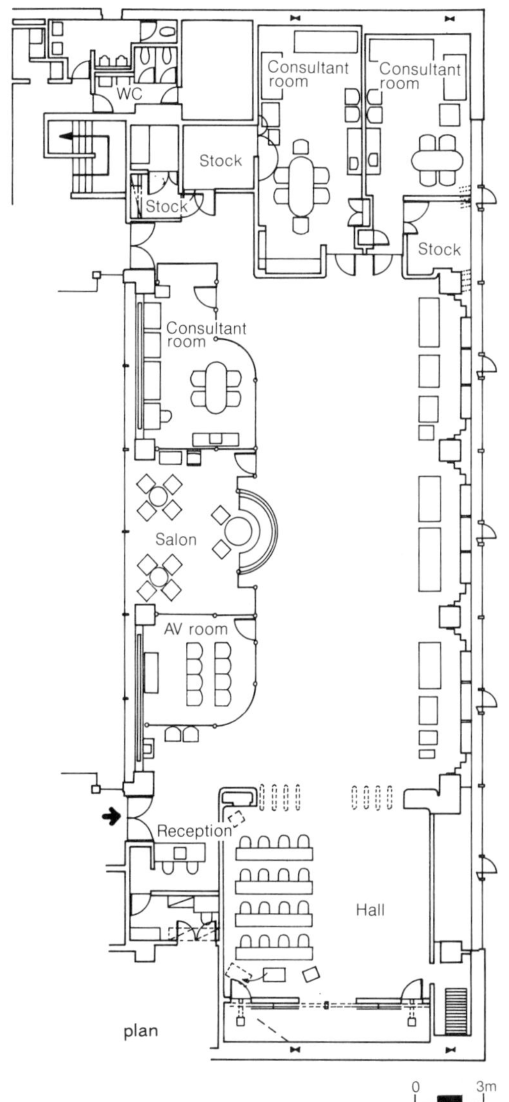

材料仕様
床／フリーアクセスフロア下地　タイルカーペット　壁面／LGS　PBt＝９＋12 下地紗貼ラッカー塗装　コンサルタントルーム・クロス貼り　柱　窓台／銅板ｔ＝1.2 焼付塗装仕上　天井／アルルック　クリアーｔ＝３シルクプリント加工及び銅板ｔ＝１焼付塗装ＰＢｔ＝９下地　紗貼り　ラッカー塗装及びクロス貼り　スクリーン／透明ガラスｔ＝10　一部サンドブラスト加工　支柱／鋼管　φ＝114.3ｔ＝3.2下地　アルルックt=3曲加工

営業内容
開店／1984年７月16日　営業時間／午前９時～午後５時　休日／毎週土　日曜日　経営者／㈱リコー

入口方向をみる　このスペースはパーティーも行なわれるので　壁面収納にはいろいろな設備が組み込まれている

医薬品会社の研修ラウンジ
トラベノール フォーラム

東京都千代田区六番町４全英ビル７階
Phone/03-237-6611

撮影／宮本隆治

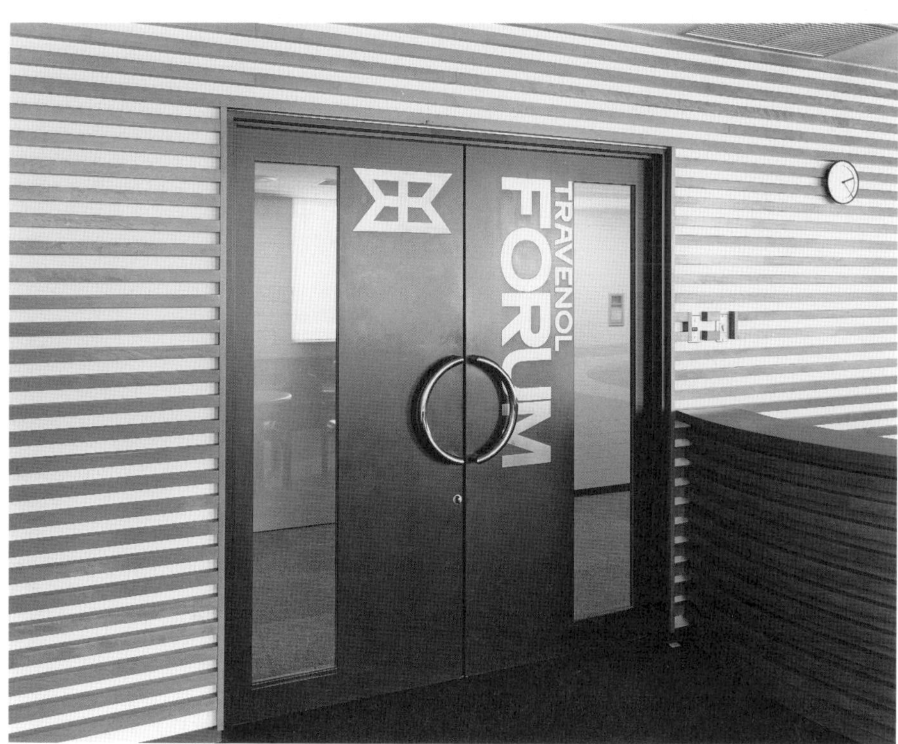

入口廻りをみる

(Photo captions)
Top / The entrance area. Since a party is held at this space, various devices are built into the wall's accommodating area.
Bottom / The entrance area.

書棚　スライドブースをみる　受付カウンターを中心に同心円とした床パターンと　それに沿った家具が配置されている
The bookshelves and slide booth. The floor pattern in concentric alignment with the reception counter, and furniture arranged along it.

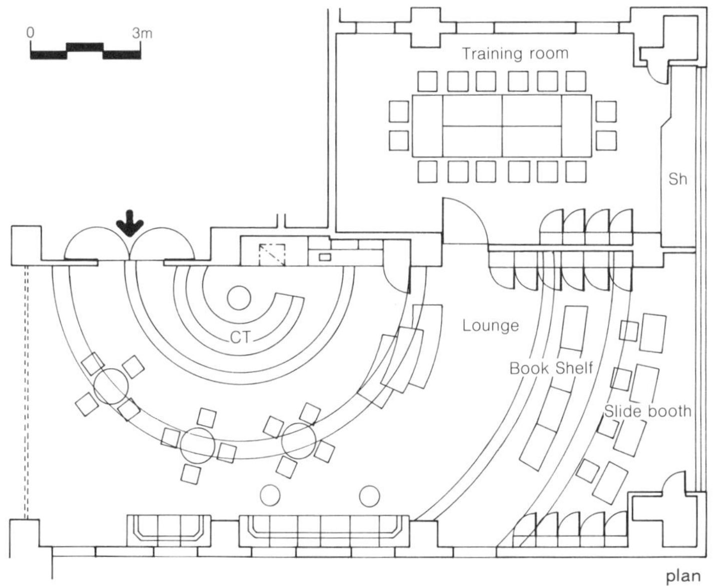

同心円をボギャブラリーとする

このスペースは　医薬品を取り扱うトラベノール㈱の企業コンセプトに沿って　外部の医療機関の人々への情報提供　連携　懇談などのできるスペースを　との意向をうけて設計されたラウンジ スペースである。スペースの性格としては堅苦しさをなくした　よりカジュアルな雰囲気を作り出したいと考え　全体配慮を　入口に配した受付カウンターを中心にした　同心円状の配置とした。この配置パターンは　アイランドカウンターやスライドブース　レファレンスデスクの形を決める上での大きなデザインボキャブラリーとなっている。天井高が通常の事務所と同じで　上下への展開がしづらいため　このように平面的に少しくずしていく方法は有効であったと思う。全体のまとめとしては　桜材の素材感を出すため　ソリッドのリブ材を立面に配して　できるだけ煉付け的なフラットな面材は収納の扉などのみにとどめて　空間に動きが感じられるよう意図した。

〈遠藤精一〉(85-9)

設計／エンドウプランニング　施工／エンドウ総合装備
面積／135.77m²　工期／1985年3月1日～4月1日

Lounge Space TRAVENOL FORUM

Use concentric circle as a vocabulary

Along with the corporate concept of Travenol Co. that is dealing with medical supplies, this space was designed as a lounge space, in reply to the request for providing a space where information may be given to people of outside medical institutes, or you may cooperate, have business talks with them.
In order to remove formality and create a more casual atmosphere, general considerations were given to the concentric circular layout centering sound the reception counter at the entrance. This layout pattern serves as a major design vocabulary in determining the shapes of the island counter, slide booth and reference desk.
Since the ceiling height is same as in an ordinary office and it is difficult to make vertical development, the plane development as made in this case seems to have been effective. As a whole, in order to give as natural a sense of cherry material as possible, solid ribs were arranged vertically and the use of flat surface materials was limited to the accommodating area doors, etc., so that you may feel dynamism in the space.

4, Rokuban-cho, Chiyoda-ku, Tokyo　Phone: 03-237-6611

Design / Seiichi Endo
Area / 135.77 m²

材料仕様
床／繊維床タイル　幅木／ソフト幅木　壁面／PBVP　一部樺材着色拭き取りウレタンペイント塗り　天井／PB & 岩綿吸音貼り　家具／樺材ウレタンクリア塗装

上／左奥廊下に添って設置されたカウンセリングルーム群　右頁下／左奥廊下よりみたカウンセリングルーム

結婚情報センター
ツヴァイ

東京都中央区八重洲2-5-1 八重洲ブックセンター8階　Phone/03-281-7281

撮影／坂東智司

Top / A group of counseling rooms installed along the inner left side corridor.
Right page, bettom / The counseling rooms viewed from the inner left side corridor.

閉鎖的な部分を両立させる

東京駅近くの「八重洲ブックセンター」8階に　大手スーパー「ジャスコ」の100%出資で結婚情報センター「ツヴァイ」がオープンした。「ツヴァイ」とはドイツ語で2（2人）を表しており　人と人との出逢いを提供し　かつ素晴らしい家庭を築いてほしいという事業姿勢がそこに表れているような気がする。

そんなイメージを大切に　基本的ゾーニングを進めていくと　動線的にロビーが重要なポイントになってきた。エントランスとカウンセリングルームの間に位置し　諸々（いろいろ）の意味で　2つのゾーンのクッションになる必要性があった。また意匠の上では　機能的な制約が比較的に少ないため自由度が大きく「ツヴァイ」という組織の象徴的な空間に凝縮することができた。

曲線の壁と円柱を中心に　疑似柱によるサークル状の内側のカコイをつけることにより　このロビーが必要な　閉鎖的な部分と開放的な部分を両立させた。またこのカコイに仕込まれた間接照明とカーペットのパターンにより　“やさしさ　人のつながり”を円形とグリーンのカラースキームで表現できたつもりである。　〈寺本昌志〉(85-4)

設計／メックデザイン インターナショナル　寺本昌志

施工／綜合デザイン　面積／590㎡

工期／1984年12月5日～24日　工費／5000万円

Marriage Information Center ZWEI

Makes closed area compatible with open area

At the 8th floor of "Yaesu Book Center" near Tokyo Station opened the marriage information center "Zwei" fully invested by one of the leading supermarket chains "Jasco." "Zwei" means two (persons) in German, and therein seems to be implied a service attitude towards offering a place for man coming across woman so that they may hopefully build a wonderful family life.

When we proceeded with the basic zoning making much of such image, the lobby gained in importance from the point of view of dynamism. Situated between the entrance and counseling room, the lobby, in various meanings, had to serve as a cushion between the two zones. In respect of design, since the functional restrictions were relatively small, allowing a high degree of freedom, the inside could be condensed to a symbolic space for "Zwei" as an organization.

With the curved wall and column in the center, and surrounded with the inside circular enclosure having quasi-pillars, this lobby could be designed so that the closed area is compatible with the open area. Additionally, by the indirect lighting and carpet pattern set in the enclosure, it was intended to express "gentleness, human relations" through the circular and green color scheme.

2-5-1, Yaesu, Chuo-ku, Tokyo　Phone: 03-281-7281

Design / Masashi Teramoto
Area / 590 m²

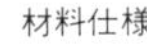

材料仕様

床／タイルカーペット貼り　幅木／堅木h＝75 ＯＰ 艶消し　壁面／ＰＢｔ＝12　寒冷紗パテしごき下地　シグマコート吹付け　天井／既存岩綿吸音板ＶＰ塗り変え　カウンター／カラーコア　円柱／結晶化ガラス

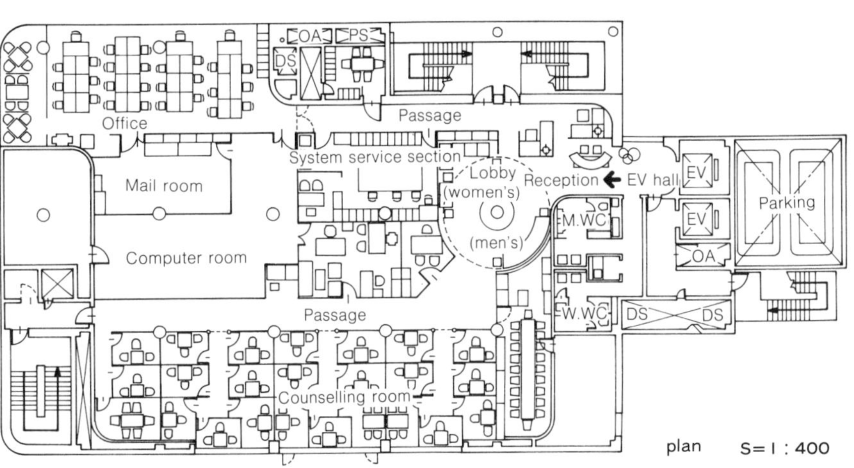

plan　S=1：400

受付カウンターよりロビーをみる　右側が女性用　左側が男性用

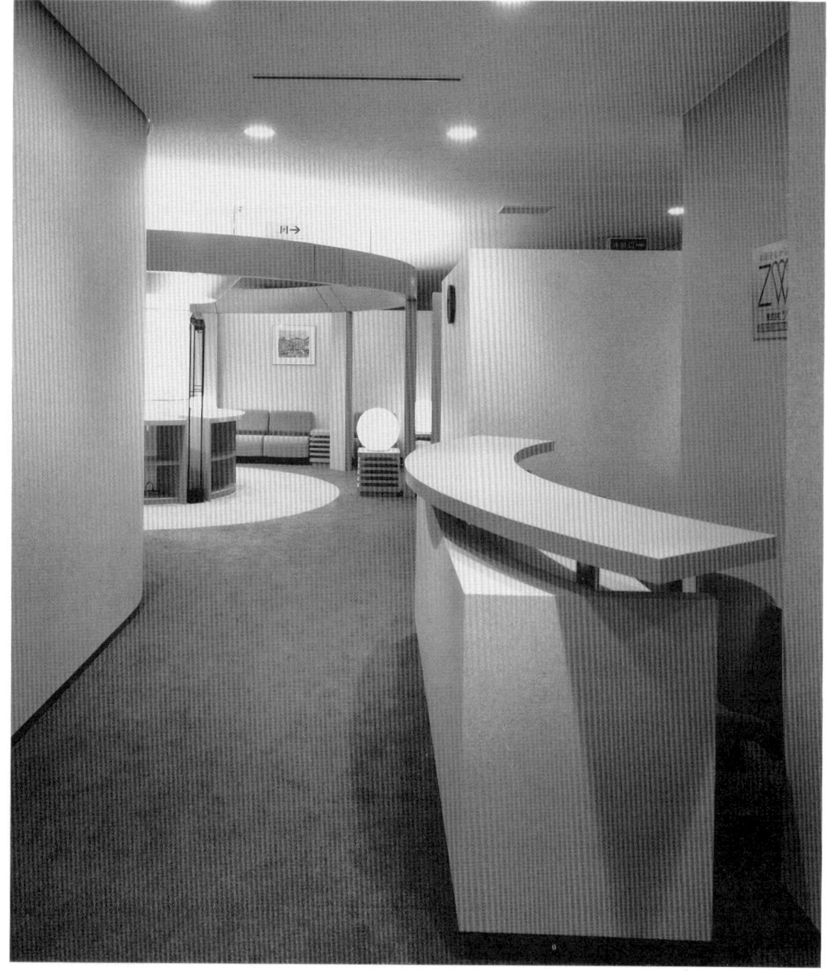

(Photo captions)
Top / The lobbies viewed from the reception counter. The left side is for ladies, and the right side for men.
Bottom / The lobbies viewed from the EV hall through the reception counter.

ＥＶホールより受付カウンターを通してロビーをみる

ファサード

The facade.

オリジナル サイクルショップ
コギー 六本木店

東京都港区六本木6-8-21 ＳＫ六本木ハイム103
Phone/03-423-0094

店内奥の自転車組立スペースをみる

The bicycle assembly space in the inner area.

撮影／狩野正和

入口部より店内全景をみる

The entire scene viewed from the entrance area.

材料仕様

サイン／塩ビパイプ(ネオン内蔵)　床／塩ビ系タイル貼り　幅木／堅木ＳＯＰ仕上　壁面／ＰＢｔ＝12ＧＬ下地寒冷紗パテしごき　ローラー仕上　天井／ＰＢｔ＝12　下地Ｒ面加工寒冷紗パテしごき　ローラー仕上　照明器具／ダウンライト　家具／甲板・大理石　什器／乳白アクリル円柱φ＝300スリムライン３色入

営業内容

開店／1983年７月21日　営業時間／午前11時～午後９時　休日／毎週木曜日　従業員／２人　主な取り扱い商品／オリジナル自転車　部品　アクセサリー　スケートボード　ローラースケート　アウトドア用品　スポーツウエア

店内奥の接客カウンター前より入口方向をみる

The entrance area viewed from the inner guest service counter.

空間全体をサイン的効果で訴求を図る

「コギーショップ」はパーソナリティーを重視し　気軽な遊び心とファッション&ツールなどというように　トータルなサイクルライフの啓蒙　ニューメディアの確立に挑戦する多店舗展開の企画である。

新しい業態の商品構成の内容は　自転車及びパーツを中心にウエア　ローラースケート　スケートボード　アウトドア用品　アクセサリー　小物　など広範囲のため商品同志が相互に関係し　共存し合ったトータルなイメージを空間内に創り出す工夫をした。

動線的にはスクランブル状の動線をとり　どの位置においても商品構成の一部が見られるよう考慮した。空間構成のマテリアルは商品構成のマテリアル(金属～布)とバッティングしないように　タブローキャンバスのファンデーションと考え　ライトグレーにし　大理石のカウンターとRC打放し(COGGEY店名打込み)の間仕切り壁など　できる限りシンプルに構成し　かつ　単調にならないようRの線と面とを配慮し従来のサイクルショップとの差別化を意識した。

また　この空間の中に曖昧な色光をとじ込めフロントと店内という概念をなくし　空間全体がサイン効果を成し　歓楽街の幾重にも重なるイルミネーションの虚像現象を創りだした。

〈山田　晃〉(84-4)

企画／ダイヤ通商㈱コギー事業部

設計／山田　晃＋超工房　有本有一

施工／きこりたち

面積／66m²　工期／1983年6月26日～7月18日

工費／1230万円

Original Cycle Shop COGGEY Roppongi

Pursues the sign effect upon the entire space

With emphasis on personality, "Coggey Shop" is a multi shop chain challenging the enlightenment of total cycle life and establishment of new media, by pursuing the casual spirit of play, fashion & tools, etc.

The product line in the new mode extends widely from bicycles & parts in the main, to wear, roller skates, skate boards, outdoor ware, accessories, and fancy goods. So, it was intended to create a total image within the space in which goods may relate to each other and coexist.

As for dynamic lines, they were arranged to scramble so that you can see part of goods from any position. As for space composition materials, in order to prevent them from batting with goods arrangement materials (metal or cloth), they were regarded as the foundation of tableau canvass using light grey. By using marble for the counter and RC as placed for the partition walls (bearing the name "COGGEY"), the arrangements were as simplified as possible. Additionally, in order to prevent them from becoming monotonous, it was consciously attempted to differentiate this shop from the conventional cycle shops, by taking account of radiused lines and planes. Additionally, by confining vague colored light within this space, the conceptual division between the front and inside was removed so that the space as a whole may produce a sign effect, giving rise to a virtual image phenomenon like illumination in layers at an amusement street.

6-8-21, Roppongi, Minato-ku, Tokyo
Phone: 03-423-0094

Design / Akira Yamada
Area / 66 m²

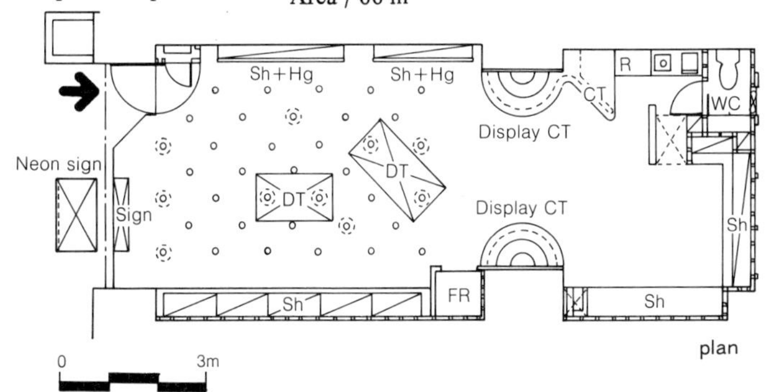

2階より1階売場をみる　The 1st floor selling area viewed from the 2nd floor.

カー＆カーグッズ
オートラマ 磐田店

静岡県磐田市今之浦2-8-2　Phone/05383-5-1251

正面外観をみる　The front appearance.

車輌進入路側外観をみる　The appearance of the vehicle incoming way side.

撮影／西沢　豊

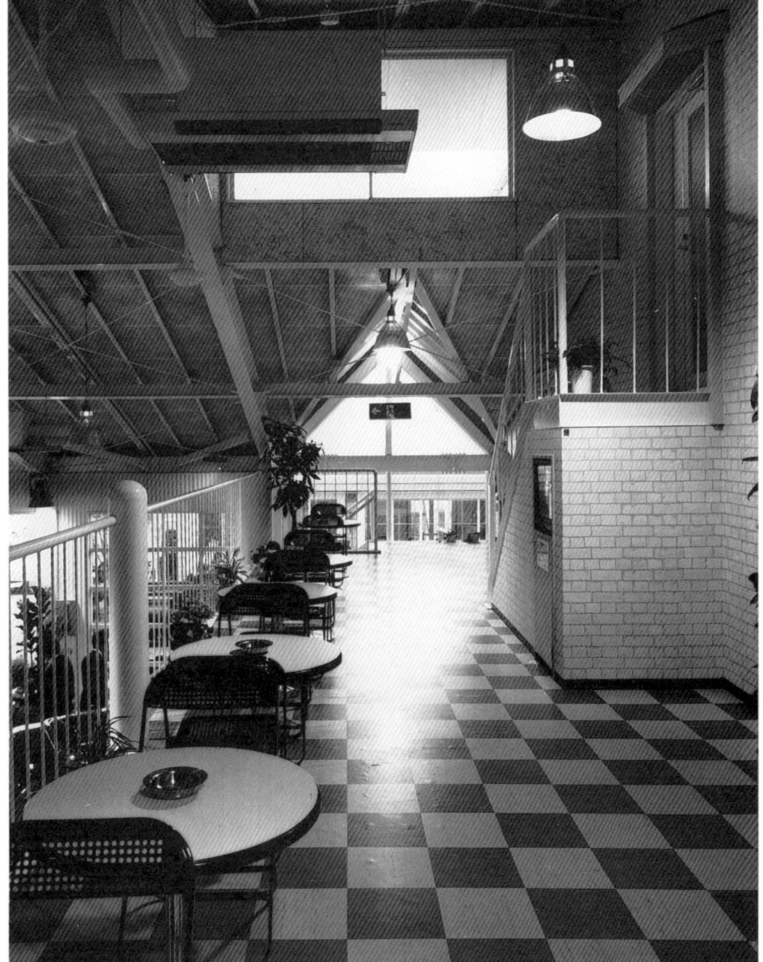

2階商談スペースをみる　The business talk space at the 2nd floor.

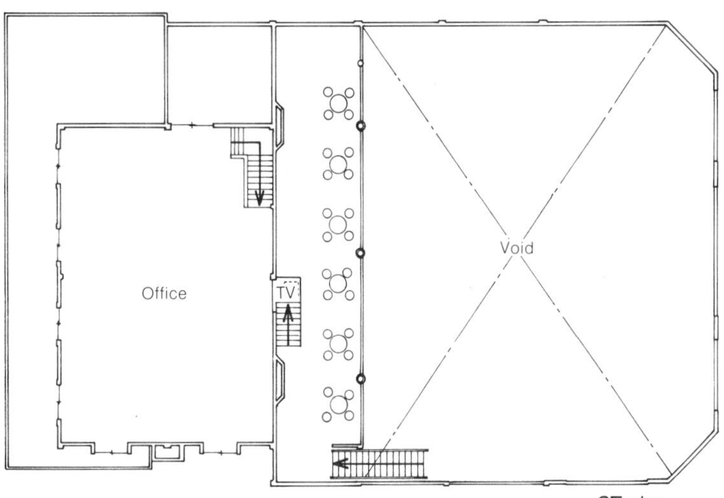

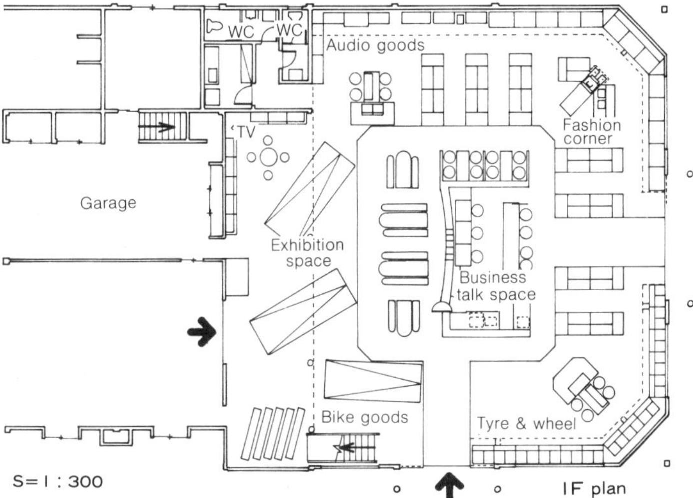

予感を具現化する

モータリゼーションの周辺状況の変化　新たな業態の成立を以前から予感させていました。こうした変化のなかで　新たな業態の開発と提案を具現化したのが「オートラマ磐田店」といえます。この「オートラマ磐田店」は　オフデューティー コミュニケーションを目指した「バーンビレッジ イワタ」のキーステーションとしての機能　内容を持つ施設です。「バーンビレッジ イワタ」はファストフード　カフェテリア　インテリアグッズ　サーフショップ　多目的ホールなどから構成されています。また　アメリカの放送（CNNニュース）を直接受信し　リアルタイムの情報発信も行っています。

この新しい生命体は　自身の中に既にインプットされている増殖指令に基づいて　新たな業態への道を歩んで行くことでしょう。

〈吉川準治〉(86-4)

企画／エンジニアリング　フジ　吉川準治

設計／建築・新貝一級建築設計事務所

　内装・エンジニアリング　フジ　佐藤　憲　マック太田

施工／建築・平野建設　内装・エンジニアリング　フジ

構造・規模／S造　地上2階建

面積／敷地・3035.12m²　建築・512.91m²　床・1階473.16m²　2階186.15m²　合計659.31m²

工期／1985年6月5日～11月1日　工費／9625万円

Car & Car Goods AUTORAMA Iwata

Materialize a presentiment

The changes occurring around the motorization have made us feel a presentiment since a while ago that a new-type shop may come into being. It may be said that "Autorama Iwata" has materialized the development and proposal of a new-type shop. This "Autorama Iwata" is equipped with functions and contents of a key station of "Burn Village Iwata" which is aimed at off-duty communication. "Burn Village Iwata" consists of fast food, cafeteria, interior goods, surf shop, multi-purpose hall, etc. It also receives American broadcasting (CNN) directly, and sending information in real time.

This new living body, according to the multiplication command already inputted in itself, will continue to grow towards a new mode of operation.

2-8-2, Imanoura, Iwata City, Shizuoka Prefecture
Phone: 05383-5-1251

Design / Ken Sato
Area / Site 3035.12 m^2, Building 512.91 m^2,
Floor: 1st floor 473.16 m^2, 2nd floor 186.15 m^2;
Totalling 659.31 m^2

材料仕様

屋根／石綿瓦　外壁／スチール貼り石綿サイディング　外部床／2丁掛けタイル貼り　サイン／杉板OP&ネオン&アクリル内照式看板　床／塩ビ系タイル&合成樹脂系タイル　幅木／ラワンt=150P　壁面／小波スレート貼りEP&古煉瓦タイル貼りEP　天井／木毛セメント板OP　什器／角パイプ&スチールメッシュOP　カウンター／トップ・メラミン化粧板　腰・多彩模様吹付け塗材　商談テーブル／楢合板染色クリア塗装

営業内容

開店／1985年11月3日　営業時間／午前10時～午後8時　休日／毎週水曜日　経営者／㈱オートラマバーン　鈴木順一　従業員／12人　主な取り扱い商品／日本フォード社　新車　中古車　車用品全般　バイク　バイク用品

カラフルな自動車　バイクに呼応する中央商談カウンターの化粧柱　梁を見上げる
Looking up at the decoration pillars and beams at the central business talk counter corresponding to the colorful automobiles and bicycles.

入口より店内をみる

The inside viewed from the entrance.

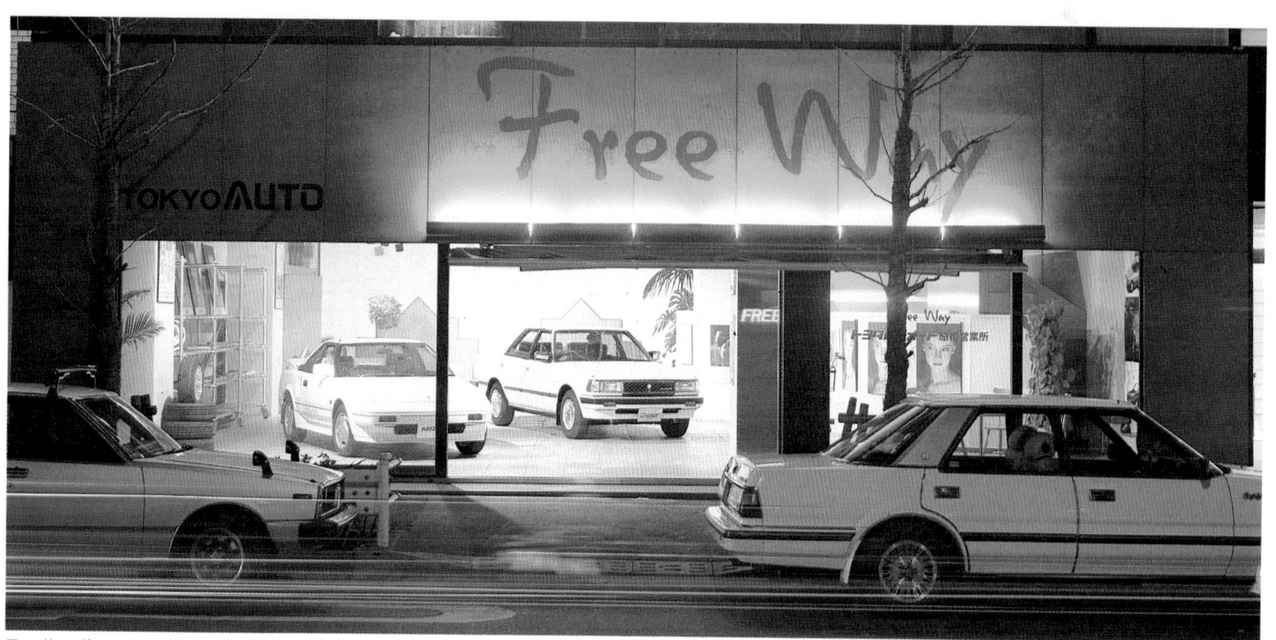

ファサード

The facade.

ショールーム

フリーウェイ トヨタ東京オート原宿営業所

東京都渋谷区神宮前3-25-14　Phone/03-478-6611

撮影／北田英治

店内奥の商談コーナーをみる

The business talk corner at the inner part.

材料仕様

ゲート／亜鉛合金板パネル　開口部／アルミサッシ　床／プレキャスト　コンクリート 600×400　家具／ベンチ&椅子・楢材着色ポリウレタン艶消しクリア仕上　テーブル・天板：鉄板 t＝15 ＯＰ 脚：コンクリート打放し　展示用曲面壁／表側・プラスター仕上　裏側・コルク貼り　その他／72インチビデオスクリーン　システム

営業内容

開店／1984年11月27日　営業時間／午前9時～午後7時　休日／なし　経営者／トヨタ東京オート㈱　従業員／8人　主な取扱商品／トヨタ車：チェイサー　エムアール2 スプリンター　スターレット　ライトエースなど

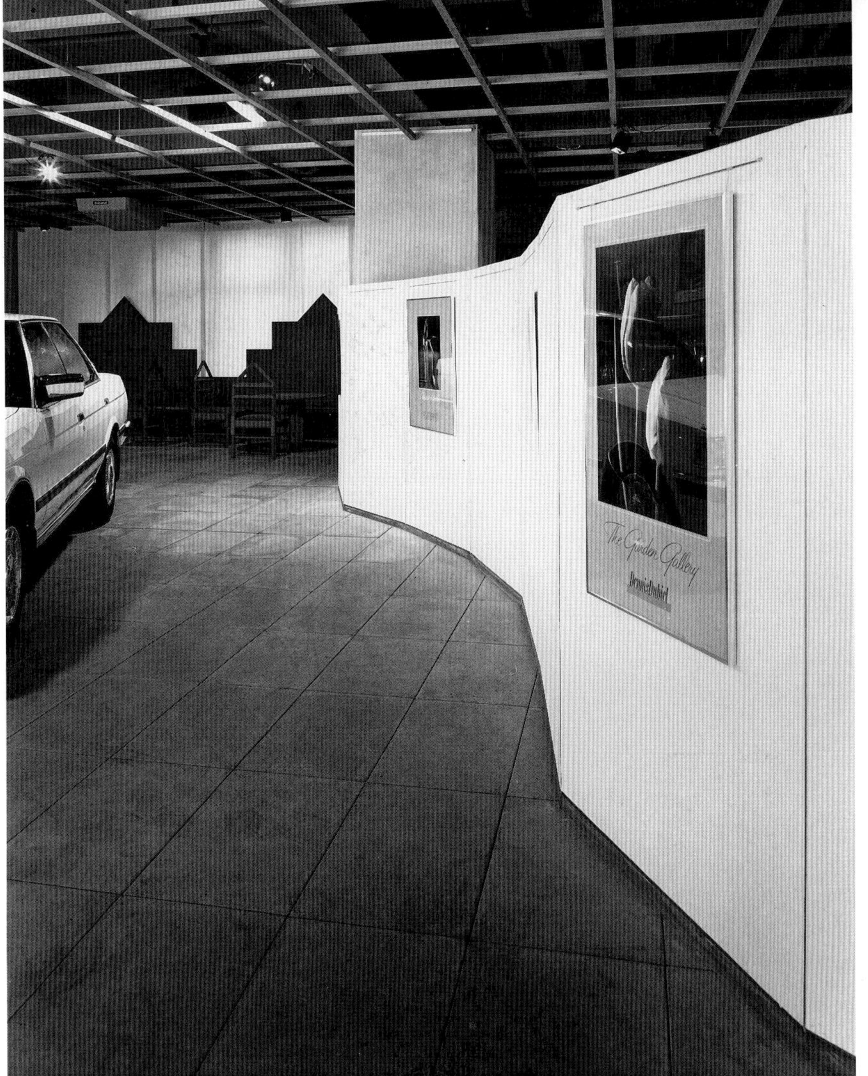

シヨールームと事務スペースのパーティションをみる　壁面はギャラリーに開放
The partition between the showroom and office space. The wall surface is open to the gallery.

車を中心としたギャラリー スペース

「フリーウェイ」は原宿の明治通り沿いにあり　隠田神社から青山(外苑前)に至る道筋に至る道筋に入る少し手前に位置する。

「フリーウェイ」の役割は　単に車のショールームとしてのみでなく　この立地特性を先取りすることにある。それゆえ私達は　ファッション情報発信拠点としての　未完のスタジオづくりを目指した。その最初の目標は　車の持つ本質的な美しさを損なうことのないスペースをということである。ショールームを構成しているものは　あくまで付属的なものにすぎず　中心になるのは車であり　それを取り囲むギャラリー(街の人々)でありたい。

床や壁の質感は　車がそこに存在するのを不自由にしてはならない。天井もいわゆる“天井面”という仕切りは存在させず　マルチパーパスの木材を交差させ　必要な場所に照明機材を取り付けた。伊藤清忠氏デザインのグレーに着色された大型ベンチは　商談のためのコーナーという重要な用途を持っているが　椅子だから座るという目的のみではなく　車の背景としての街のシルエットでもあり　大型ビデオスクリーンのためのフレーミングでもある。　〈宮城　睦十岡本　紘〉(85-6)

設計／嶋田宮城建築設計事務所　宮城　睦
協力／伊藤清忠(家具)
施工／双葉工業　面積／178.34m²
工期／1984年10月15日～11月27日

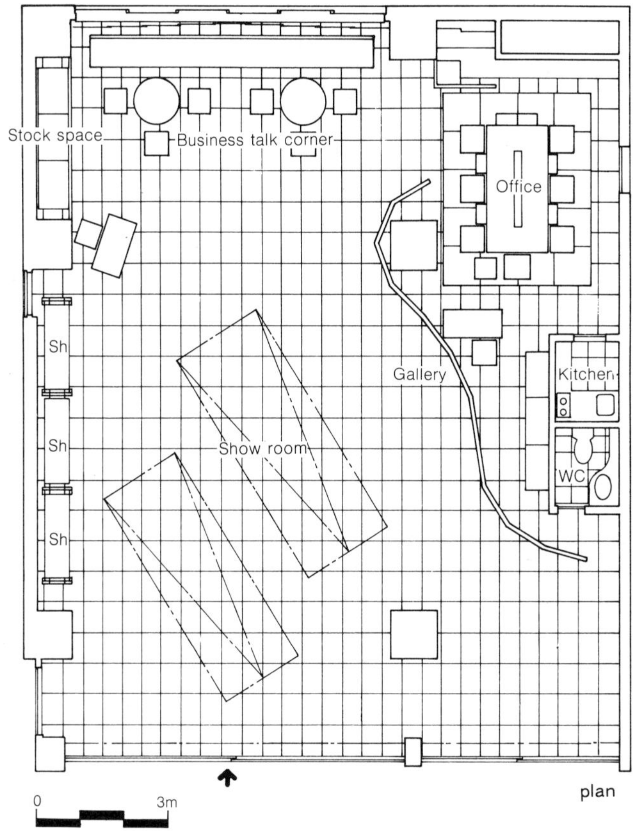

Car Showroom FREE WAY

A gallery space mainly for cars

"Free Way" stands along Meiji Street, Harajuku, a little in your side of the course leading from Onda Shrine to Aoyama (Gaienmae).

The role of "Free Way" lies not merely in serving as a car showroom, but also in grasping the locational characteristics of this area ahead of the times. Thus, we aimed at creating an unfinished studio as a center that sends fashion information. The primary objective was to secure a space not damaging the intrinsic beauty of cars. The elements constituting the showroom are basically accessories – cars and their gallery (people) should hopefully be in the main. The walls and floor should not have a sense of quality that makes the presence of cars unnatural. As for the ceiling, too, we have removed the partition – the so-called "ceiling cover." Instead, we arranged multi-purpose lumbers to intersect with each other, and installed lighting apparatuses where necessary.

A large grey-colored bench, designed by Mr. K. Itoh, has an important use – a corner for business talks – but its purpose is not simply for sitting but it also serves as a silhouette as the background of cars, and as a framing for a large video screen.

3-25-14, Jingu-mae, Shibuya-ku, Tokyo
Phone: 03-478-6611

Design / Mutsumi Miyagi
Area / 178.34 m²

インフォメーション前の9面マルチTVをみる

9-set multi TV in front of the information corner.

カー ショールーム
マツダロータリー 御堂筋

大阪市南区八幡町28 第3松豊ビル Phone/06-212-4117

撮影／山田誠良

パブリックスペースより店内全景をみる

The entire inside scene viewed from the public space.

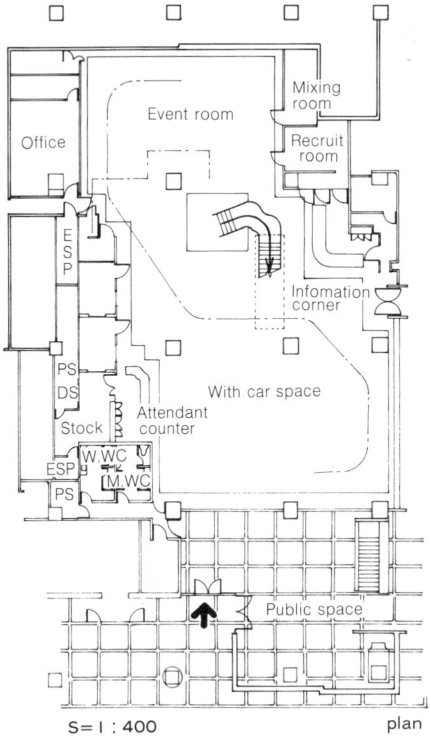

Mixing room
Event room
Office
Recruit room
ESP
Infomation corner
PS
DS
With car space
Attendant counter
Stock
W.WC
ESP
M.WC
PS
Public space
S=1 : 400
plan

上 下／アテンダント カウンターバックに写し出されたマルチイメージ

(Photo captions)
Top, bottom / Multi images reflected on the attendant counter back.

ファサード

The facade.

光と映像のショールーム

この「マツダローリー御堂筋」のスペース全体の構成は"パブリック"を意図している。御堂筋の歩道の隣接したスペースは　通行者に対するさまざまなサービス装置が季節とともに変化する。(アイスクリーム 花屋 カフェ…) 奥まったスペースを主体に各種イベントやシンポジウム　カルチャー教室など　マルチ パーパスに展開されるイベントが　タイムリーに企画される。車の展示は　スポーツやレジャーなどといった生活感と一体化した展示とし　もっとも多くても4台程度という　従来型の車メーカー ショールームとは一味違う展示を意図している。床は木を主体とした　石とのコンプレックスの構成　壁面のスチールパネルの冷たさをやわらげている。9台のマルチビデオ　スクリーンがスペースの演出に対応して　スペース全体をカバーする天井面のレールをモノレール状に自走する。夜間はスペース全体の壁面スチールパネルをスクリーンにして　15台のプロジェクターから種々の環境映像が自動的に流れ出す。床面に埋め込まれた"エアポートライト"が　これに同調して　またたきを始める。

〈秋山茂樹／乃村工芸社〉(86-12)

多目的スペースに対応する9面マルチTV

天吊りのレール上を動くマルチビジョンシステムを採用したのは　ショールーム自体が多目的のものであり　床にレールを走らせるとどうしてもマルチビジョンのボリュームがかさみ　デザイン的にも目障りですし展示物の障害にもなるからです。マルチテレビはできるだけ軽くなるようにスケルトン構造にしたのですが　それでも1.2tほどあります。貸ビルで　建築工事が7割方進んだところから　われわれが関与し始めたので　この重量には多少の不安が残りましたが　問題なく完成しました。6ヵ所に映像信号用のコネクターがあり　モーターでレール上をそこまで移動させ　マルチテレビのケーブルを接続します。マルチテレビ本体も180°回転します。FM電波で信号を送ることも考えたのですが　予算上の問題から(FMだと約3000万円 実施方式だと約800万円)この方法に落ち着きました。

〈山崎尚人／乃村工芸社・文責編集部〉(86-12)

設計／田中一光デザイン室　乃村工芸社
協力／エムジーエス(照明) 田中一光デザイン室(グラフィック)
施工／乃村工芸社　面積／930㎡
工期／1986年1月15日～5月3日　工費／5億円

Car Showroom MAZDA ROTARY Midosuji

A showroom with light & image

The overall configuration of this "Mazda Rotary Midosuji" space is aimed at "public." At the space adjacent to the pavement of Midosuji Street, various pedestrian service devices change with season (ice cream, flower shop, café, etc.). With the inner space in the main, various events are timely held, including various symposiums and culture schools. Cars are displayed in an atmosphere of sports or leisure where cars are used daily. Thus, only 4 cars are displayed at most, differentiating this showroom from the conventional types of car makers' showrooms. The floor mainly consists of wood, accented with stone, softening the coolness of steel panel walls. The multi video (9 sets) screen runs along the rail on the ceiling covering the entire space, responding to the space presentation. At night, over the wall surface steel panels of the entire space as the screen, various environmental images automatically come out from 15 units of projector. "Airport lights" buried in the floor begin twinkling aligning with them.

28, Hachiman-cho, Minami-ku, Osaka City　Phone: 06-212-4117

Design / Ikko Tanaka
Area / 930 m^2

材料仕様

床／単層フローリング　御影石本磨き及びバーナー仕上　幅木／御影石本磨き　壁面／鋼板メラミン焼付け塗装　天井／岩綿吸音板及びスチールメッシュ　照明器具／ダイクロスポット　家具／モビリア　フィリッツハンセン　家具・什器／ステンレス黒染め及び大理石

営業内容

開店／1986年5月10日　営業時間／午前11時～午後7時　休日／なし　運営管理／㈱アドインターナショナル スタッフ／9人

PART 3 リビング Living

中央階段前にディスプレイされたグローブ ソファ(L180×H145×D114cm)と照明器具(152×305cm)
The globe sofa (L180 x H145 x D114 cm) and lighting apparatus (152 x 305 cm) displayed in front of the central staircase.

インテリア グッズ シンク ビッグ

東京都渋谷区渋谷2-9-9 ローズベイ青山ビル1階 Phone/03-797-0499

撮影/平沢 敞

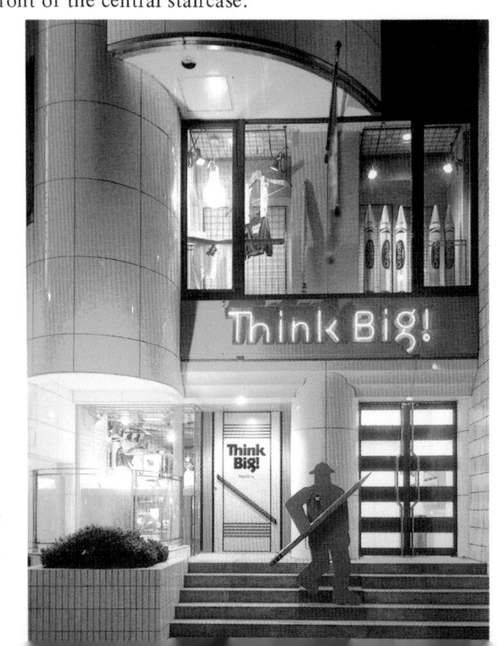

ファサード
The facade.

Crayola
CRAYON
These are miniature models of "Think Big"
接客コーナー兼ねたディスプレイスペースをみる　歯ブラシH145cm　クレヨンH142cm
The display space also serving as a guest service corner. A toothbrush (145 cm), and a crayon (142 cm).

"モノ"との出会いの場

キャンベルスープの缶を大きく表現することによって　人間が本来大きな物に対する憧れと欲望をポップアートの世界で初めて表現した　アメリカを代表するアーチスト・アンディ ウォーホール。彼は　人々の心の中に大きさの持つ意味を訴え　感動を与え　人気を得た。そして　アートの世界の経過の中から２人のアーチストによって「シンク ビッグ」のでっかい商品が　ニューヨーク・ソーホーで誕生した。
ニューヨーク・ソーホー地区の倉庫街。そこは作品と語り合える場　モノと出合える場として　アーチストたちのアトリエが　自然発生的に集まった地域であり　建築物の特性を活かし　作品と空間の調和を創り上げ　いつしか表現の場として脚光をあびてきた。こうした環境の中から生れた「シンク ビッグ」のものたちは　ただ単に物を大きくしただけではなく　手に持てるほどの大きさ　重さであり　モノを持つ満足感と喜び　そして温かさを与えてくれるモノたちである。
こうした「シンク ビッグ」の商品との出合いの場として　設計上のポイントになったのは　基調色が白と黒ということから　モノトーンをベースにしたプレーンな空間設定であり　色彩　素材計画であった。また　ファサードのデザインは「シンク ビッグ」そのものをメッセージとして使える接点であり　重要なポイントとなった。　〈柳沢武彦〉(86-4)

設計／柳沢武彦　施工／乃村工芸社商業施設開発事業部　藤縄充昭
面積／１階・104㎡　２階・104㎡　合計208㎡
工期／1985年10月１日～11月１日　工費／3200万円

Interior Goods THINK BIG

A place where you can encounter "things"
Andy Wolhaul, an artist representative of America, who, for the first time in the world of pop art, expressed man's intrinsic longing and desire for big things, by expressing Gambel soup's can massively. He created an appeal to the meaning of bigness, thus moving people and gaining popularity. Thus, in the changing course of the world of art, "Think Big," with big goods, was brought into being by two artists in So·Ho, New York.
A warehouse street in So·Ho. There, as a place where you can encounter "things," and talk with artistic pieces of work, artists' ateliers have gathered naturally. By effectively utilizing the features buildings, this space has been harmonized with the pieces of artistic work, eventually being spotlighted as a place for expression. The things at "Think Big," which were born in these circumstances, are not mere enlarged ones, but can be grasped by your hands, and are heavy, giving you a pleasure of possession and warmth.
In creating such a place for encountering goods of "Think Big," design, coloring and material plans were intended to setting a plane, monotonous space by using black & white as the basic tone. The facade was designed by using the very "Think Big" as a message, thus serving as an important point of contact.

2-9-9, Shibuya, Shibuya-ku, Tokyo　Phone: 03-797-0499

Design / Takehiko Yanagisawa
Area / 1st floor 104 m^2, 2nd floor 104 m^2; Totalling 208 m^2

奥のディスプレイ壁をみる　鉛筆H177cm　レコードΦ86cm

The display wall at the back. A pencil (177 cm), and a record (φ86 cm).

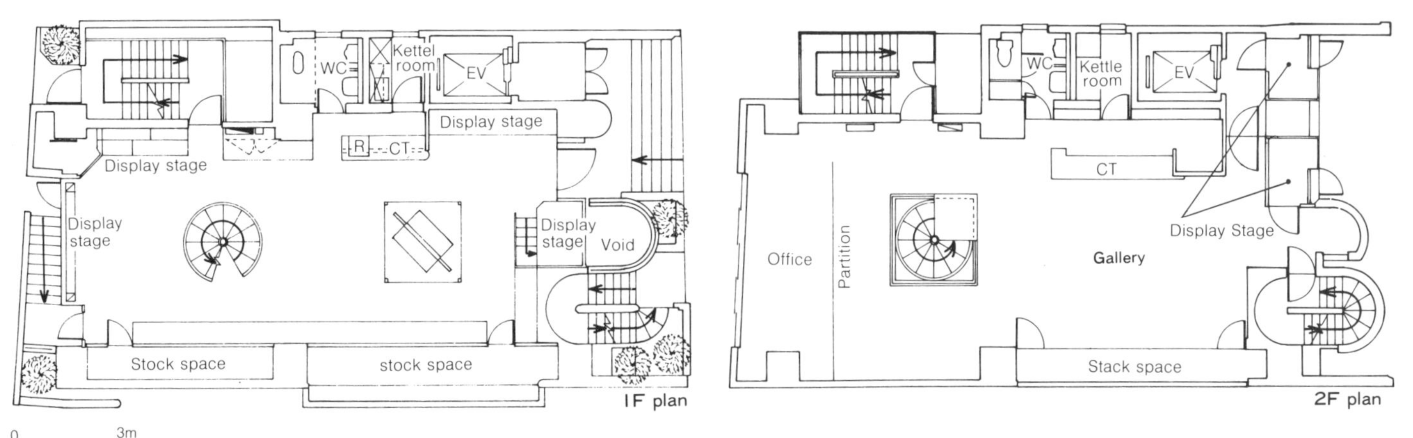

材料仕様

外壁／スチールメラミン焼付塗装　外部床／大理石貼り　サイン／スチールメラミン焼付塗装　チャンネル文字　ネオン管入り　床／楢フローリング貼り　一部集成材貼り　天井／ＰＢ下地　寒冷紗パテしごきＶＰ塗装　パイプ25×40メラミン焼付塗装　什器／メラミン焼付塗装

営業内容

開店／1985年11月14日　営業時間／午前10時30分～午後７時30分　休日／なし　経営者／㈱新星　従業員／サービス５人　主な取り扱い商品／ベルトウォッチ２万6000　クレヨン１万4000　マティーニグラス２万　レコード１万6000　鉛筆３万6000　歯ブラシ５万6000～６万

ハウス ウェア モミの木

仙台市大和町4-2-15 Phone/022-237-5656

1/2の勾配天井と中２階を設け展示品と空間との調和を図る

今までの"物"と"工事"だけではなく ユーザーとの対話や生活情報提供を図り トータルな形での増改築需要に対応しようという目的で 既存建物の手前に新築した。

建築面では ほぼ正方形に近い形態 あまりにもおさまりすぎたワクは かえって窮屈な感があるので 正方形を崩すことから始めた。まずアプローチ部に 半円形を突き出した。次に 周りの環境とのバランスを考えると２層にした。その結果 店内には新たな空間が出現した。

展示品が 空間の大きさに負けないよう 高い天井は1/2勾配天井とし 床面積の1/4に中２階を設ける(このスペースはイベントスペースとして利用) ことで縦への変化を与えた。

また 外から内 内より外へのアプローチとして天井より２種類のトップライフを設けることで 光の変化も採り入れ ここち良い空間を演出した。

〈小磯勝則／インチーム〉(86-11)

Housewares Shop MOMINOKI

½ incline ceiling and mezzanine create a space harmonizing with articles displayed

In order to go beyond the conventional scope of "thing" and "work," this building was constructed in front of the existing building, with a view of offering a place for conversation with users and living information, and thereby meeting the needs for extension/rebuilding in a total manner.

Structurally, it is almost square. However, since too much adherence to exact layout and framing makes us feel stiff, we set about collapsing the square pattern. First, we provided a semicircular projection at the approach area. Then, in view of a balance with the surrounding environment, we provided two layers, thus bringing a new inside space into being.

In order to prevent articles displayed from being overwhelmed by the expanse of space, the high ceiling is designed with a ½ incline, and a mezzanine (used as an event space) was installed over ¼ of floor space, thereby giving a longitudinal accent.

Additionally, by providing two types of top light from the ceiling as an approach from outside to inside and from inside to outside, a variation of light was introduced, thus producing a comfortable space.

4-2-15, Yamato-cho, Sendai City
Phone: 022-237-5656

Design / Katsunori Koiso
Area / Site 2547.84 m^2, Building 156 m^2,
Floor: 1st floor 148 m^2, 2nd floor 37 m^2;
Totalling 185 m^2

撮影／平沢 敞

入口よりキッチン ダイニングをみる
The kitchen and dining room viewed from the entrance.

ファサード
The facade.

ファブリケーションコーナーよりラルフローレンコーナーをみる　住宅風のつくりの中でハウスウェアを陳列している
Ralph Lauren corner viewed from the fabrication corner. House ware is displayed in a residential atmosphere.

2階の商談　イベントスペースをみる

The commodity/event space at the 2nd floor.

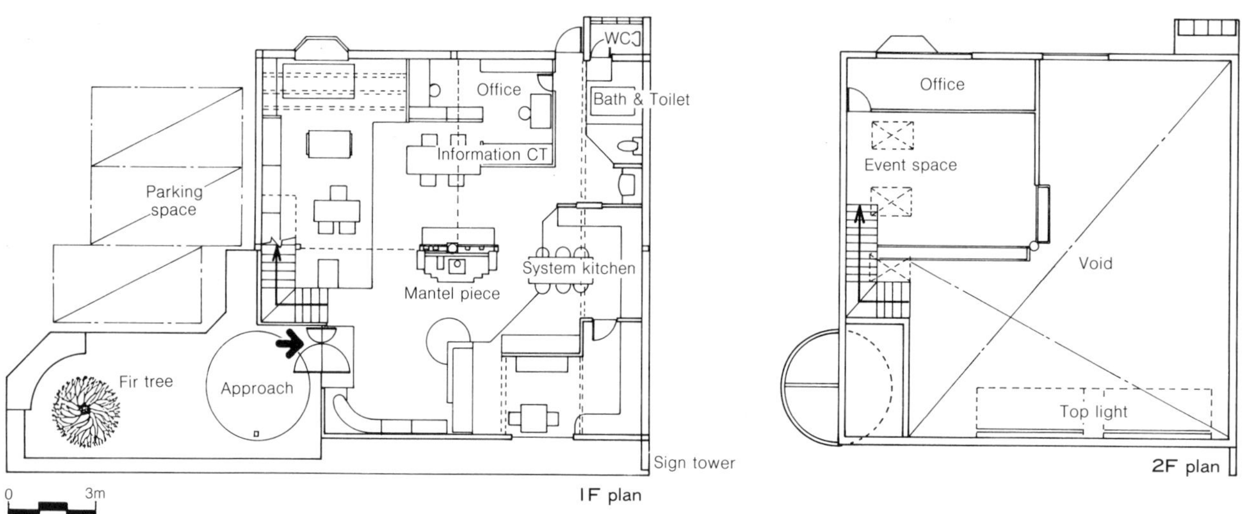

材料仕様

屋根／耐久性フッソ樹脂塗装鋼板　外壁／ＡＬＣ板吹付け塗装　外部床／炻器質タイル貼り　インターロッキングブロック敷き　サイン／スチール板にスコッチカルフィルム貼り　ネオン管内蔵　床／楢フローリング貼り　カーペットタイル貼り　Ｐタイル貼り450角 ラミネートビニールフローリング貼り　幅木及び腰／米松及びタモ材染木ＣＬ　壁面／ＰＢｔ＝12下地クロス貼り　天井／ＰＢｔ＝12下地クロス貼り　一部ルーフウインド　照明器具／ＨＩＤ　混合ランプ　家具及び什器／米松及びタモ材染木ＣＬ　ポリウレタン合板　カウンター／タモ材板目時代仕上げ　テーブル／大理石

営業内容

開店／1986年７月12日　営業時間／午前10時～午後６時　休日／毎週火曜日　経営者／ゴロク建材㈱　主な取り扱い商品／ラルフローレンハウスウエアホームファニシング　ファブリケーションファブリック

正面外観をみる

The front appearance.

インテリア プラザ キス(KISS)

松山市畑寺3-11-31　Phone/0899-43-7164

撮影／山田誠良

1階奥のＷＣ前より展示スペース全景をみる

The entire display space viewed from WC at the inner part of the 1st floor.

1階奥のコーディネート コーナーをみる

The coordination corner at the inner part of 1st floor.

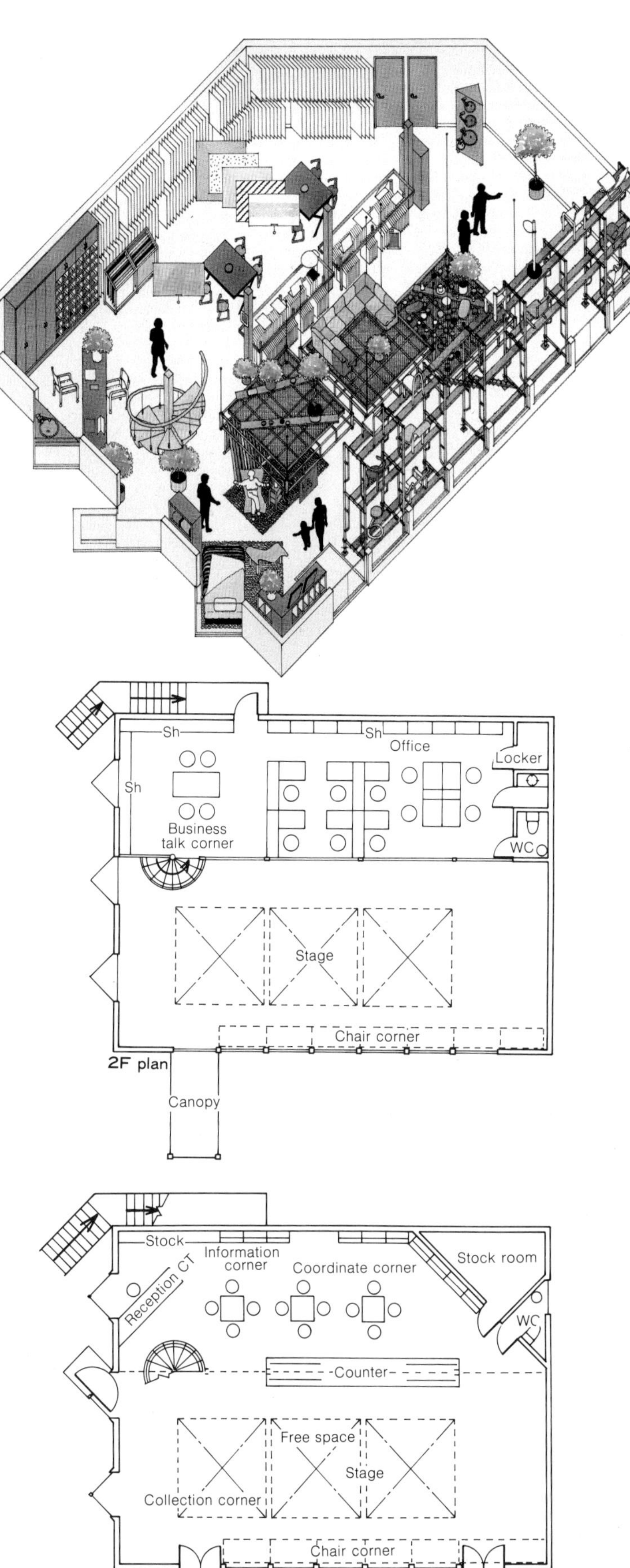

畳工場を再生したハイテックで可変的なインテリアショップ

「キス」はKoeki Information Secretary Serviceの略で 松山市の郊外に位置し コーエキ㈱が母体となっている。

30坪ほどのショールームには カーテン カーペット 壁紙 建材などサンプルが 2000点近く集められ 壁面には50脚近くのチェアが並んでいる。

50坪のフリースペースでは 商品や素材も ひとつの情報として常に新商品 新素材をプレゼンテーションしたり 講演会や各種イベントを通じてデザイナーの良きパートナーとして役割を果たしている。

今までのように業種 業態 アイテムにとらわれず 空間を構成する素材やパーツの知識や情報を積極的に集め 整理して提供することが ユーザーにとってもプラスになるという認識の上で 運営されている。

建物は 畳工場を再生したもので 高さを活かして 様々なイベントを行うため 3.2m²角の舞台用照明を組み込んだステージが 自在の高さで 固定できるようになっている。

チェアコレクションのディスプレイ台も 建築の足場を使用し 移動 追加が可能となっている。 〈原川公一〉(85-8)

設計／フジエテキスタイル 原川公一
施工／建築・大二建設＋イヨ重建 内装・コーエキ
面積／敷地・600m² 建築・266.66m² 床・1階266.66m² 2階100m² 合計366.66m²
工期／1984年9月11日～10月15日 工費／2770万円

Interior Plaza KISS

A high-tech, variable interior shop born by rebuilding a Japanese mat factory

An abbreviation of Koeki Information Secretary Service, and stemming from Koeki Co., Ltd., "KISS" is situated in the suburbs of Matsuyama City.

At the showroom about 97 m² wide, nearly 2,000 sample pieces of curtain, carpet, wall paper, building material, etc. are displayed, and there are nearly 50 chairs on the wall.

At the free space (162 m²), goods and materials are always displayed as a kind of information, and presentation of new products and materials is made, while various events, including a lecture meeting, are held, thus serving as a good partner of designers.

Differing from the conventional display space which has been apt to be limited to specific type of business, mode of operation and items, this space is managed according to the policy that it will be beneficial also to users, if we positively collect information or knowledge of materials and parts that constitute the display space, and pigeonhole and supply it to users.

The building was born by rebuilding a Japanese mat factory. By utilizing the height, a moving stage with built-in 3.2 x 3.2 m square lighting is designed so that it can be fixed at any desired level.

The chair collection display stand can be moved or extended by means of the building scaffold.

3-11-31, Hatadera, Matsuyama City
Phone: 0899-43-7164

Design / Koichi Harakawa
Area / Site 600 m², Building 266.66 m²,
Floor: 1st floor 266.66 m², 2nd floor 100 m²;
Totalling 366.66 m²

材料仕様
屋根／石綿セメント 外壁／木片セメント 外部床／砂利敷き 一部モルタル鏝押え サイン／スチールメラミン焼付けネオン入り 床／モルタル鏝押え 目地1800×1800ピッチ 屋根及び天井／木毛セメント板 照明器具／投光器 舞台用スポット 家具／椐合板ラッカー塗装 昇降ステージ／スチールパイプフレーム金網張りメラミン焼付け ジャンボカウンター／トップ・腐食ガラス 脚・スチールメラミン焼付け

営業内容
開店／1984年10月15日 営業時間／午前10時～午後7時 休日／毎週水曜日 経営者／コーエキ㈱・明関安雄 従業員／16人 客単価(持ち帰り商品)／5000～3万円 主な取り扱い商品／素材・フジエテキスタイル 川島織物 ワコール 家具・パルッコ カルテル カッシーナ イデー その他内装工事全般

プラスチック製品
プラスチックプラザギンザ

東京都中央区銀座4-12-18 日章興産ビル1階
Phone／03-546-0336

古い構造を先かし　シックなカラーを使用
この店は　店名が示すとおりプラスチック素材の商品群を扱うスペシャリティショップで“プラスチックで生活のすべてを考える”をテーマにしている。
ライフスタイルのあらゆる場面に登場する　これらプラスチック商品は　海外商品の構成比を70％とする約3000のアイテム。この素材のみを扱う店としては　世界的にも大変ユニークなものである。
店舗設計としては　こうしたユニークな性格を際立たせるために“ベーシック　オーセンティック”をデザイン　コンセプトとした。店内は　古い構造を生かし　コンセプトにぴったりのテーマカラー・インディゴブルーとグレーを基調にシックな雰囲気にまとめ　外装もグレーシックがよく似合うように　ギリシャ産の白い大理石とした。　〈松風正幸〉(86-4)
設計／松風正幸　安東早苗　施工／商工美術
面積／137.1㎡
工期／1985年7月1日〜8月31日

Plastic Goods Shop
PLASTIC PLAZA GINZA

Use chic colors to match the old structure
As the name suggests, this shop is specializing in product lines of plastic materials, pursuing the theme "think about every aspect of living through plastic."
These plastic goods appear in every life-style scene. Displayed here are about 3,000 items, with about 70% occupied by overseas goods. Specializing in plastic goods, this shop is very unique even in the world as a whole.
In order to accentuate the uniqueness, the shop design employed "basic, authentic" as its concept. As for the interior, in order to match with the old structure, we created a chic atmosphere using the theme colors – indigo blue and grey – as the basic tone, just fitting the concept. The exterior was also finished with white Greek marble so that it matches well with the chic grey color.

4-12-18, Ginza, Chuo-ku, Tokyo
Phone: 03-546-0336

Design / Masayuki Matsukaze
Area / 137.1 m^2

撮影／北田英治

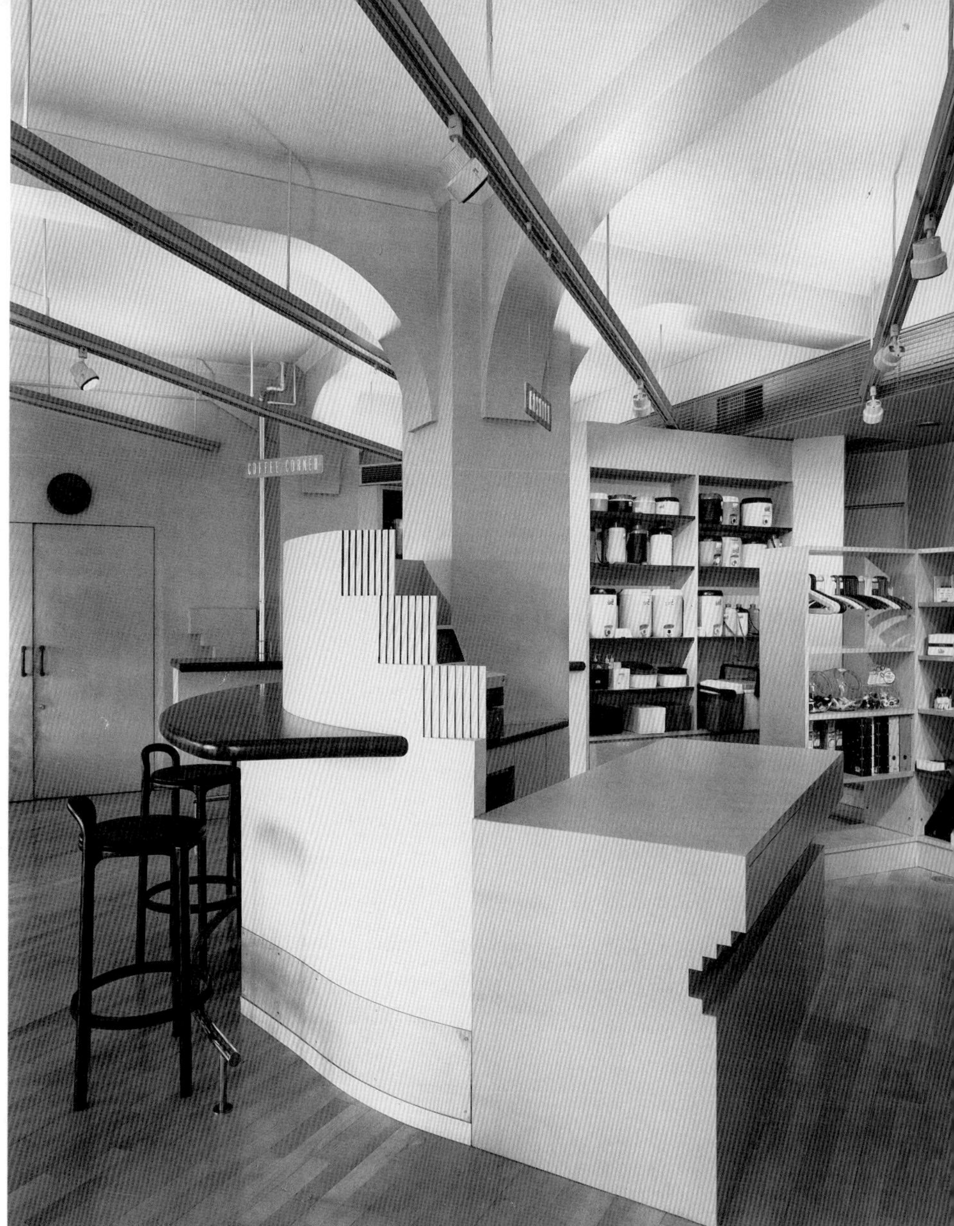

喫茶スペースとサービスカウンターをみる　The tea house space and service counter in the left side.

ファサード　The facade.

右奥より店内をみる　天井はもとの構造を生かし　特注のダクトライトシステムを使用

The inside viewed from the inner right side. The ceiling employs a special ordered duct light system by utilizing the former structure.

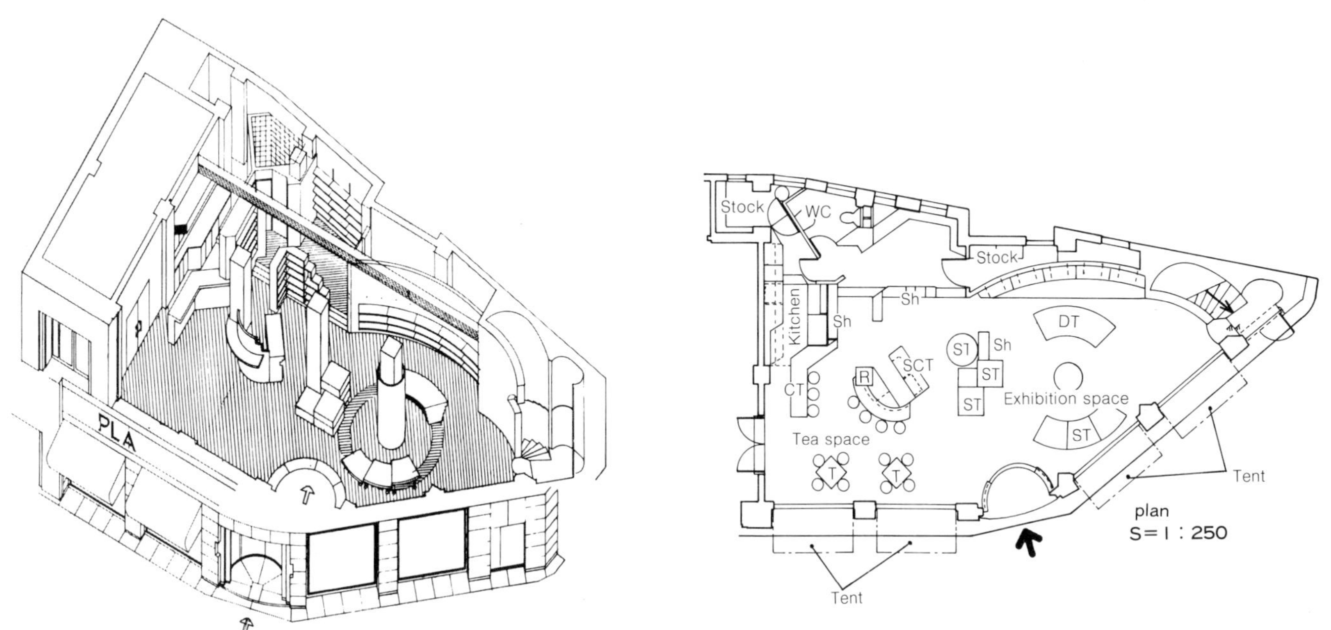

材料仕様

外壁／ギリシャ産白理石水磨き仕上げ　外部床／黒御影石ジェットバーナー仕上げ　サイン／アクリル内部照明　床及び幅木／フローリング貼り　エントランス・黒御影石水磨き＋本磨き仕上げ　天井／プラスター下地ＶＰ　照明器具／ダクトライト特注システム　家具／木製　一部メラミン単板貼り

営業内容

開店／1985年９月27日　営業時間／午前10時～午後８時　休日／毎週水曜日　経営者／アポロサービス㈱　従業員／正社員３人　アルバイト４人　合計７人　客席数(喫茶)／15席　客単価(喫茶)／300円　主な取り扱い商品／プラスチック製品及びその複合製品20～30万　カルテル社(伊)　マーバデザイン社(西独)　クラウンコーニング社(米)　レデ グッチーニ社(伊)　ボバム社(デンマーク)　ヘラー社(米)　ゲディー社(伊)　他　主なメニュー(喫茶)／コーヒー　紅茶　ジュース各300　シンビーノ350　ミルク250

店内より見返す　構造体と微妙なズレをもった柱や梁がイリュージョンを生む
Looked back from inside the shop. The pillars and beams having delicate gaps from the structure give rise to illusions.

エプロン＆ハウスウェア
アヤ

京都市中京区高倉通り御池上ル柊町571　Phone/075-221-2952

撮影／渡部　渡

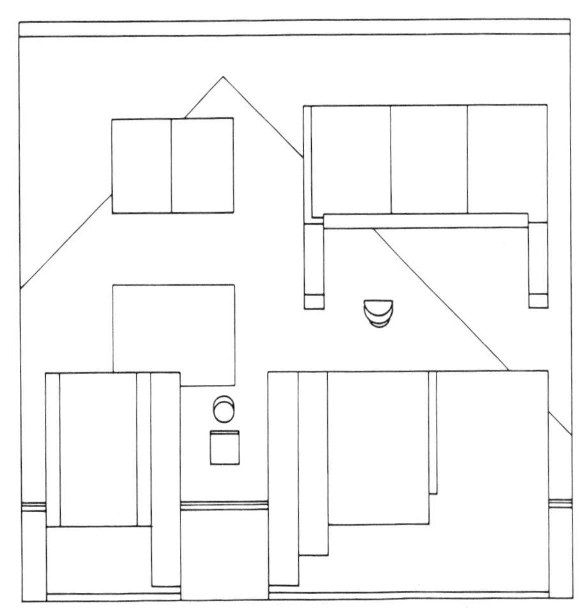

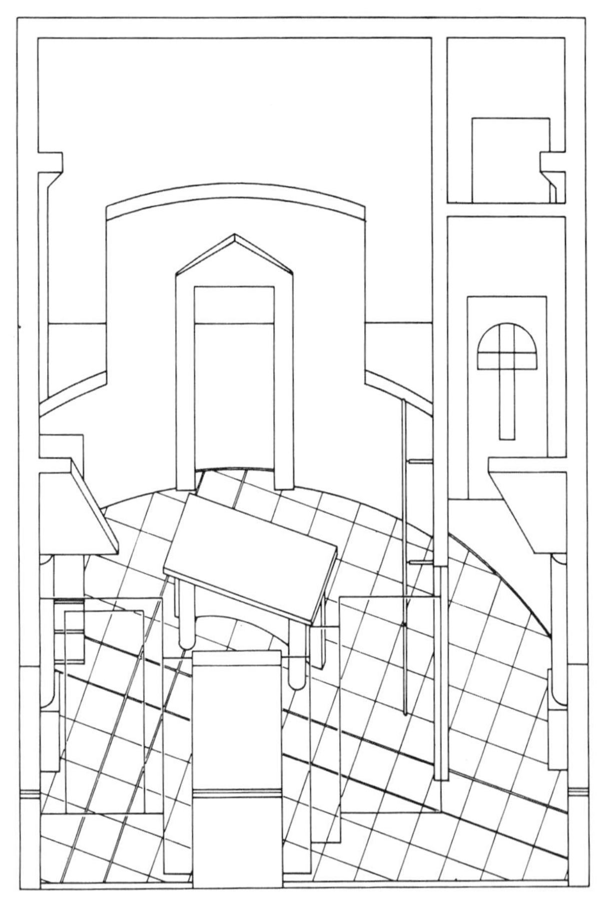

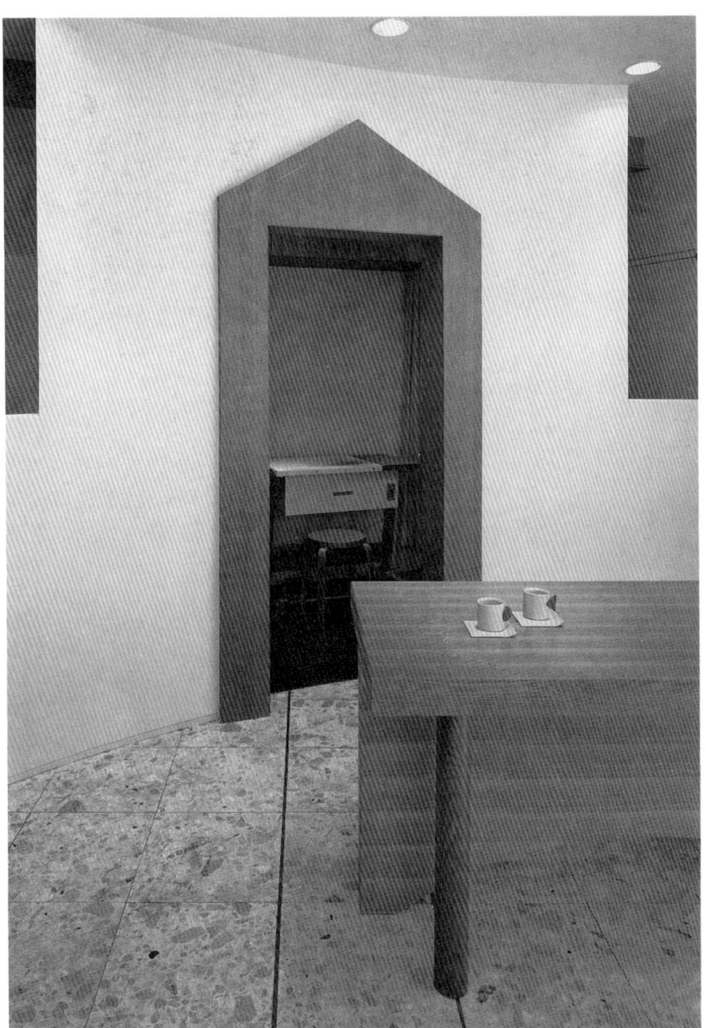

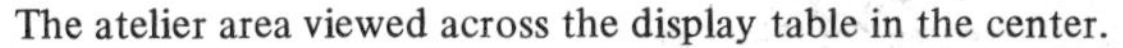

中央のディスプレイテーブル越しにアトリエ方向をみる
The atelier area viewed across the display table in the center.

ファサード

The facade.

幾何学的な錯覚で空間の拡がりをひきだす

店舗　アトリエ　通路の3つの要素からなるブティックである。総面積が30m²に満たない空間の中に　それぞれ独立し　なおかつ1つの空間として意識されるように構成されている。平面計画は　正方形　三角形　円弧の幾何学的形態から成り　構造体との微妙なズレによるイリュージョンで　面積的な条件をカバーしようとしている。断面計画は　エントランス部の天井高を低く抑えることで　内部の拡がりを目指している。そして立面においてはHouseをイメージするものが　意識下での時間的空間的拡がりを換起すべく　各所に配置されている。　〈山口正博〉(84-7)

設計／ビー・アソシエイツ　山口正博　施工／ＭＩ建築工芸
面積／28.6m²　工期／1984年3月16日～4月17日

Apron & House Wear AYA

Uses geometric illusions to give an expansive space image

"Aya" is a boutique that consists of shop, atelier and aisle. Within the space less than 30 m² in total area, these three elements are arranged independently of each other, but can make you recognize as an integral space.

The floor plan consists of square, triangle and arc – geometric shapes – and by means of illusions caused by gaps with structures, spacial limitations are made up. As for the cross-sectional layout, by lowering the height of ceiling above the entrance area, it was intended to create an expansive inside space. As for elevation, in order to arouse a sense of expanse in both time and space at the subconscious level, those imaging a house are placed here and there.

571, Hiiragi-cho, Takakuradori, Nakagyo-ku, Kyoto City
Phone: 075-221-2952

Design / Masahiko Yamaguchi
Area / 28.6 m²

材料仕様

外壁／モルタル下地　ボンタイル吹付け　スチールサッシ透明ガラス　テンパーライトドア　外部床／テラゾタイル貼り400角　一部真鍮目地　ゴムタイル貼り　床／テラゾタイル貼り400角(一部真鍮目地)ゴムタイル　壁面及び天井／ＰＢ下地　寒冷紗パテしごきＶＰ塗装　家具／楢練付けＣＬ塗装

営業内容

開店／1984年4月21日　営業時間／午前11時～午後7時　休日／毎週日曜日　祭日　経営者／林みほ　従業員／1人　客単価／5000円　主な取り扱い商品／エプロン1500～5000　ハウスウェア／3000～2万

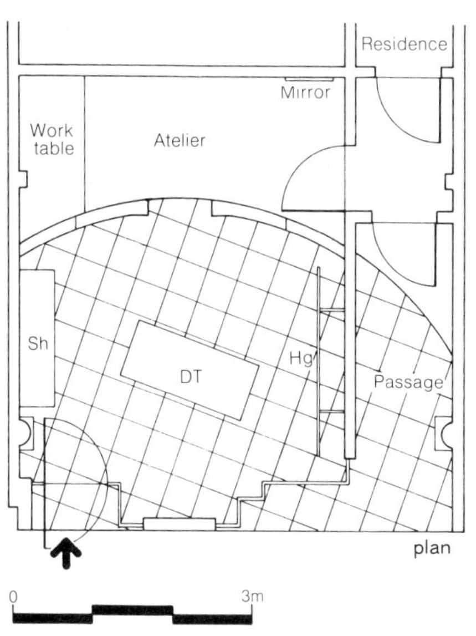

左奥より店内をみる

The shop viewed from the inner left part.

ファサード

The facade.

AVショップ コール 日吉店

横浜市港北区日吉本町1774　Phone/044-61-0185

撮影／池亀孝一

商談コーナーをみる　The business talk corner.

店内右方向をみる　The right side of the shop.

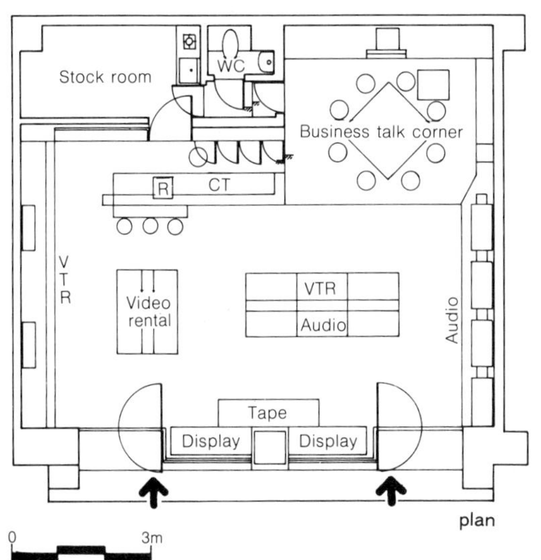

若い女性をターゲットにした地域密着型AVショップ

「コール」という愛称で呼ばれているこの店は　ソニーの販売チャンネルの新たな方向を求めてスタートした店である。

グレーとベージュのチップが混入された　黒く太いが　柔かな緑どりで切り取られたファサードは　雑然とした街並に対して　アイデンティティを明解に示すものであり　都市との関連性を否定するものではない。

店内を構成するひとつひとつの素材や形態は　それ自身では意味をもっていないが　それは線や面になり　点を含めて空間的な繋がりをもち調和され　全体像を浮かび上がらせている。そうして生み出されたニュートラルで居住性の高い空間は　子供たちやお年寄りに対しても寛容であるばかりでなく　ハードな商品群の中でも寛ぎとやさしさを与えてくれる。

クオリティーの高さや洗練されたイメージというものは同時に機能的で　制御された環境をつくり出すことでもある。そして　このようなコンセプトの設定は　技術力によって成長してきた企業にこそ可能なのかも知れない。

〈諌元孝通〉(86-7)

企画／ソニー　長尾　清　AD／サン・アド　橋本　薫
設計／諌元孝通　施工／サン・アド　山下安孝
面積／72.2m²(倉庫・便所9.8m²)
工期／1985年9月1日～21日

AV Shop CALL Hiyoshi

A community-rooted AV shop targeting young ladies

Endearingly named "Call," this shop was opened seeking after a new course of Sony's selling outlet.

The black and thick with grey and beige chips mixed in, but cut out in gentle green, the facade definitely shows its identity against the disorderly street, not rejecting relations with the surrounding urban environment.

Each material or shape constituting the inside has not a meaning by itself, but as a whole these materials and shapes make up a line or plane, creating an overall image in harmonious spacial connections, including dots. The neutral, highly habitable space created in that manner is generous not merely to children and old people, but also gives comfortableness and gentleness even in the midst of hard product groups.

High quality and refined images are also designed to create a functional, controlled environment. This type of concept setting may be possible only by an enterprise that has grown with its technical capability.

1774, Hiyoshi-honcho, Kohoku-ku, Yokohama City
Phone: 044-61-0185

Design / Kaoru Hashimoto
Area / 72.2 m^2 (Warehouse · Lavatory 9.8 m^2)

材料仕様

外壁／石綿セメント板下地　模様塗料吹付仕上げ　外部床／タイル貼45角　サイン／スチール抜文字アクリル裏あて模様塗料吹付仕上げ　床／エンボスゴムタイル貼り　一部楢フローリング染色ウレタン吹付塗装　壁面／ＰＢ下地　ＡＥＰ　一部スリットミラー貼り　一部モルタル金鏝押え　天井／ＰＢ下地　クロス貼り　家具／メラミン化粧板及びタモ材染色クリア仕上げ

営業内容

開店／1985年９月27日　営業時間／午前10時～午後10時　休日／毎週火曜日　経営者／ソリッドプラザ・竹中武男　従業員／４人　アルバイト２人　合計６人

婚礼家具
松井家具

奈良市南市町17-1　Phone/0742-22-2775

シンプルな建物の形態とメタリックな表情を目指す

この建物は　本店の倉庫を解体し　ブライダル館として別館を建て　本店との店舗の一体化を図るためにつくられた。

外装は　鉄骨造の構造的な特徴を明確に視覚化し　内外の壁の仕上材として選択したスレートの小波板を　メタリックな表現として洗練化するために　継目を重ねあわせる通常のジョイントを排し　横貼りとしたうえで　継目を消去するディテールにした。

スレートには　シルバーのペイントを吹き付け鉄骨の梁や柱の黒と赤のラインと対比させることによって　周囲の歓楽街の状況とは逆に　シンプルな建物の形態とメタリックな表情にした。

内部は　窓を上部にとることにより　周囲の状況を拒絶し　独立化を図り　家具を展示する状況をつくった。この建物は　周囲の状況にたいするアンチテーゼとしての意味も含んだ計画である。

〈武市義雄〉(85-5)

設計／ＲＥＡ建築工房　武市義雄
施工／山中建設
構造・規模／Ｓ造・地上２階建
面積／敷地・169.89m²　建築・139.48m²　床・１階136.24m²　２階149.76m²　合計286m²
工費／3561万円

Bridal Furniture MATSUI-KAGU

Aimes at a simple building shape and a metallic appearance

This building came into being as a bridal furniture space by demolishing the warehouse of the main shop. As an annex, it is designed to integrate with the main shop.

The exterior is designed to definitely visualize the structural features of ferroconcrete framing. In order to refine the ripple-patterned slates chosen as the inside/outside wall finishing material to give a metallic expression, usual seamed joints were not used; instead, seamless, side-cover finish was employed.

Over the slates is spray-painted in silver color, and by contrasting it with black and red lines of steel-frame beams and pillars, the building was simply designed with a metallic appearance, as opposed to the surrounding amusement streets.

As for the inside, by providing windows at upper parts, the surrounding circumstances were rejected, making the inside independent so that furniture may be displayed. This building was designed so that it also implies an antithesis against the surrounding circumstances.

17-1, Minamiichi-machi, Nara City
Phone: 0742-22-2775

Design / Yoshio Takeichi
Area / Site 169.89 m^2, Building 139.48 m^2,
Floor: 1st floor 136.24 m^2,
2nd floor 149.76 m^2;
Totalling 286 m^2

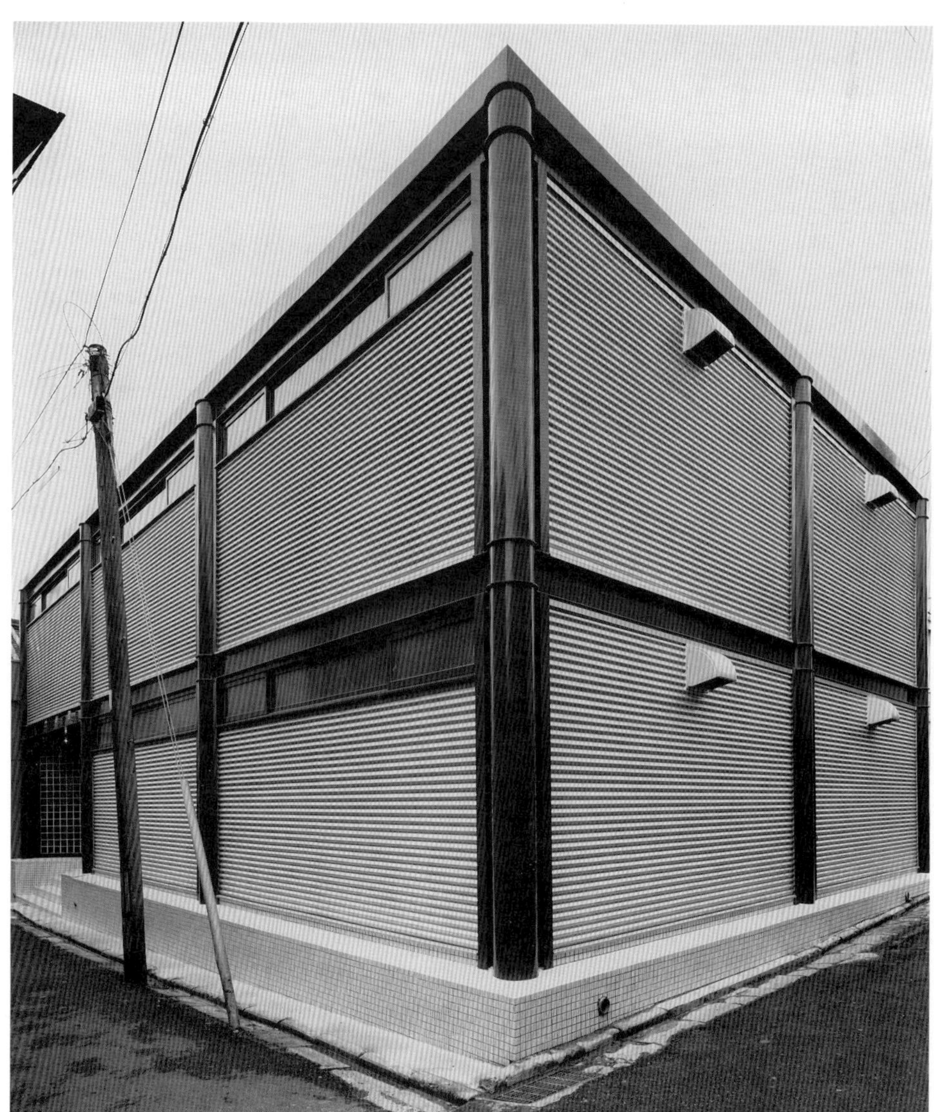

S造小波スレートｔ=6.3横貼りの外観　Steel framed ripple-patterned slates (t = 6.3, side-covered).

入口廻りをみる　The entrance area.

撮影／川元　斉

2階階段より店内をみる

The shop looked into from the 2nd floor staircase.

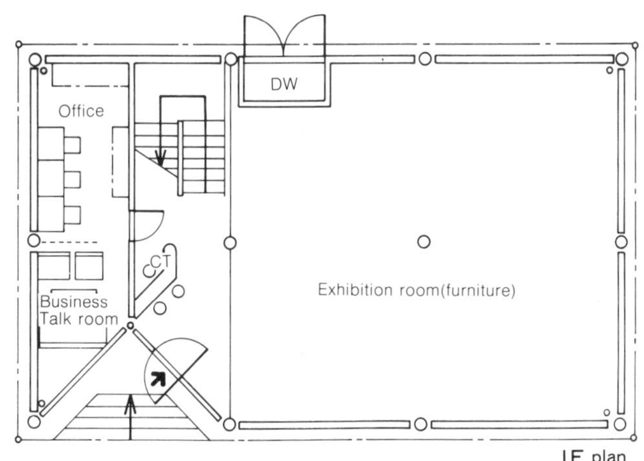

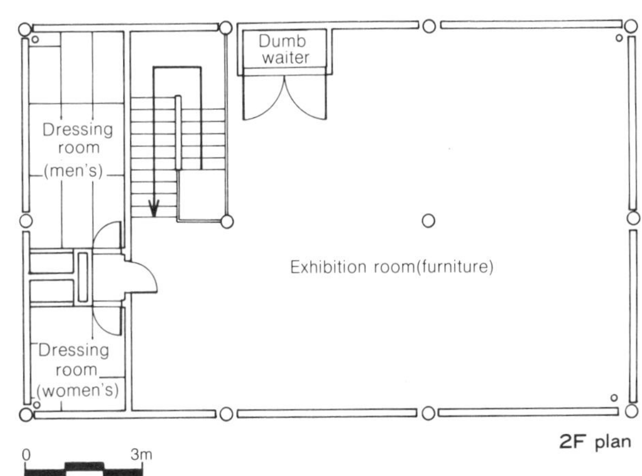

材料仕様

屋根／耐久カラー付シート防水　外壁／岩綿スレート小波板ｔ＝6.3 横貼りＶＰ吹付け　スチールサッシ　一部ガラスブロック　外部床／磁器質タイル貼り45角　サイン／ステンレス文字　床／パイルじゅうたん　毛足ｔ＝６貼り　一部磁器質タイル貼り45角　幅木／スチール120×40×3.2ＯＰ　壁面／岩綿スレート小波板ｔ＝6.3横貼りＶＰ吹付け 天井／Ｖ型デッキプレートｔ＝1.6　ｔ＝1.2ＯＰ　照明器具／ビームランプ　カウンター／トップ・米松集成材　腰・ＲＣ打放し

営業内容

開店／1984年12月１日　営業時間／午前10時～午後８時　休日／毎週木曜日　経営者／松井英夫　従業員／サービス13人　主な取り扱い商品／婚礼家具一式

AVステーション
CSV 渋谷

東京都渋谷区神南1-15-5　Phone/03-462-0133

素材　色ともニュートラルなNUDE空間

この店は　新しいタイプのオーディオ ヴィジュアル ショップとして企画された。
オーディオやCD　ビデオ等のソフトだけでなく　シンセサイザーやコンピューターを始めとする新しい音づくり　映像づくりに重点を置きそのためにはFM放送スタジオ　ビデオ編集室　オーディオサロン　ハードの製作工房など　若者が使いながら創作活動をしていく拠点を目指した。また　よりコミュニケーションの場を拡げるために　大きなステージを利用したコンサート　オブジェ　ギャラリー等の企画も用意した。
店内は　これらの要望をどうするかでスタートし　各売場ごとに店長をおき　彼自身のアイディアを尊重していく方法をとった。
全体を"NUDE"と考え　個々の売場で　その特徴を発揮するという方針をとった。そのため　床　壁面　天井は　どれもニュートラルな素材を選び　色もモノトーンに押えた。

〈入江経一〉(86-7)

設計／基本・入江建築設計事務所
　　実施・東京井関
施工／第一建設
面積／1階・312m² 2階・336m² 合計648m²
工期／1985年10月20日～11月29日
工費／3000万円

AV Station CSV Shibuya

A nude space neutral in both material and color

This shop was planned as a new-type audio-visual (AV) shop. Here, not merely software (audio, CD, video, etc.) but also hardware (synthesizers, computers, etc.) is stressed to create new sounds and images. As a step in this direction, this station is aimed to serve as a center where young people can make creative activities, while using an FM broadcasting studio, video editing room, audio salon, hardware workshop, etc. Also, in order to expand the place for communications, a large stage can be used for concert, objet gallery, etc.
The inside layout was made to meet those requirements. Chiefs are assigned the respective selling corners, and their own ideas are made much of.
By regarding the entire shop as a "nude" space, are allowed each selling corner to give full play to its features. For this purpose, the floor, wall and ceiling were all finished with neutral materials using a moderate monotone.

1-15-5, Jinnan, Shibuya-ku, Tokyo
Phone: 03-462-0133

Design / Keiichi Irie
Area / 1st floor 312 m², 2nd floor 336 m²;
Totalling 648 m²

撮影／鳴瀬　亨

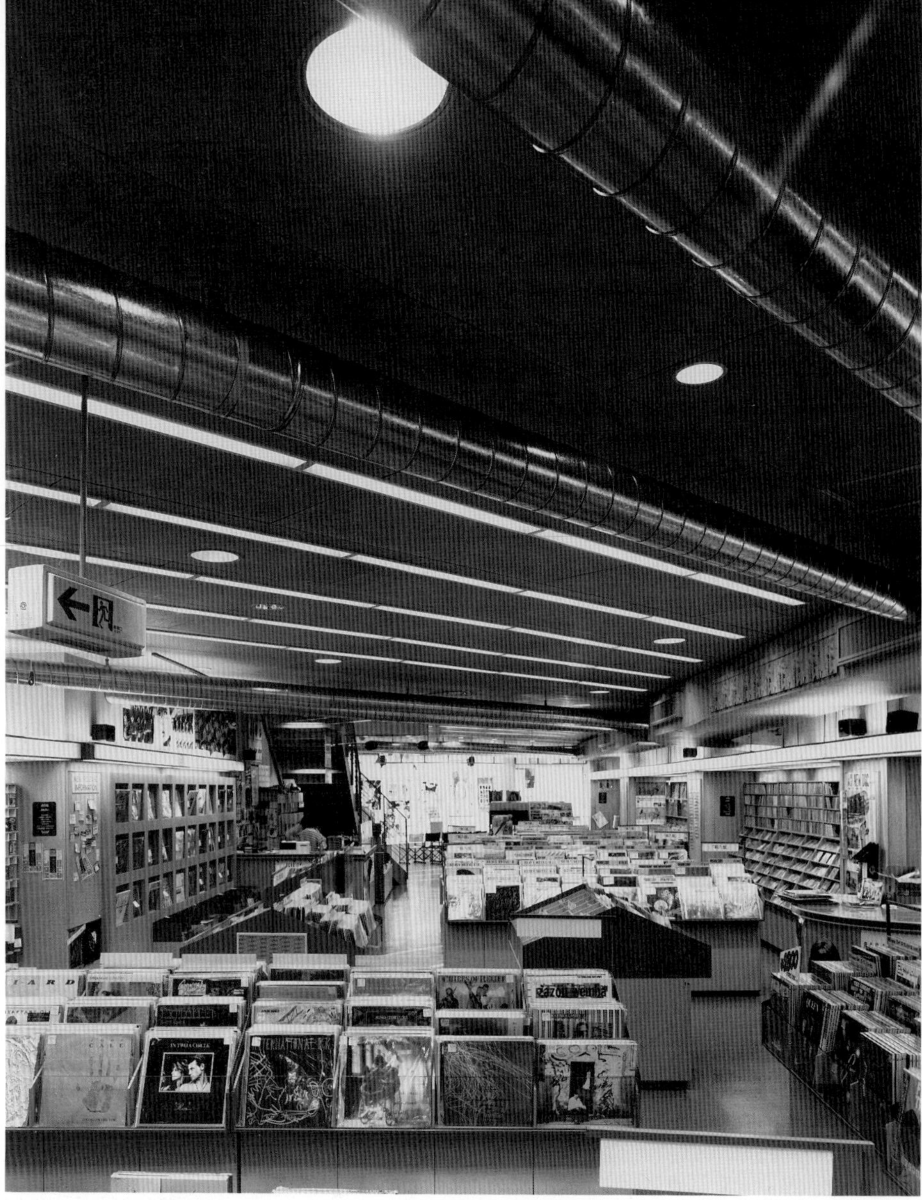

1階奥より入口方向をみる　The entrance area viewed from the inner part of the 1st floor.

ファサード　The facade.

1階入口にある吹抜けギャラリーホールをみる　CSVにかかわる作品の発表の場
The stairwell gallery hall at the entrance to the 1st floor – a place for announcing works related to CSV.

２階全フロアをみる

The entire 2nd floor.

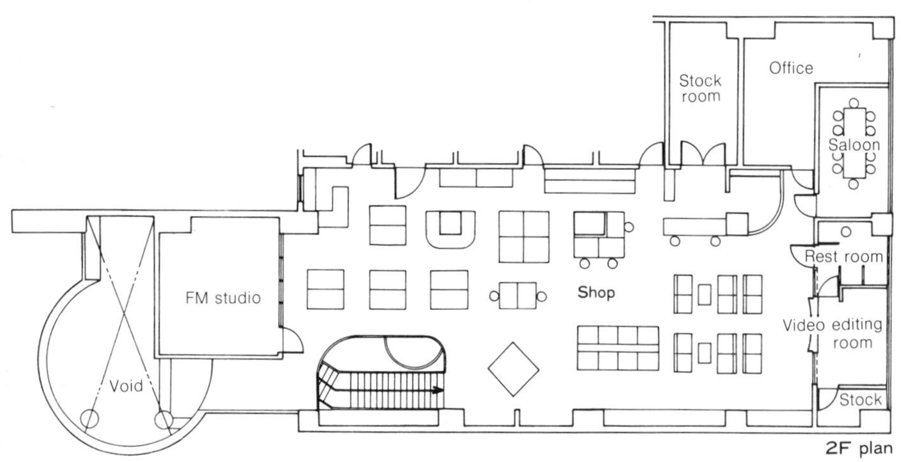

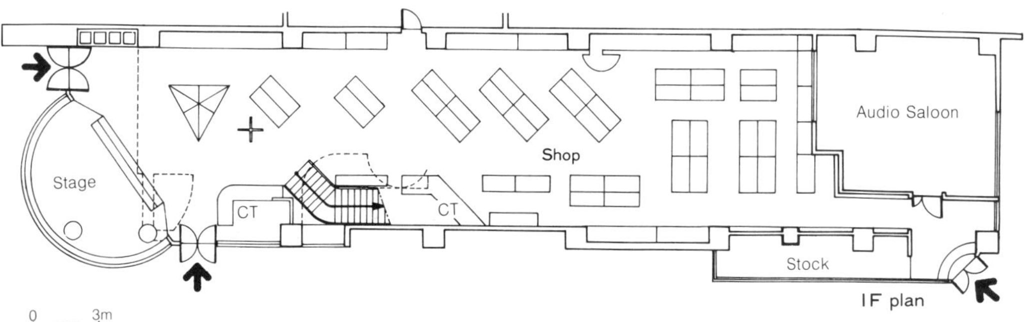

材料仕様
床／１階・塩ビ床シート　２階・フローリンググレーステインワックス仕上げ　壁面及び天井／フレキシブルボードｔ＝６

営業時間
開店／1985年11月29日　営業時間／平日・午前11時～午後８時　土　日　祭日・午前10時～午後８時　経営者／ＣＳＶ渋谷　従業員／15人　パート及びアルバイト10人　合計25人

ブティック＆グッズ ヴィブ

仙台市中央2-3-24 Phone/0222-65-2862

精神的にリッチな感覚が感じられる空間

今回「ヴィブ」を誕生させることは　次々に展開されるファッションビル　高感度ブティックの中で　これからの大型専門店のあり方を問われるプロジェクトであり　また　それは単に目新しいということだけではなく　常に鮮度を保ち　ハイレベルでの精神的にリッチな感覚を　空間にいる人達に感じてもらうことも目的であった。

それには　ストレートに心地良さを感じてもらうことと伴に　柔らかな刺激を与えることではないかと考え　トップライトの導入と空間をスケルトンすることにした。トップライトにより　注がれる自然の光は　素朴なコンクリートの空間に柔らかさを与え　床に敷かれた木と　壁や天井に取り付けられた間接照明は　温かさを演出してくれた。

どこにでもある素材で構成した空間ではあるが　いつ訪れても　新鮮な気持ちになれるような気がする。

〈堀田　明〉(85-7)

企画／ランドスケープアットワーク　小寺崇志
設計／建築・ランドスケープアットワーク 堀田 明
丹青社建築センター　田久保宗光
内装・ランドスケープアットワーク 堀田 明
海津規子
施工／丹青社仙台支店
面積／1階228.11m² 2階189.99m² 3階28.37m²
合計446.47m²
工期／1984年8月1日～11月15日
工費／1億1900万円

Boutique & Goods VIVE

A space where you can feel mentally rich

In bringing "Vive" into being, we intended to propose what a desirable future large specialty shop should be, amidst the situation in which fashion buildings/high sensitivity boutiques are appearing one after another. Our aims also lay not merely in seeking a novel sense, but also in always keeping freshness so that those in this space can feel a sophisticated, mentally rich sense.

To this end, we thought it necessary to make people feel pleasant straightly, and also stimulate them gently, thus introducing a toplight and skeleton space. The natural light coming through the toplight gives softness to the simple, concrete space, while the wood flooring and indirect lighting mounted on the wall and ceiling produce warmth. Although this space is composed of materials available everywhere, it seems that we can feel refreshed whenever we drop in this space.

2-3-24, Chuo, Sendai City　Phone: 0222-65-2862

Design / Akira Hotta
Area / Site 252.52. m^2, Building 228.11 m^2,
Floor: 1st floor 228.11 m^2,
2nd floor 189.99 m^2, 3rd floor 28.37 m^2;
Totalling 446.47 m^2

撮影／平沢　敞

アーケード街からみたファサード　The facade viewed from the arcade street.

入口より1階ブティックコーナーをみる The 1st floor boutique corner viewed from the entrance.

2階グッズコーナーの中央を縦貫するスカイライトをみる

The skylight transversing the center of the 2nd floor goods corner.

2階グッズコーナーより入口上部吹抜けとスカイライト部をみる **The skylight above the stairwell of the entrance area viewed from the 2nd floor goods corner.**

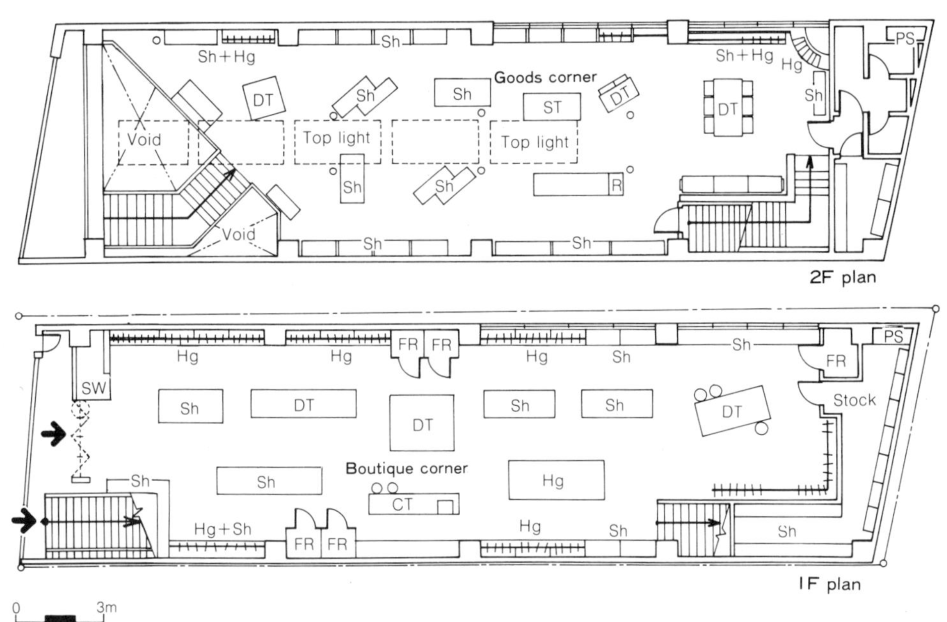

材料仕様

屋根／トップライト・網入りガラス　外壁／コンクリート打放し　ファサード・御影石パターン貼りバーナー仕上げ　外部床／御影石タイル貼り 100 角サイン／コンクリート打ち込み文字　床／松材フローリング貼り200×400染色ウレタン塗装仕上げ　壁面コンクリート打放し　天井／1階・コンクリート打放しVP　2階・LGS組み　PB貼り下地AEP　家具／1階・タモ材染色ウレタン塗装　2階・パイン材オイル仕上げ

営業内容

開店／1984年11月21日　営業時間／午前10時30分～午後7時30分　休日／なし　経営者／㈱モア　従業員／11人　客単価／婦人服1万3000円　グッズ1500円　主な商品／トレンドレディースファッションウェア　1階・フロムニル　ムービングブルー　エスト　アトリエメイク　モーヌ　2階・ヨーガンレール(サニタリー)　ビーハウス(テーブルウェア)　ストロー(ナイトウェア)

家電 ラヂオ 鳴浜

名古屋市南区鳴浜町6-1　Phone/052-611-4307

内部と外部との自然な還流

「ラヂオ」は　もともと駐車場として使用していた2階建の建物の1階部分をショップにしたものである。当然　エクステリアも手掛けたが　特別にオーバーアクションはしていない。むしろ何もしない方が　町の中の存在として自然だと考えたからである。どうしても無視できない柱や梁の要素は　インテリアと一体としてとらえた。

プランの中には　事務処理をするためのオフィスやキッチンもレイアウトしてあるが　何よりも　交差点のコーナーにある条件を利用して　角に独立したショーウインドを設け　その両側を導入部として　インテリア的エクステリアゾーンを確保したことが　ショップ全体として的確な役割を果したと思っている。

〈岡本輝男〉(86-9)

企画／中京三洋住宅機器販売　犬飼章夫
設計／デザインスタジオ　オカモト　岡本輝男
施工／光洋社　面積／156m²
工期／1986年4月28日～5月28日
工費／2023万円

Electric Goods Store RAZIO Naruhama

Natural flux and reflux between inside and outside

"Razio" came into being by redecorating the 1st floor of a two-storied building which was previously used as a parking place. Naturally, we undertook the exterior, but did not give an excessive expression to it. Because we felt it better to leave the exterior untreated so that this space may exist naturally as part of the town. The pillars and beams – elements that cannot be ignored – were treated in one piece with the interior.

In the layout are included an office or kitchen. By utilizing the locational advantage that this building is at the corner of a crossing, an independent show window is provided at the corner. With both sides of it as an introduction, an exterior zone like an interior was secured. This seems to be playing an accurate role in the entire shop scheme.

6-1, Naruhama-cho, Minami-ku, Nagoya City
Phone: 052-611-4307

Design / Teruo Okamoto
Area / 156 m^2

三角形の独立したショーウインドをみる　The triangular independent show window.

ショーウインドをみる　The show window.

撮影／加斗タカオ

入口よりガラススクリーンを通してみる

The shop viewed through the glass screen from the entrance.

店内奥よりみる

The inner part of the shop.

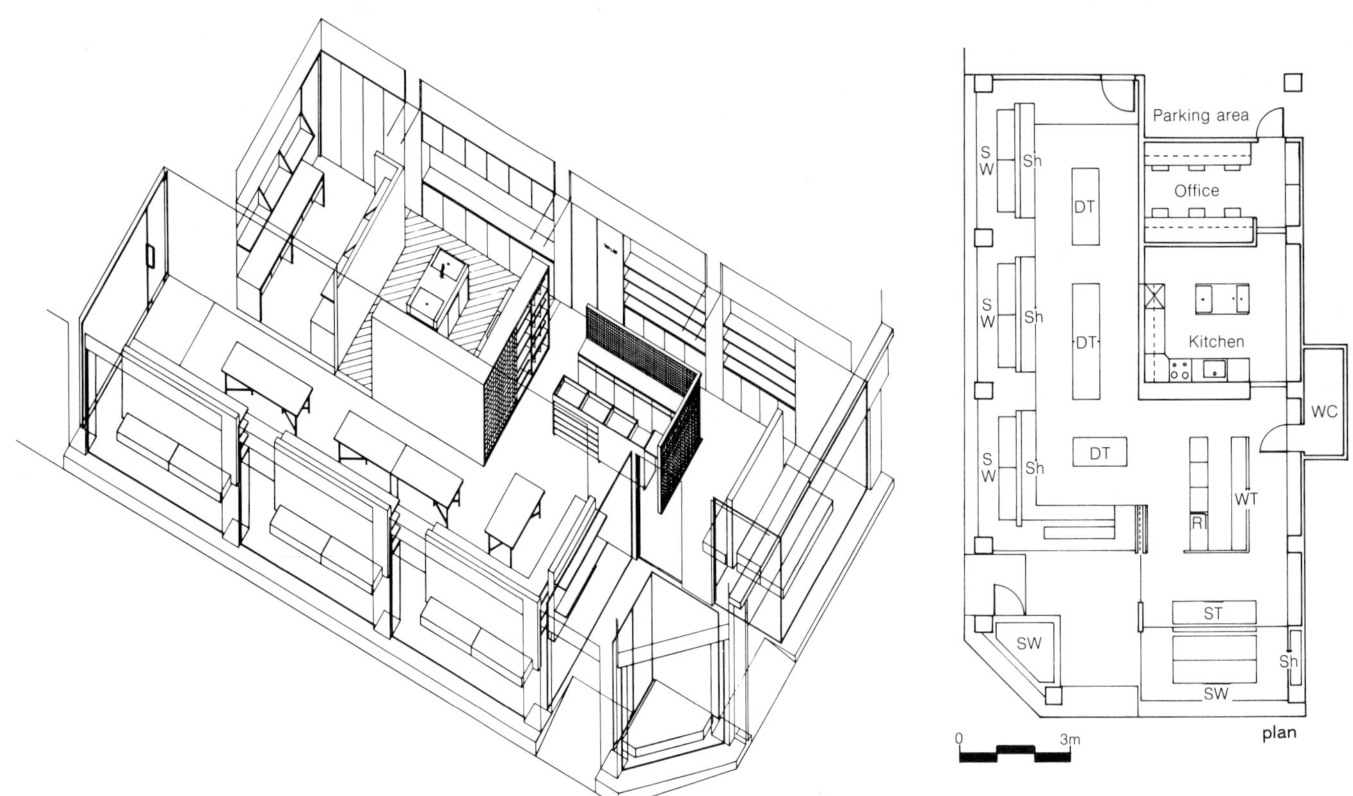

材料仕様

外壁／モルタル下地ＶＰ　外部床／タイル乱貼り　サイン／スチールメラミン焼付け　床／モルタル金鏝仕上げ(墨入り)　一部タイル乱貼り　一部キッチン部分楢フローリング貼り　幅木／スプルスＶＰ　壁／硅酸カルシウム板及びＰＢ　ＥＰ吹付け　天井／既存ＥＰ　スクリーン／モルタル　タイル乱貼り　什器／桐合板ラッカー吹付け

営業内容

開店／1986年６月７日　営業時間／午前10時～午後８時　休日／毎週水曜日　経営者／高見義夫　従業員／３人　パート及びアルバイト３人　合計６人　主な取り扱い商品／家庭電化製品　システムキッチン　システム家具　インテリアグッズ

ディスプレイ什器の上下は収納スペース
The upper and lower parts of display utensils serve as storage spaces.

レジカウンター脇のランプ類コーナーをみる
The lamps corner beside the register counter.

ワイヤメッシュで覆われたファサード　**The facade covered with wire mesh.**

フィルターにより既存の建築を変換

秋葉原の　お世辞にもきれいとは言えないペンシルビルの改装。間口５ｍそこそこ。鰻の寝床のように細長い。隣りの「リビナ マヤギワ」の改装に伴って出てくる廃材をできる限り利用するという条件。

「リビナ店」の方は　イタリア家具のショールームのように　ゆとりのある売場構成。そしてビシッと割り付けられたアルミパネルの外装。どうみても　最初から勝ち目はない。

そこで“下手な厚化粧はやめよう”というのが出発点。既存の内装をはがすと　粗々しいジャンカだらけのコンクリートが現れた。これはそのまま見せることにした。種々雑多の電球や電池　これも並べられるだけ並べることにした。しかし　ただ見せたり露出したりするのでなく　その前に透明なフィルターのようなものを立て　それによって　その裏のものの意味を変換する――そんな変換器のような建築を目指した。

〈隈　研吾〉(85-7)

設計／隈　研吾＋ＴＬヤマギワ研究所
施工／ダイワ
面積／58㎡
工期／1985年３月１日～４月１日
工費／2500万円

バルブ
リビナ ヤマギワ バルブショップ

東京都千代田区外神田1-5-2　Phone/03-253-5111

撮影／本木誠一

入口より店内奥をみる

The inner part of the shop viewed from the entrance.

Bulb Shop LIVINA YAMAGIWA BULB SHOP

Converts the existing building with filters

This shop came into being by redecorating a pencil building that is far from being beautiful. The frontage is as short as 5 m, and the inside is very narrow. It utilizes as much waste materials as possible that become available along with the redecoration of the adjacent "Livina Yamagiwa."

Like an Italian furniture showroom, "Livina" has spacious selling corners. And the exterior finely finished with aluminum panels. In all respects, this bulb shop has no chances of winning. Thus, our starting point was: "Let's eschew from painting the face poorly." When the existing interior was removed, a coarse concrete surface appeared. We decided to leave it exposed. We also decided to place various kinds of bulb and battery as much as possible. However, we wished to convert the meaning of those goods by placing transparent filters before them – instead of simply exhibiting or exposing them. Thus, we intended to create a building like a converter.

1-5-2, Sotokanda, Chiyoda-ku, Tokyo Phone: 03-253-5111

Design / Kengo Kuma
Area / 58 m^2

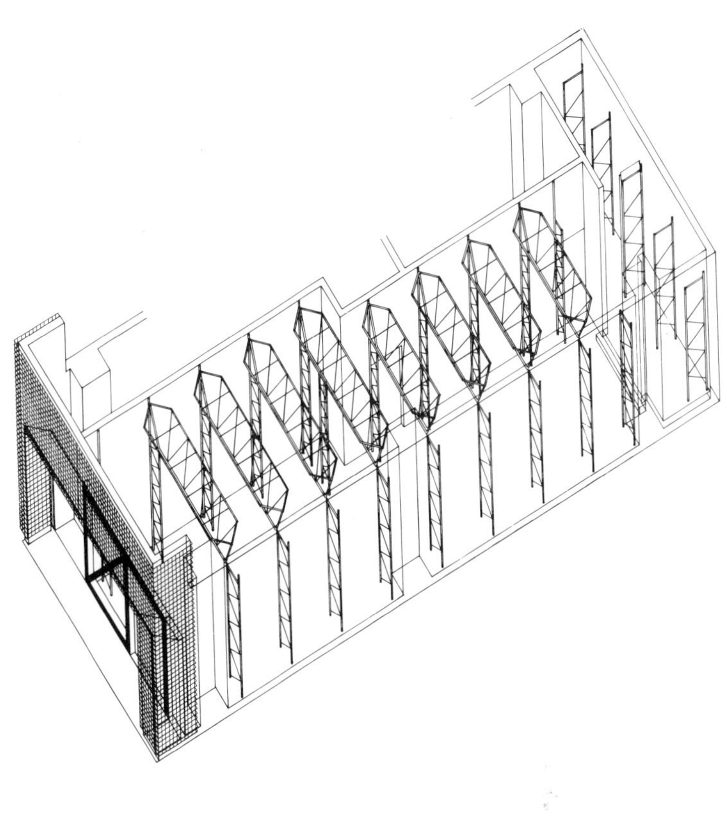

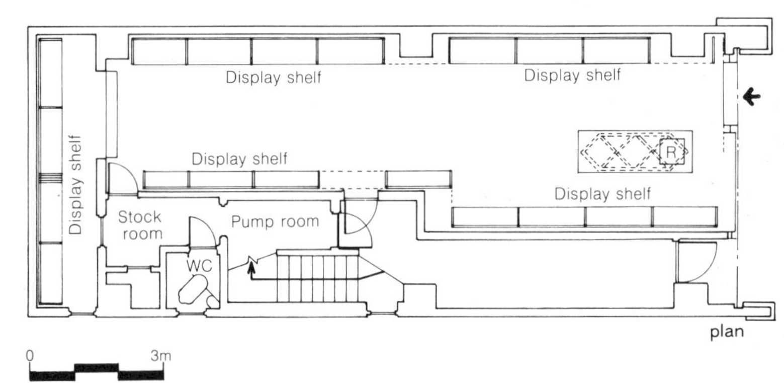

材料仕様
外壁／モルタル刷毛引き　既存タイルＳＯＰ塗りの上ワイヤメッシュ50×50×φ=4 メラミン焼付仕上げ　床／ゴムタイル貼り サイン／スチールメラミン焼付塗装の上電飾サイン　床／ゴムタイル貼り　壁面／コンクリート打放し(既存)　一部モルタル刷毛引き　天井／コンクリート打放し(既存)の上スチール製トラス　メラミン焼付仕上げ　照明器具／スチール製トラスにハイクリプトン球取付け　レジカウンター上部・モーカルソケットＨＩＤ球取付け　什器／トラス型スタッドに可動棚板　下部キャスター付収納ワゴン　カウンター／スチール製トラス　フレーム・フロートガラスｔ＝12

営業内容
開店／1985年４月４日　営業時間／午前10時～午後７時(金　土は７時30分)　休日／なし　経営者／ヤマギワ㈱　従業員／３人　主な商品／一般電球　舞台用電球　工場用電球　乾電池　懐中電灯　配線用パーツ

ゲートからデッキを通してドーム方向をみる

The dome area viewed from the gate through the deck.

グリーンショップ 新晴園

東京都三鷹市新川1-13-26　Phone/0422-43-5211

撮影／本木誠一

内部照明により陰影を浮び上がらせるドームの夜影

A night view of the dome whose shade rises up by internal lighting.

花壇からパーゴラ風の木製ドームを俯瞰する

Overlooking the wooden dome of a pergola style from the flower bed.

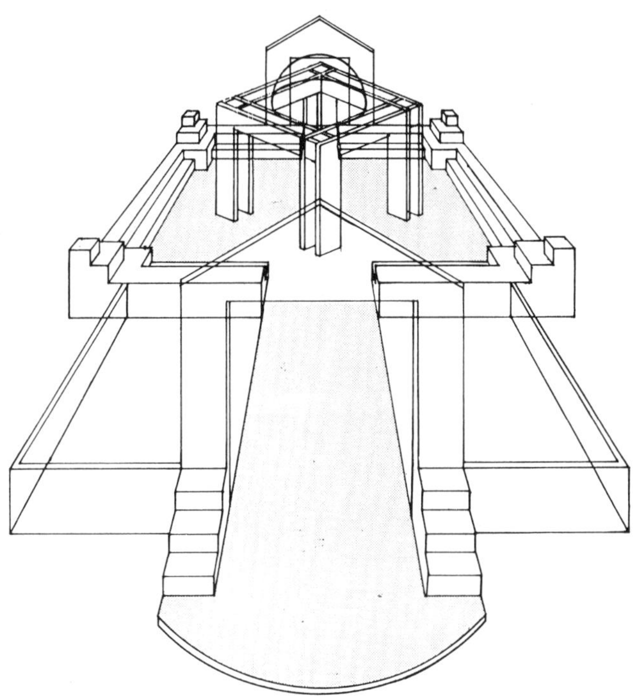

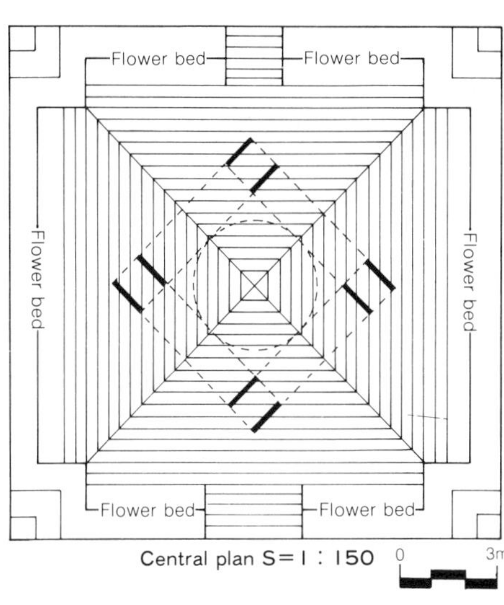

Central plan S=1 : 150

木製の格子ドームを通して内部に降りそそぐ木洩日

A dim light pouring into the shop through the wooden latticed dome.

正12角形の格子ドームがつくり出す光と影

この施設は　広い敷地に恵まれた郊外型のグリーショップの中にあるスペースで　いわば“くつろぎの場”である。
ややもすると　無機質になりがちな粗末な温室建築に囲まれ　時として忘れがちな自然のうるおいを呼びもどそうと　考案された30坪ほどのスペースである。部材は一種類で　その断面は2インチ×4インチのランバー材の2つ割を使っている。これを縦　横15cmの格子状に組み　所定のモジュールにしたがってパネル化し　それを集合化して空間をつくった。昼……降り注ぐ太陽の光が　格子の網の目の隅々に射し込み　吹く風が　かすかな音をたてて　このスペースを通過していく。外部から射し込む光が“こもれび”に変わるのとは対象的に　夜は内部から発する人工照明による陰影が　ドームの先端から夜空に散っていく。建築と呼べるかどうかわからない　この空間に　うっかりすると見のがしてしまう些細な出来事が毎日毎日くり返し起きている。〈白鳥健二〉(85-9)

設計／アトリエ・コスモ　施工／大市工務店　構造・規模／W造・平家建
面積／103.68㎡　工期／1985年4月1日～30日　工費／350万円

Florist SHINSEIEN

Light and shadow produced by 12-lateral latticed dome

This facility is a space in a suburban green shop blessed with a wide site, and may be said to a "resting place."
It is a space about 97 m^2 wide devised to call back the grace of nature into this location which is surrounded by humble hothouses which tend to become inorganic. The member is of one kind – 2 x 4 inches (cross section) of lumber. These lumbers are latticed in 15 x 15 cm format, and by making them available as panels according to the preset modules, a space was created by assembling them.
In the daytime, the sunlight pours down, coming in through every mesh of lattice, and the blowing wind passes through this space making an indistinct sound. In contrast to the light coming in from outside getting "dim," at night, the shade due to artificial lighting coming from inside scatteres away from the top of the dome into the night sky. At this space which may not be fully recognized as an architecture, various minor things, which tend to be overlooked, are occurring day after day.

1-13-26, Shinkawa, Mitaka City, Tokyo　Phone: 0422-43-5211

Design / Kenji Shiratori
Area / 103.68 m^2

材料仕様
屋根・外壁及び外部床／スプルス材　パイン材によるランバー

営業内容
開店(増築)／1985年5月1日　営業時間／午前9時～午後7時(夏)　午前9時～午後6時(冬)　休日／1～3月と6～9月は毎週水曜日　上記以外の期間はなし　経営者／宇田川晴敏
従業員／6人　客単価／1500円　主な取り扱い商品／花　観葉植物　庭木　園芸用品全般

ファサード

The facade.

フラワーショップ

ゴトウ花店

東京ヒルトンインターナショナル店

東京都新宿区西新宿6-6 東京ヒルトンインターナショナル
地下1階　Phone/03-342-0510

撮影／平沢　敞

接客カウンターより壁面ディスプレイをみる

The wall display viewed from the guest service counter.

入口より店内全景をみる

日本的な空間を現代感覚で

東京ヒルトンホテルの地下1階「ヒルトピア ショッピングアーケード」に この店はある。ショップコンセプトは このホテルの持つインターナショナルなイメージを背景にし "日本的空間を現代感覚で"を基本に置いた。

花の持つそれぞれの色 美しさを念頭に置き カラーコンディションを白と黒のバランスでまとめ またこの個性的な色合いを大切にするために フォルム全体をシンプルにし 直線と曲線の変化で 全体の空間演出をした。

照明計画は 演出照明として 全体のトーンを崩さずに 間接照明でソフトにまとめた。

〈青山 学〉(85-5)

設計／ＳＰプランニング 青山 学 一條幹人

施工／ＳＰプランニング

面積／38㎡(うち作業場10㎡)

工期／1984年6月5日～7月10日 工費／1505万円

The entire inside scene viewed from the entrance.

接客カウンター

The guest service counter.

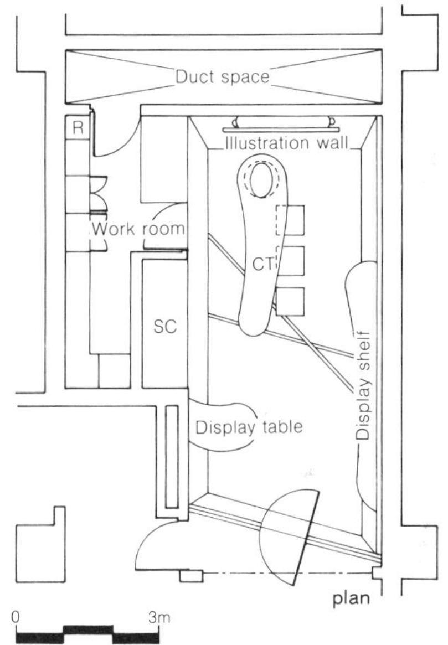

材料仕様
床／黒御影石　一部チーク材埋込み　壁面まわりチーク貼り　壁面及び天井／ＰＢ下地　ＶＰ
接客カウンター及び棚／榀合板ウレタン塗装

営業内容
開店／1984年９月11日　営業時間／午前10時～午後８時　休日／なし　経営者／㈱ゴトウ花店
従業員／サービス２人　作業場17人　合計19人　客単価／6000円　主な取り扱い商品／四季の切り花　フラワー関連グッズ

Flower Shop GOTO Tokyo Hilton International

Presents a Japanese space with a modern sense

Within "Hilton Shopping Arcade" at the 1st basement of Tokyo Hilton International, stands this shop. Against an international image of this hotel as the background, we set the shop concept at "a Japanese space with a modern sense."

Keeping the colors and beauty of each flower in mind, we arranged the color condition in a balance of black and white. Additionally, in order to accentuate this characteristic tone, the form as a whole was simplified, and the overall space was presented by using variations of straight line and curve.

As for the lighting plan, indirect lighting was employed to produce a soft atmosphere without affecting the overall tone.

6-6, Nishi-shinjuku, Shinjuku-ku, Tokyo　Phone: 03-342-0510

Design / Manabu Aoyama
Area / 38 m^2 (working space 10 m^2)

バス&トイレショールーム
エクサイト

東京都港区赤坂1-12-32 Phone/03-505-0311

「サイト2ーデコール」コーナーをみる
"Site 2" corner.

世界のバス&トイレプラザのショールーム

「エクサイト」は イナックスが"トイレ&バスは快適空間であるべき"との主張を 欧米10ヵ国30メーカーの製品と情報によって発信しようと企画したものである。それは 生活空間におけるトイレ バス環境を より快適な"第三の空間"として活性化させていくための生活美提案の基地である。「エクサイト」のデザインは そうした考え方を"風景の領域""抽象と具象"といった二元的世界の中に息づく"庭園"の第三性に重ね合わせ その"景観"を形成している。

全体の構成は 展示空間とサービス空間の2つに区分されている。

こうして構成される"景観"は 18世ヨーロッパの回遊式庭園の様々な景観を記号化したフローリング デザインと 建築設備 照明 音響装置の それぞれを相貫する立体トラスフレームのシーリングデザインによって パッケージしている。 〈田中俊行/空環計画研究所〉(86-12)

企画/イナックス パオス
設計/空環計画研究所 田中俊行
施工/森ビル商事 乃村工芸社
面積/約1500m²
工期/1986年8月1日~9月30日
工費/6億4000万円

「サイト3ーレシオ」コーナーをみる
"Site 3" corner.

撮影/本木誠一

「ギャラリー」より「カフェ」をみる
"Café" viewed from "Gallery."

「インフォサイト」コーナーをみる

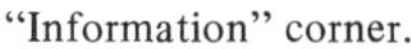
"Information" corner.

中央の「サイト１ーテクスタク」をみる

"Site 1 corner" in the center.

「サイト1ーテクスタス」をみる　中央は500個のライトが水の波紋を描くオプチカルポント
"Site 1 corner." An optical pond where 500 lights in the center draw ripples of water.

Showroom XSITE

A showroom of world's baths & toilets
"Xsite" was launched by Inax to assert that "toilet & bath" should be a comfortable space, by showing the products and information of 30 manufacturers in the U.S. and 9 European countries. It implies a station to propose a desirable toilet/bath environment to be activated as a more comfortable "third space." "Xsite" is designed to exist lively in the dual world of "scenery and domain" and "abstraction and concretion," thereby presenting this space as a "garden" in the dual "scenery."
The overall composition consists of two segments – display space and service space. The "scenery" thus composed is packaged by the flooring design which symbolizes various kinds of European gardens in the 18th century, and the ceiling design of solid trass frames penetrating the architectural facilities, lighting and acoustic devices.

1-12-32, Akasaka, Minato-ku, Tokyo
Phone: 03-505-0311

Design / Toshiyuki Tanaka
Area / about 1500 m^2

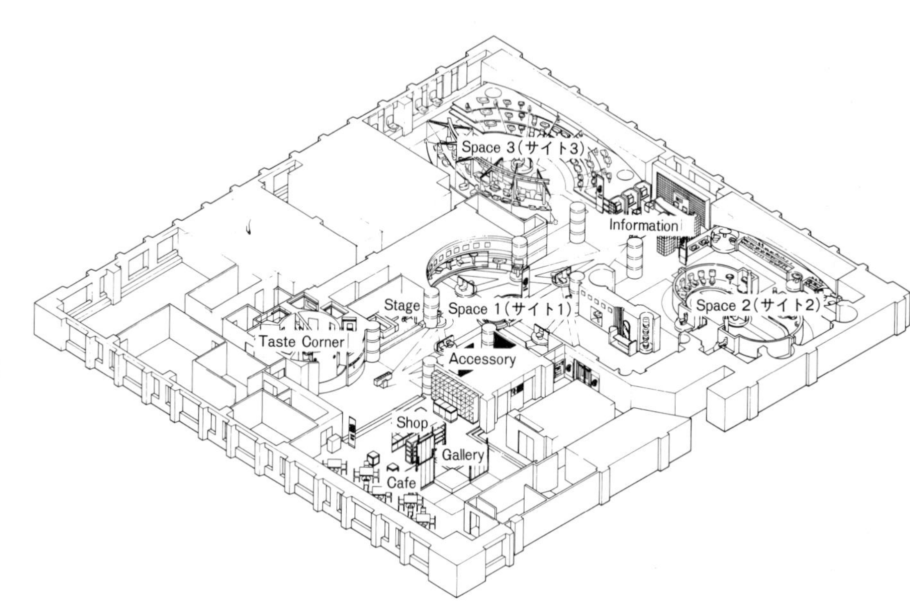

材料仕様
床／タイル貼り600角　一部昇降板　壁面／結晶化ガカス ラスタータイル貼り　スチールメラミン焼付け塗装鏡面仕上げ　スチールフレームガラスブロック積　天井／岩綿吸音板リブ貼り　一部あらわし天井部スチールパイプ組み　メラミン焼付け塗装　椅子／インターデコール　チェアーズ　ロックストーン

営業内容
開店／1986年10月15日　営業時間／午前11時～午後7時　休日／毎週日曜日　祭日　経営者／㈱イナックス　従業員／8人　主な展示商品／バス　トイレ関連商品

エステート&エージェント
バードランド

東京都渋谷区神宮前3-27-22　Phone/03-402-9535

店内に軽いジャズがながれる店(オフィス)
㈱バードランドは　建築　インテリアの設計　施工　不動産業を営む会社である。
この建物を設計するにあたって　まず考えたことは　マンションの一室で　膨大な資料に埋もれ　スリッパをパタパタと履き　本当に"夢"がクリエートできるのだろうか？ただ"信用"という看板のみにぶらさがっているのでは　この業界は進展しない。ここは　あくまでもオフィスではなく　ショップなのである。ショップという意識が　業界の"らしさ"を大きく変えていくことであろう。
ショップの三大要素である"音　光　色"を　とてもシャープに演出した。ドアを開けると軽いジャズが流れ　十分な明かりと　白をベースにスパイスカラーとして　取り入れたブルー系の色。ただし「バードランド」のレイアウト　内装は年に何回かは変わる。何故ならば素材も色もレイアウトも　自分たちで実験し体験するためである。特に"素材"は必ず実験してからクライアントにすすめる。"提案できる新しさ"と"プロとしての責任"を　このガラス張りのクリアなショップの中で見せていきたい。

〈三咲まどか／バードランド〉(86-9)

設計／バードランド　向井真也　施工／藤工芸
面積／48.5㎡　工期／1985年7月1日～10月15日

Estate & Agent Office BIRD LAND

A shop (office) in which a light jazz is on air
Bird Land Co., Ltd. is a company covering architecture, interior design, installation and real estate business.
In designing this building, I wondered if a "dream" can be created really in a room of mansion-style apartment house, wearing slippers. If it merely depend on the sign of "reputation," this trade will not develop. This is not an office, but a shop. Awareness as a shop will cause a great change in the nature of this trade.
"Sound, light, color" as the three major elements of shop were presented very sharply. Opening the door, you hear a light jazz on air. With ample light, white as the basic color is spiced with blue colors. However, the layout and interior of "Bird Land" change several times a year. Because they wish to experiment with and experience in the use of materials, colors and layout by themselves. As for "Materials," among others, they make it a rule to recommend clients to adopt them, only after experimenting with them. It is hoped that "newness that can be proposed" and "responsibility as a professional" be exhibited in this glassed, clear shop.

3-27-22, Jingumae, Shibuya-ku, Tokyo
Phone: 03-402-9535

Design / Shinya Mukai
Area / 48.5 m²

撮影／平沢　敞

ファサード

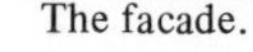
The facade.

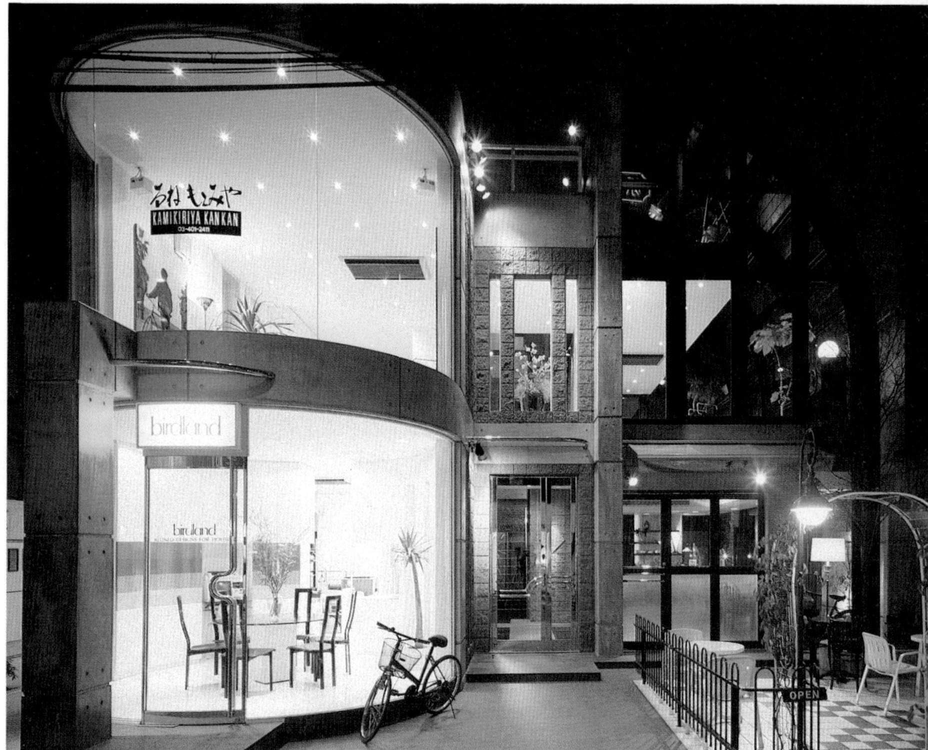

「バードランド」のあるビルの全景
An overall view of the building in which "Bird Land" is open.

オフィススペースよりみる
A view from the office space.

材料仕様
開口部／強化ガラスｔ＝10アール加工　床／大理石400角　幅木／ビニール幅木　壁面及び天井／ＰＢ下地ＶＰ塗装　什器／楊合板ウレタン吹付け塗装

接客スペースを通してみる

A view across the guest service space.

同社経営による「カフェ ド 茶香」

"Café" run by the same company.

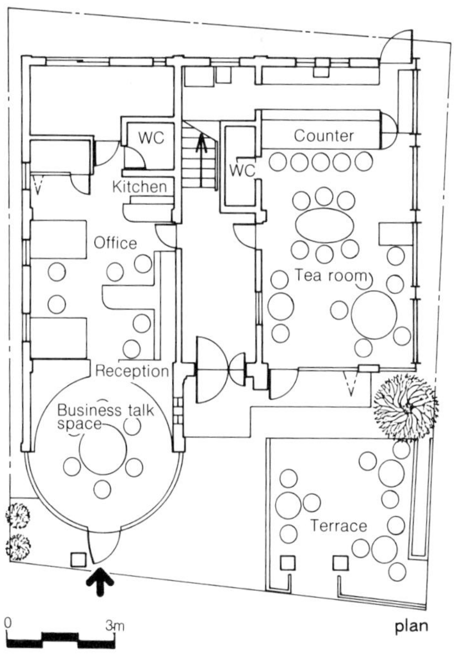

営業内容
開店／1985年10月16日　営業時間／午前10時～午後7時　休日／毎週日曜日　経営者／㈱バードランド・三咲まどか　従業員／10人　主な取り扱い業務／不動産業務及び設計・施工

外観全景をみる　手前が既存棟　奥が新築棟　The entire appearance. The conventional building in your side, and the new building in the inner area.

デベロップ＆エステート エージェント
グリーンホームズ

東京都渋谷区神宮前1-1-26　Phone/03-405-8876

撮影／平沢　敞

小さなデベロッパーのための　大きな意味を持つ　小さなオフィスとプレゼンテーションスペース
空間ほど高い付加価値を持っているものは　ざらにはなく　また　これほど高い価値を付加できるのも　そうはない。
街の遊撃手。都市空間演出家。平面が立体になり環境になる。こんなプロセスをアクションしていくことが　ぼくらの"正しい姿勢"でありたい。そんなプロセスの中で　多岐に渡って展開していく高い付加価値を　ビジュアル化していくことができるとしたら　それが　ぼくらの"正しいプレゼンテーション"になるのではないか――そう考えて始めたのがこのデザイン。
〈新津正昭／デザイン・ラボ〉(86-9)

企画／グリーンホームズ＋デザイン・ラボ
設計／建築・アモ(AMO)設計事務所
　　内装・デザイン・ラボ
施工／新建設
構造・規模／S造・地上3階建
面積／敷地・129.92㎡　建築・108.15㎡　床・1階96.95㎡　2階106.98㎡
　　3階67.41㎡　合計271.34㎡
工期／1985年1月下旬～6月上旬

Develop & Estate Agent Office GREEN HOMES

A small office having a large meaning for small developers, and a presentation space
It is not everything that has such a high added value than space, and it also is not everything to which such a high value can be added.
A "short" in the town. A city space producer. A plane becomes a solid which then becomes an environment. To act on such process would hopefully be our "correct posture." If we could visualize a higher added value developing in many directions along such process, we might be able to make "correct presentation" – hence we set about this design.

1-1-26, Jingumae, Shibuya-ku, Tokyo　Phone: 03-405-8876

Design / Masaaki Niitsu
Area / Site 129.92 m^2, Building 108.15 m^2,
Floor: 1st floor 96.95 m^2, 2nd floor 106.98 m^2,
3rd floor 67.41 m^2; Totalling 271.34 m^2

相談コーナーをみる

The consulting corner.

材料仕様

外壁／レンガタイル貼りＡＥＰ塗装及び化粧木片セメント板　外部床／寄木フローリング ココナッツタイル500角貼り及びカーペット　幅木／木製ＯＰ　壁面及び天井／総寒冷紗ＡＥＰ塗装　家具／カッシーナジャパン　アルフレックス　モビリア

営業内容

開店／1985年６月20日　営業時間／午前９時～午後７時　休日／毎月第２土曜日　日曜日　従業員／18人　主な取り扱い業務／建物の企画　設計及び売買　仲介　コンサルティング　その他不動産に関する一切の業務

吹抜け上部通路より応接室をみる

The reception room viewed from the aisle at an upper part of the stairwell.

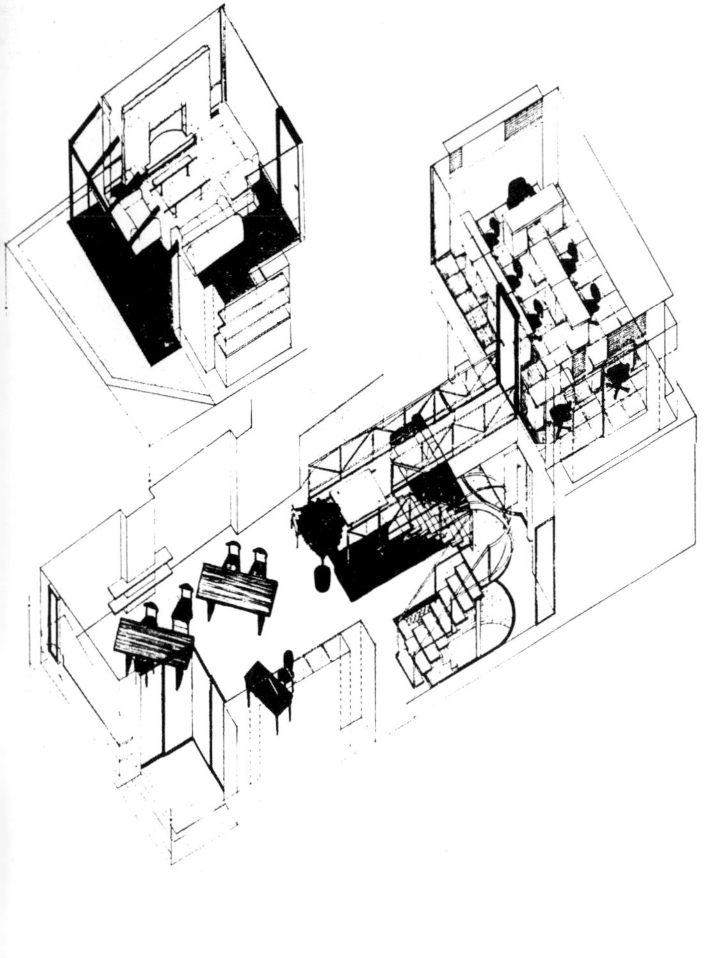

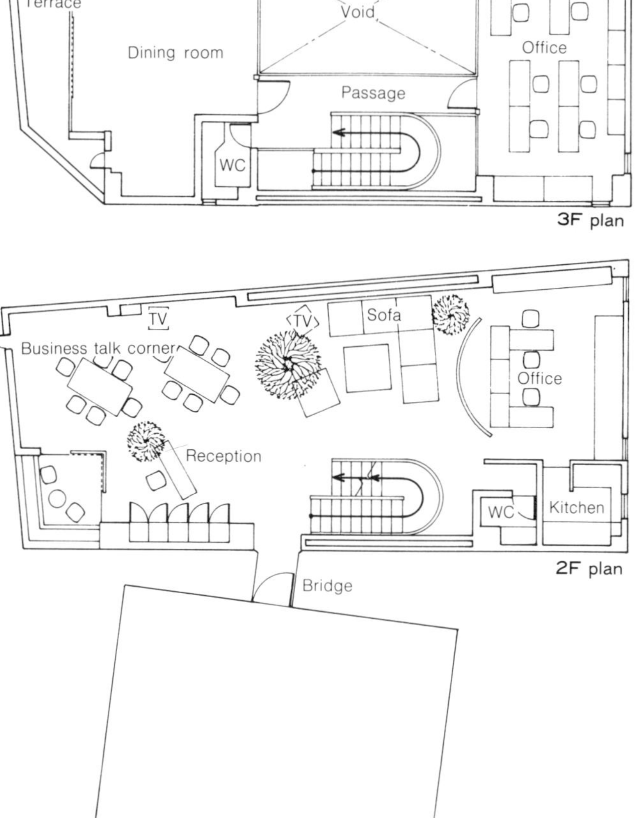

入口よりカウンターテーブルをみる

The counter table viewed from the entrance.

ショールーム

テクスチャー ショールーム

東京都渋谷区猿楽町9-8　Phone/03-477-2711

撮影／白鳥美雄

マンションの地階通路に面した入口廻り

The entrance area facing the basement aisle of a mansion-type apartment house.

奥よりカウンターテーブルを通して入口方向をみる

The entrance area viewed from an inner part across the counter table.

材料仕様

床／石材サンプル(25種類)ランダム貼り　壁面及び天井／染色(4色)アルミ角パイプ70×30ルバー組み　カウンター／脚・桛材クロス合板組み構造　トップ・アルミ t ＝12腐食仕上げ　熱線吸音ガラス2枚合わせ

営業内容

開店／1986年4月10日　営業時間／午前11時～午後7時　休日／毎週日曜日　祭日　経営者／㈱ヨコタデザイン・ワークスタジオ

入口左側より全景をみる　The entire appearance viewed from the left side of the entrance.

右側壁面収納棚の扉を開けた状態　The door of the storage shelf on the right side wall is opened.

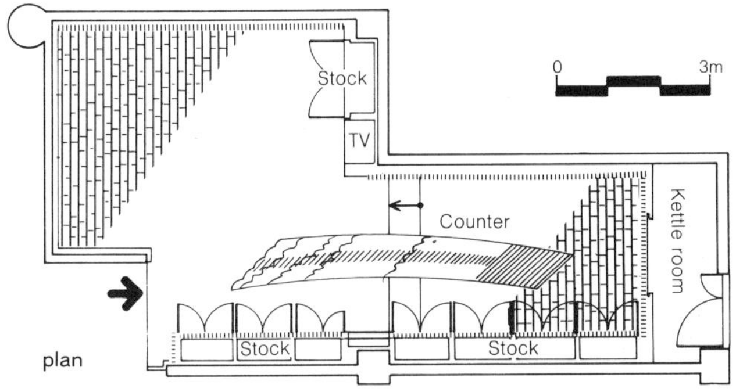

三者三様のコンセプトが一つのスペースに拮抗する

このショールームは３人のデザイナー・北岡節男氏(ウォール&シーリング) 横田良一氏 (フロア) 藤江和子氏(ファニチュア)が最初の打ち合わせの時に分担を決めて以来　顔を合わせることもなく　独自にデザインを進めて完成したものである。

このスペースは「ヨコタデザイン・ワークスタジオ」のショールームで　エキジビションも行えるギャラリー　広報活動のためのプレスルーム　クライアントとの打ち合わせ及びプレゼンテーションルーム　プロダクツ製品のための展示スペースという４つの役割を持った多目的スペースである。

デザイン事務所が　このようなスペースを持つことは　日本では珍しいが　欧米ではあたりまえのことである。歴史の違いといってしまえばそれまでであるが　自分のデザイン姿勢を一貫したものとして　積極的にプレゼンテーションするためにも　必要スペースであろう。新しい試みで誕生したこの「テクスチャー ショールーム」が　どのように機能していくか　デザインだけではなく　他の側面にも注目してみたい。

〈編集部〉(86-7)

企画／ヨコタデザイン・ワークスタジオ
設計／北岡節男(ウォール&シーリング)
　　横田良一(フロア)　藤江和子(ファニチュア)
施工／美留土
面積／52.9㎡(うち湯沸室4.7㎡)
工期／1985年11月11日～11月16日(インテリア)
　　1986年２月１日～３月31日 (ファニチュア)

Showroom TEXTURE Showroom

Three unique design concepts contend with each other

This showroom was completed by incorporating unique concepts of three designers – Mr. Setsuo Kitaoka (wall & ceiling), Mr. Ryoichi Yokota (floor), and Ms. Kazuko Fujie (furniture) – who have not met since the first arrangement by which they fixed their shares of work, and have thereafter proceeded with their own design.

This space is a showroom of "Yokota Design Work Studio," and a multi-purpose space consisting of a gallery where an exhibition can also be held, a press room for PR activities, a presentation room that also serves as a place for arrangements with clients, and a products display space.

In Japan this type of spacious design office is very rare, but quite usual in the U.S. and Europe. We may simply attribute it to the difference in history, but this showroom may be said to represent a positive attitude towards consistent presentation of one's own design concept in such a wide space. It is worth watching how this "TEXTURE Showroom" born as a new attempt will develop functionally not merely in respect of design, but also in respect of other aspects.

9-8, Sarugaku-cho, Shibuya-ku, Tokyo
Phone: 03-477-2711

Design / Setsuo Kitaoka, Kazuko Fujie, Ryoichi Yokota
Area / 52.9 m² (mini-kitchen 4.7 m²)

エフェクトスペース　実際の使用状況を再現して演出効果を確かめる
The effect space where light presentation effects are confirmed by reproducing an actual state of use.

ショールーム
ライティング ラボ

東京都港区海岸1-15 鈴江ビル4階　Phone/03-438-0400

撮影／白鳥美雄

実験室を超えるスペースを目指す

商業空間をクリエイトしている人たちに　光の演出効果を見てもらえるスペースとして　東京・竹下桟橋のロフト街に「ライティング ラボ」がオープンした。660m²天井高5.8mのこのラボは4つのスペースで構成されている。

ここでは　光のデータを測定し　設計に役立てることはもちろんであるが　重要な役割として"光効果"を"実験室"の範囲から"社会との関わり"まで拡げること　オーバーな表現をすれば　現代の文化との関わり方について　色々と試みる空間として　様々な人たちの協力を得ながら模索していくことを目指している。

インテリア設計の立場も　この点を有効に表現できるように　実験スペースはシンプルにして　機器を移動させたり　間仕切りを取り付けたり機能のセグメント化を　色々な立場で表現できるようにシステム化されている。ロビースペースは　打ち合わせをしたり　お茶　酒を飲みながら光の効果を体験でき　そこからの景色は港　海で　大変美しく　昼も夜も光の変化を楽しませてくれる。　〈阿久根正次＋高取邦和〉(84-12)

企画／大光電機　設計／スーパーポテト＋TACT DAIKO
グラフィック／田中一光デザイン室
施工／山田建設　面積／1階・660m²　2階・120m²　合計780m²
工期／1984年4月1日～9月4日

サインスペース　サインの視認性を実験できる

The sign space where visibility of sign is experimented with.

Showroom LIGHTING LABO

Aims at a space which goes beyond a labo

At a loft street in Takeshita Sanbashi, Tokyo, opened "Lighting Labo" as a space where commercial space creators can see light presentation effects. 660 m^2 in area and 5.8 m in ceiling height, this labo consists of four spaces.

Here, not merely data on light is measured to help in design, it is also intended to expand "light effects" from the scope of a "laboratory" to "social relations" – or, when exaggerated a little, it is intended to use this space for various attempts in relation to the modern culture, while seeking cooperation from various people in various fields.

As for interior design, in order to effectively express this point, the experimental space was simplified for systemized arrangements through movement of devices, installation of partitions, segmentation of functions, etc. At the lobby space you can make arrangements, experience the light effects while having a tea or liquor, and enjoy beautiful scenery outside – port and sea – with varying changes of light night and day.

1-15, Kaigan, Minato-ku, Tokyo　Phone: 03-438-0400

Design / Super Potato & Tact Daiko

Area / 1st floor 660 m^2, 2nd floor 120 m^2;　Totalling 780 m^2

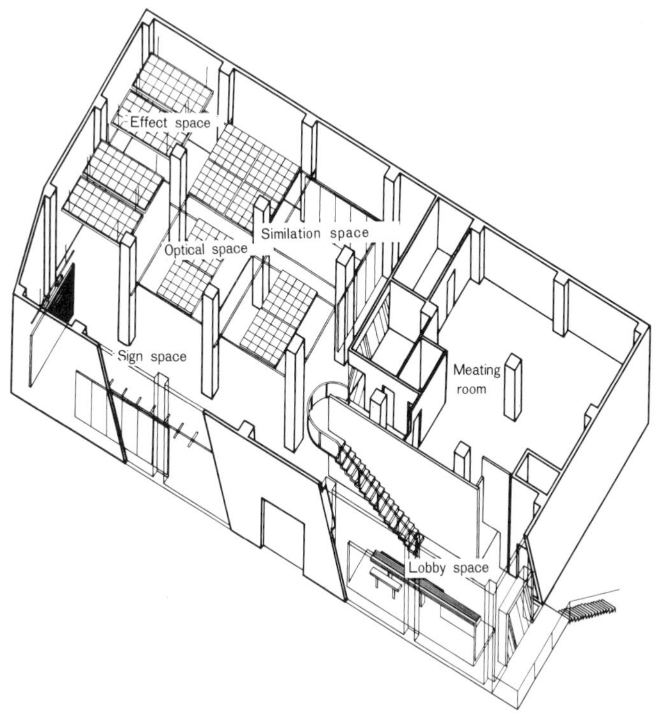

オプティカルスペース　各種ベースライトを点灯させた状態で天井をスライドさせて照明効果を比較検討をする

The optical space where, with various kinds of base light at on, the ceiling is slided to comparatively examine the effects of lighting.

ロビースペース　海の見えるレセプションバー

The lobby space with a reception bar from which the sea is visible.

材料仕様

床／コンクリート既存塗装仕上げ　壁面及び天井／コンクリート既存塗装仕上げ(白)　照明／スライド・昇降天井照明＋ベースライト　什器／可変型間仕切り　カウンター廻り／黒御影石及び積層材及び縁甲板及びステンレスＨＬ板貼り

営業内容

開店／1984年９月５日　営業時間／午前９時～午後６時　休日／毎週日曜日　祭日　経営者／大光電機㈱

透明ガラス張りの見通しの良いファサード

The transparent glassed facade from which you can easily look into the shop.

布

小倉 布 アネックス

福岡県北九州市小倉北区大手町3-1
コープ野村第1土居ビル1階
Phone/093-561-8152

撮影／岡本公二

入口左側より店内をみる

The inside viewed from the left side of the entrance.

店内奥より全景を俯瞰する

在るがままといった感じの店づくり

「小倉 布 アネックス」は小倉の繁華街から少し離れた紫川沿いのマンションの1階にある。

「布 アネックス」の名の通り 六本木「布」の姉妹店である。店では テキスタイルプランナー・新井淳一氏のオリジナルの布「㈱布」で企画された様々なオリジナル製品が売れている。また 単に布を売るだけでなく布を使ったインテリア ディスプレイなどの企画やデザインについても相談にのるという かなり幅の広い機能を持った店である。また十分あるスペースを利用して 一部をギャラリーとして使用している。

店づくりにあたっては あまりデザインをしないという方向ですすめていった。一方ローコストという問題もあったが なるべくありきたりの素材を使って あまりデザインせず 何となくボソッとしていて 在るがままといった感じの店になるよう心掛けた。 〈須田和由〉(86-11)

企画／新井淳一 設計／須田和由 施工／今岡富雄

面積／91.26㎡ 工期／1986年6月5日〜20日 工費／845万円

he entire inside overlooked from an inner part of the shop.

店内奥の接客コーナーをみる　The guest service corner at an inner part of the shop.

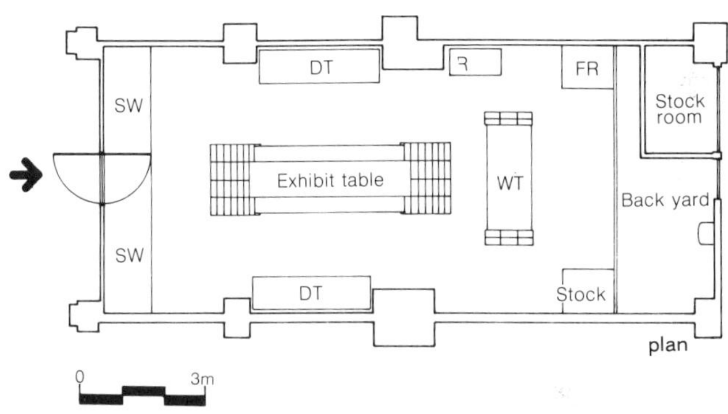

材料仕様
外壁／スチールサッシ　ガラスFix 床／楢フローリング　一部モルタル　壁面／モルタル金鏝　天井／軽量鉄骨下地SOP　照明器具／スポットライト　ダウンライト　什器／ブロック積み　棚／桜一枚板　フィッティングルーム／布

営業内容
開店／1986年６月25日　営業時間／午前11時～午後７時　休日／毎週木曜日　経営者／布・アネックス 小倉 従業員／３人　客単価／２～３万円　主な取り扱い商品／新井淳一のオリジナル布　㈱布で企画した布製品

Fabric Kokura NUNO Annex

Shop making in a natural style

"Kokura Nuno Annex" is at the 1st floor of a mansion-type apartment house along River Murasaki which is a little apart from the amusement streets in Kokura City.

As the name "Nuno Annex" shows, it is a sister company of "Nuno" in Roppongi. Here, a variety of original products, designed by Mr. Junichi Arai, textile planner, and offered by Nuno Co., Ltd., are available. This shop not merely sells pieces of cloth, but also gives advice about planning and design of interior display using pieces of cloth. Thus, it has very wide functions. Part of the wide space is utilized as a gallery.

In shop making, we made it a policy to minimize the design. Meanwhile, partly to reduce the cost, we used as ordinary materials as possible, so that this shop becomes as plain and natural as possible.

3-1, Otemachi, Kokurakita-ku, Kitakyushu City, Fukuoka Prefecture
Phone: 093-561-8152

Design / Kazuyoshi Sudo
Area / 91.26 m^2

ファサード　ギャラリー空間を構成するパーティションとスクリーン

The facade. The partition and screen composing the gallery space.

店内奥より入口方向をみる
The entrance area viewed from an inner part of the shop.

垣間見ることによる期待感

従来のテーブルウェア ショップでは 商品が大量に陳列され ショップフロントも開放的であった。しかし この「サボア ヴィーブル」のように 大型商業施設の中にあっては 商品の量の多さをもって訴求するには いささか抵抗があった。加えて この店では 六本木の「サボア ヴィーブル」(六本木アクシス3階) の連携のもとに 計画されたこともあって 思いきって“ギャラリー”性を打ち出すデザインとした。この“ギャラリー”性を形成するのが 正面ガラスパーティションと八字型のスクリーンである。閉鎖的とも思えるこのスクリーンによって ファサードは他店との差別化を 内部は落ち着いた空間を創り出せたと思っている。パーティションとスクリーンの間は ディスプレイスペースで 常時陳列商品のエッセンスが飾られ 少しずらして設けられたスクリーンの間から垣間見られる商品との連携によって 閉鎖的な中にも期待感を演出している。　〈辻健次郎／文責・編集部〉(85-12)

企画／吉左右　宮坂一郎　設計／アーキテクトディザイン　辻健次郎
施工／白水社　面積／41.7m²　工期／1986年7月16日

テーブルウェア
サボア ヴィーブル

東京都世田谷区玉川3-17-1　Phone/03-707-4368

撮影／大竹静市郎

ディスプレイ スペースを通して店内をみる

The inside viewed through the display space.

Tableware SAVOIA VIVRE

Allows you peeping expectantly

At the conventional tableware shops commodities have been displayed in large quantities, and the shop-front has been somewhat open. However, in the case of shops like "Savoia Vivre" which are within large commercial facilities, we felt it a little hesitant to create an appeal with the massive quantity of goods alone. Additionally, in cooperation with "Savoia Vivre" (at the 3rd floor of Axis, Roppongi) in Roppongi, we hammered out a design stressing the "gallery" space. This feature was expressed by the front glass partition and <-shaped screen. By this screen that may be said to be closed, it is believed that the facade could help differentiate this shop from other shops, and a composed space could be created inside. Between the partition and screen is a display space where the essence of displayed goods is always present so that they may be peeped through the screen provided a little shiftedly. Thus, in a closed space you can see goods expectantly.

3-17-1, Tamagawa, Setagaya-ku, Tokyo　Phone: 03-707-4368

Design / Kenjiro Tsuji
Area / 41.7 m^2

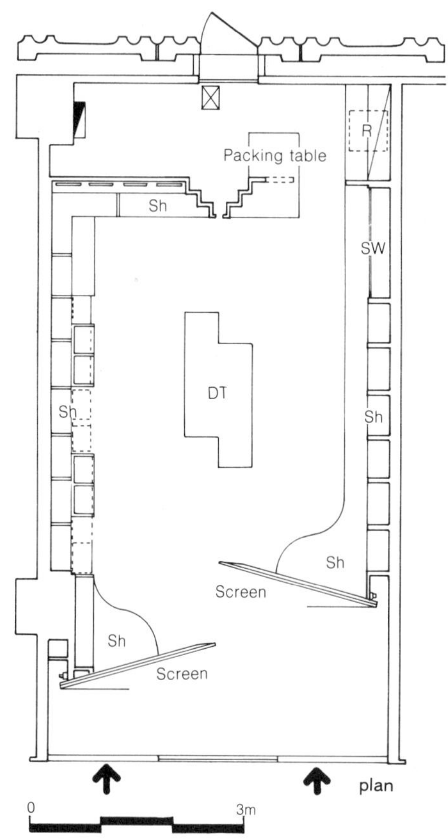

材料仕様

床／ラワンｔ＝９＋ｔ＝９下地　ホモジニアスビニール床タイル貼り　壁面／ＰＢｔ＝12下地シグマルト吹付けＶＰ　天井／ＰＢｔ＝12下地　ＶＰ　スクリーン／木下地　アルミシート仕上げ

営業内容

開店／1984年８月５日　営業時間／午前10時～午後９時　休日／なし　経営者／㈱吉左右　従業員／３人

プレゼンテーションスペースをみる　8面ある3角形のユニットがそれぞれ上下に可動する
The presentation space. Each of eight triangular units moves up and down.

ショールーム
ショーケース パン

東京都港区南青山3-11-10　Phone/03-404-5445

外観全景　**The entire appearance.**

撮影／小笠原　昌 & 鳴瀬　亨

中央のスペースフレームを通して奥のオフィスをみる

The inner office viewed through the central space frame.

阿部紘三デザインのオフィス用ビッグテーブルをみる

The big office table designed by Kozo Abe.

2階の喫茶スペース
The tea salon space at the 2nd floor.

20世紀終焉の無代創知

今　多様なものが同時に存在する時代である。気分が有生し　モノが寄生する。そして時代は気分を演出する。
考えてみれば忙しい時代――省エネの時代――質の時代――そして　こだわり　美の時代へ。その中で'81年に文化や価値を提示したメンフィスの運動がある。時間(歴史)と空間(場所)をとびこえヨーロッパ文化のみに留まらず　東洋の文化をも　そのボキャブラリーとして収集することによりインターナショナルなスタイル(地球的様式)を生成させた。今世紀末に向かって　広義のデザインは　終への喝采を受けようとしている。"Yes!"であれ"No"であれ"好き"であれ"嫌い"であれ……。SHOWCASE PAN TOKIO。この無機質な空感。考えてみれば　ごくありふれた"何んでもなさ"。しかし緻密に計画された平面分割と変幻自在　そして　緊張感と期待感　ふとした精神的安定感を与えるのは何だろう。原始から共生してきた石のせいかもしれない。人は石を敬い　石で戦い　石で守り　石で文化を創ってきた。20世紀終焉の無代創知　PANは"素の空間"20世紀のタイムカプセル　そして21世紀へのノアの箱舟でもある。
〈柳田健一〉(85-11)

設計／柳田健一　施工／エンジニアリング・フジ
面積／191m²　工期／1985年6月1日～26日

材料仕様
外壁／磁器タイル貼り100角 オーニング　ステンレス鏡面仕上げ及びＨＬ　外部床／黒御影石ジェットバーナー及び磨き仕上げ　サイン／ステンレス　スコッチカル貼り　シルクスクリーン文字　床／黒御影石ジェットバーナー及び磨き仕上げ　可動可変ステージ／トップ・寄木貼り　フレーム(スチールハンマートーン)　壁面／コルクリートパネル　ステンレスフィーバー混入　磨き仕上げ　一部黒御影石磨き仕上げ　天井／ＲＣ打放しＶＰ　一部ＰＢ貼り　照明器具／スポット及びウォールウォッシャー型ＤＬ　家具／壁面収納壁・突板合板貼り　ウレタン塗装鏡面仕上げ　素材ディスプレイ台／ラッカー研磨き　テーブル／突板合板貼り　ウレタン塗装　鏡面仕上げ　カウンター／ウレタン塗装　鏡面仕上げ

営業内容
開店／1986年6月27日　営業時間／午前10時～午後6時　休日／毎週日曜日　祭日　経営者／㈱フジ　従業員／6人　アドバイザースタッフ／阿部紘三　石上申八郎　パオロ パルッコ　ステファノ ステファニ　ラウラ デ ロレンツォ　主な商品と取り扱い業務／パルッコ　ザノッタ　カルテルなどのヨーロッパ家具及びオリジナル家具と新素材　スペースデザインの企画　設計　施工

Showroom SHOWCASE PAN

A timeless stage towards the end of 20th century

Now, we live in the days where various things exist simultaneously. Moods thrive, various things live upon them, and the times present moods.
We have long lived in the busy times – the age of energy conservation – the age of quality – and are entering the age of particularism and beauty. In this current of the times is the movement of Memphis that suggested a new-type culture and values in 1981. Going beyond time (history) and space (place), this movement intended to collect not merely the European culture, but also the Oriental culture as its vocabulary, thus generating an international style (global ritual). Towards the end of this century, design, in its wider sense, is being applauded for its coming to an end – whether you say "Yes!," or "No!," or "I like" or "I don't like" it . . . .
"Showcase Pan Tokio" – this inorganic, vacant space. Very plain, "being ordinary." However, therein arranged carefully a division of plane and kaleidoscopic changes. And, a tension and expectations. What is it that gives our mind a sense of stability? It may be stones with which man has lived together since the primitive age. Man has respected stones, fought using stones, protected himself with stones, and created culture with stones. A timeless stage towards the end of the 20th century. "Showcase Pan" is a "space for nothingness," a time capsule of the 20th century, and also Noah's Ark towards the 21st century.

3-11-10, Minami-aoyama, Minato-ku, Tokyo　Phone: 03-404-5445

Design / Kenichi Yanagida
Area / 191 m²

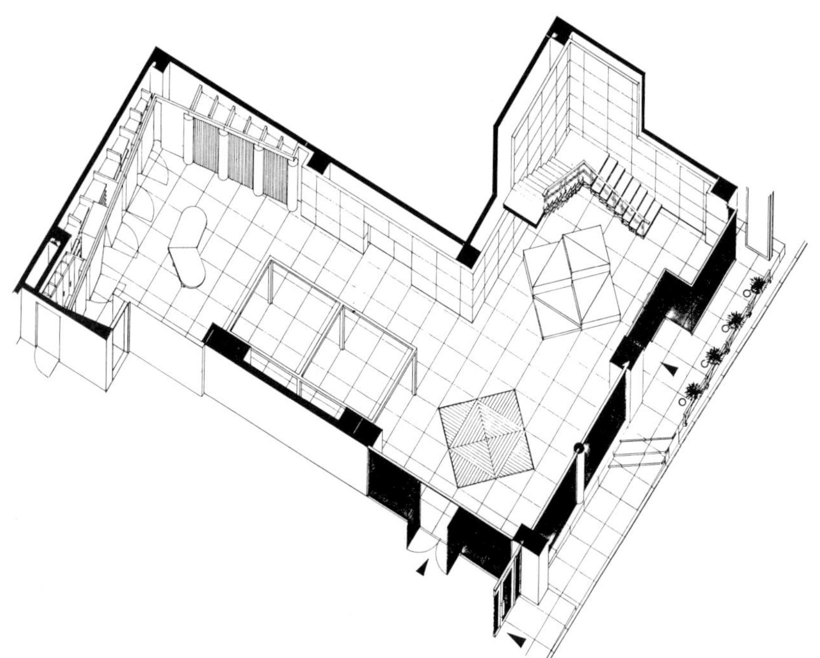

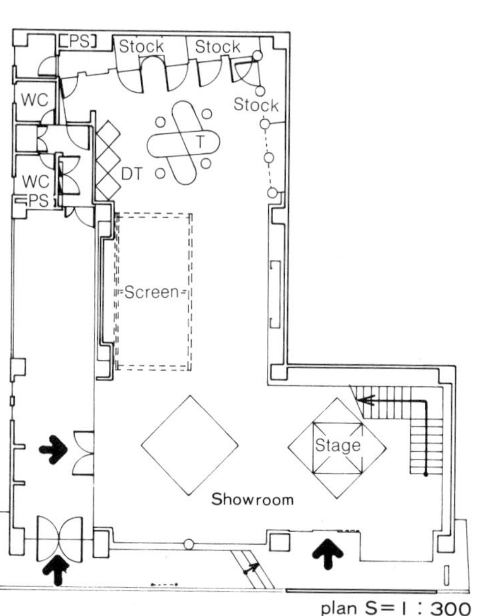

plan S＝1：300

1階中央よりチェアがディスプレイされた通路を通して階段方向をみる
The staircase area viewed from the center of the 1st floor through the aisle where chairs are displayed.

2階奥に設けられたアートギャラリー The art gallery provided at the 2nd floor.

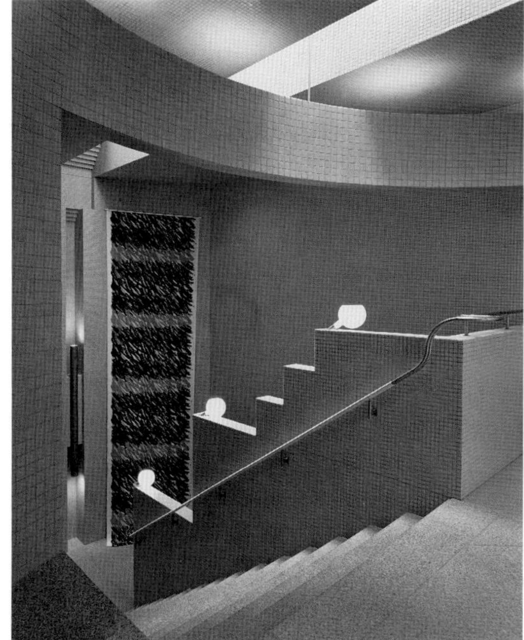
シリンダー状の階段室を2階より俯瞰する
The cylindrical stairway overlooked from the 2nd floor.

インテリアギャラリー アクタス

東京都新宿区新宿2-19-1 ビックスビル1・2階 Phone/03-356-3363

撮影/北田英治

メインの入口廻り The main entrance area.

2階コンサルティングコーナー脇より階段室方向をみる

The stairway area viewed from a side of the 2nd floor consulting corner.

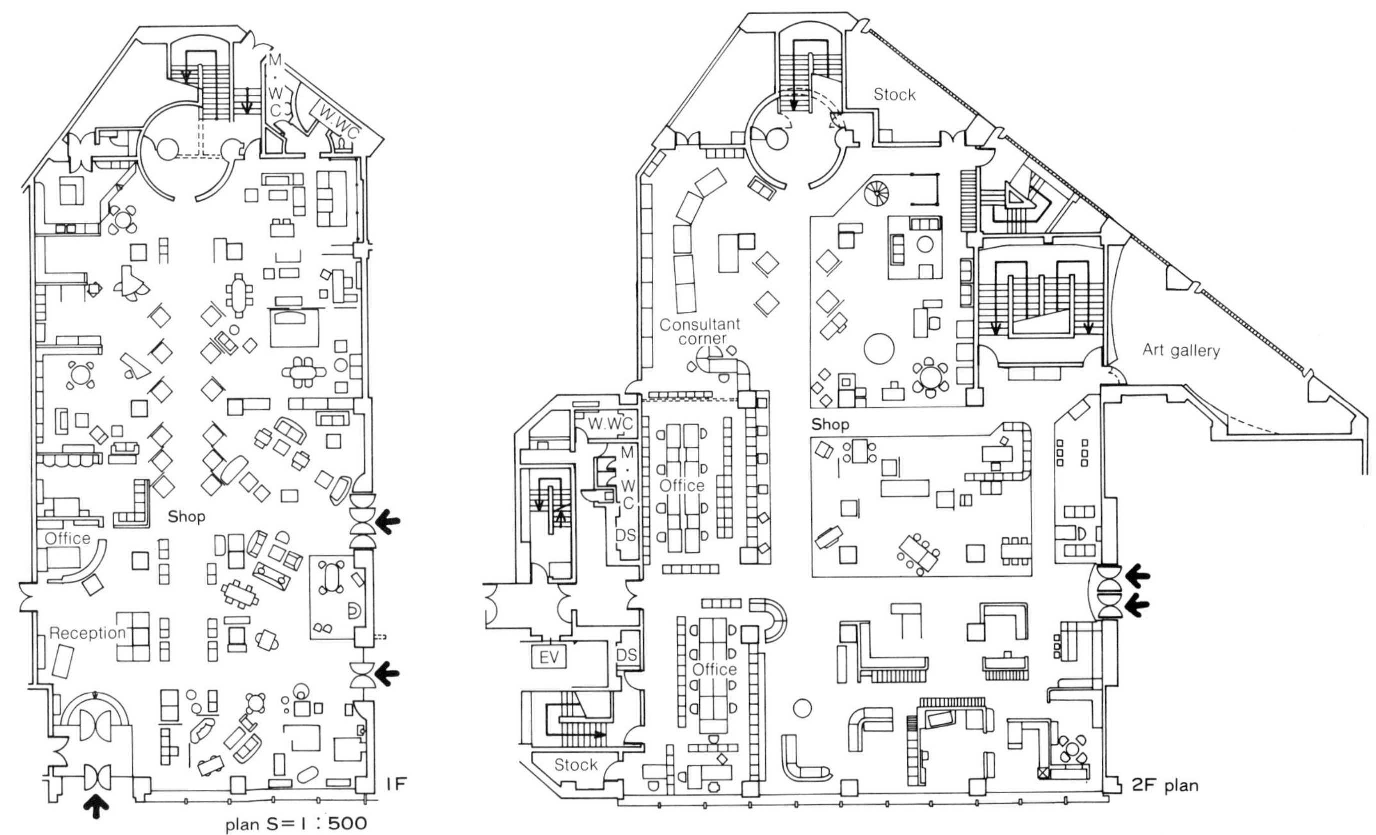

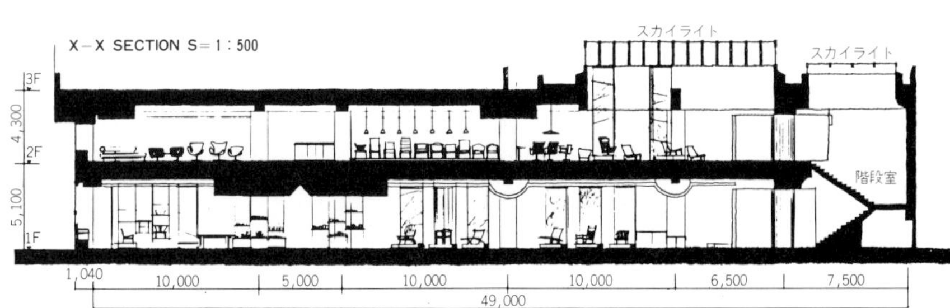

材料仕様
屋上サイン／板面アルミアルマイト加工　文字スコチカルシート貼り　入口自立サイン／米松丸太彫刻　床／楢材フローリング　階段室・黒御影石ジェット仕上げ　幅木／楢材CL　壁面／PB下地寒冷紗貼りペイント仕上げ　階段室・ガラスモザイクタイル貼り　天井／PB下地ペンキ仕上げ　照明器具／基本照明・FL間接照明　スポット照明　什器／ガラス吊棚・ゴビオン(アクタス)

営業内容
開店／1985年6月9日　営業時間／午前10時～午後6時30分　休日／なし　経営者／㈱アクタス・桐山東一郎　従業員／30人　主な商品／インターリュブケ　マークテックス　マデス　ボーゲンポール　ロルフ ベンツ　トーネット　ポルトローナ フラウなどのヨーロッパ輸入家具及び美術工芸品　アクセサリー

斬新なプレゼンテーションを可能にするための可変的システムをもつ

“インテリアギャラリー”というネーミングは　多彩な商品構成による様々なライフスタイルを展開してみせる“場”の意味である。このショップの特徴は　商品が多種多様であり　また　定常的ディスプレイにとどまらず　斬新なプレゼンテーションが常に行われるということでありその良きステージとなるために内部空間は　可変性に富んだシステムを持っていなければならない。
2000m²を超え　2層にわたる広いスペースを　どう分割し　どうアクセントをつけるかについては　商品構成の多様な変化を十分予測し　演出の手法をできる限りシンプルな形で考えた。装置は極力　原始的にした。幸い建築のスケルトンの状態では　階高がまれにみる高さを持っていたため　思い切り　この利点を生かすことを第一とした。

〈竹氏宏和／アクタス設計部〉(85-8)

設計／建築・日建設計東京　内装・喜多隼紀建築事務所　アクタス
施工／建築・五洋建設　内装・五洋建設　丹青社
面積／1階・943m²　2階・1260m²　合計2203m²
工期(内装)／1984年12月1日～1985年6月7日

Interior Gallery ACTUS

Having a variable system that makes novel presentation possible

The naming "Interior Gallery" means a "place" used to unfold various life-styles with a composition of various lines of goods. Here, not merely a regular display, but also a novel presentation are always performed. In order to serve as a good stage for such displays, the inside space must have a variable system.
As for the division of wide space extending over 2,000 m² in two layers, we simplified the mode of presentation as much as possible in expectation of wide changes in a goods composition. We also employed as primitive devices as possible. Fortunately, in the state of skeleton, since this building had an exceptional height, we tried to utilize this advantage as much as possible.

2-19-1, Shinjuku, Shinjuku-ku, Tokyo　Phone: 03-356-3663

Design / Hayaki Kita & Hirokazu Takeuji
Area / 1st floor 943 m², 2nd floor 1260 m²; Totalling 2203 m²

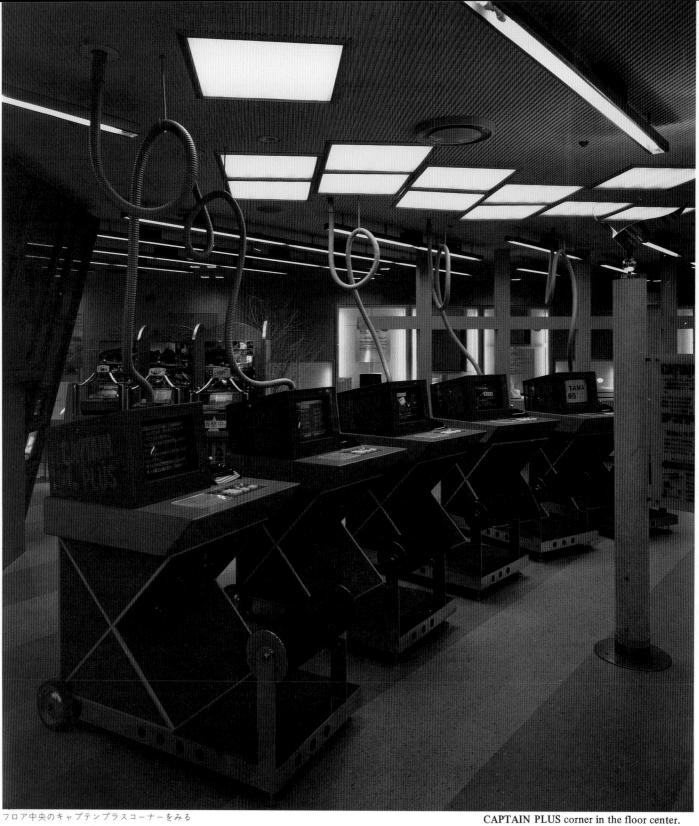

フロアの中央のキャプテンプラスコーナーをみる

CAPTAIN PLUS corner in the floor center.

ショールーム

NTTテレコムプラザ 聖蹟桜ヶ丘

東京都多摩市関戸321-3 Phone/0423-76-5000

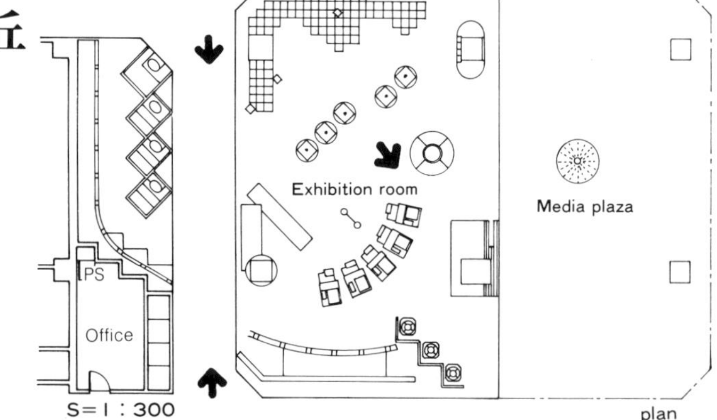

撮影／佐田山靖雄

キャプテンブースをみる

CAPTAIN booths.

多元的でイメージ豊かなメディア遊園地

このショールームは“NTTと地域の人々との新しい接点　コミュニケーションの場の創出”という基本コンセプトを展開するにあたって多元的で　イメージ豊かで　楽しみのあるエレクトロニックメディアの演出をテーマに設計が行われた。

各コーナーは　独立した固有の形　仕上げ　色彩としており　しかもランダムに配置され　あたかもオモチャ箱をひっくり返したようになった。まるで　にぎやかなメディア遊園地のように。

中心になったキャプテン端末は　若い主婦や子供ら　初心者を対象にしたキャプテンプラスと　多少機器の操作ができるレベルを対象にしたキャプテンブースがある。キャプテンブースには　パソコン通信等　他の機能も付加され　その一角には　グラフィックス等も使え　今後　地域の人達や学生のサークルにも利用してもらうIT(情報入力)コーナーもある。　〈長岡憲夫／建築センター第一建築工事課主査〉(86-7)

設計／NTT東京総支社建築センター　SUR都市建築事務所

施工／京王建設　丹青社　面積／266.67m²

工期／1986年1月15日～3月21日

Showroom NTT TELECOM PLAZA Seiseki-sakuragaoka

A plural media playland rich with images

In developing the basic concept, "creation of a new point of NTT's contact and communications with community inhabitants, we proceeded with designing this shop towards presenting plural, pleasant electronic media rich with images.

Each corner comes with an independent, characteristic shape, finish and colors, and is arranged at random. Overall, this space looked just like a toy box turned upside down – like a jay media playland.

The CAPTAIN terminals in the center consist of CAPTAIN PLUS's for beginners (young housewives, children, etc.) and CAPTAIN booths for those who are more or less experienced in machine operation. CAPTAIN booths are equipped with personal computer communications and other functions. At a corner, graphics, etc. can be used. An IT (information input) corner is also open to community inhabitants and student circles.

321-3, Sekido, Tama City, Tokyo　Phone: 0423-76-5000

Design / Norio Nagaoka
Area / 266.67 m^2

フロア中央部全景をみる　左側がコミュニケーションタワー　左奥がキャプテンプラス　右奥がテレフォンテーブル
The entire view of the floor center. The communication tower in the left side. CAPTAIN PLUS at an inner left part. The telephone table at an inner right part.

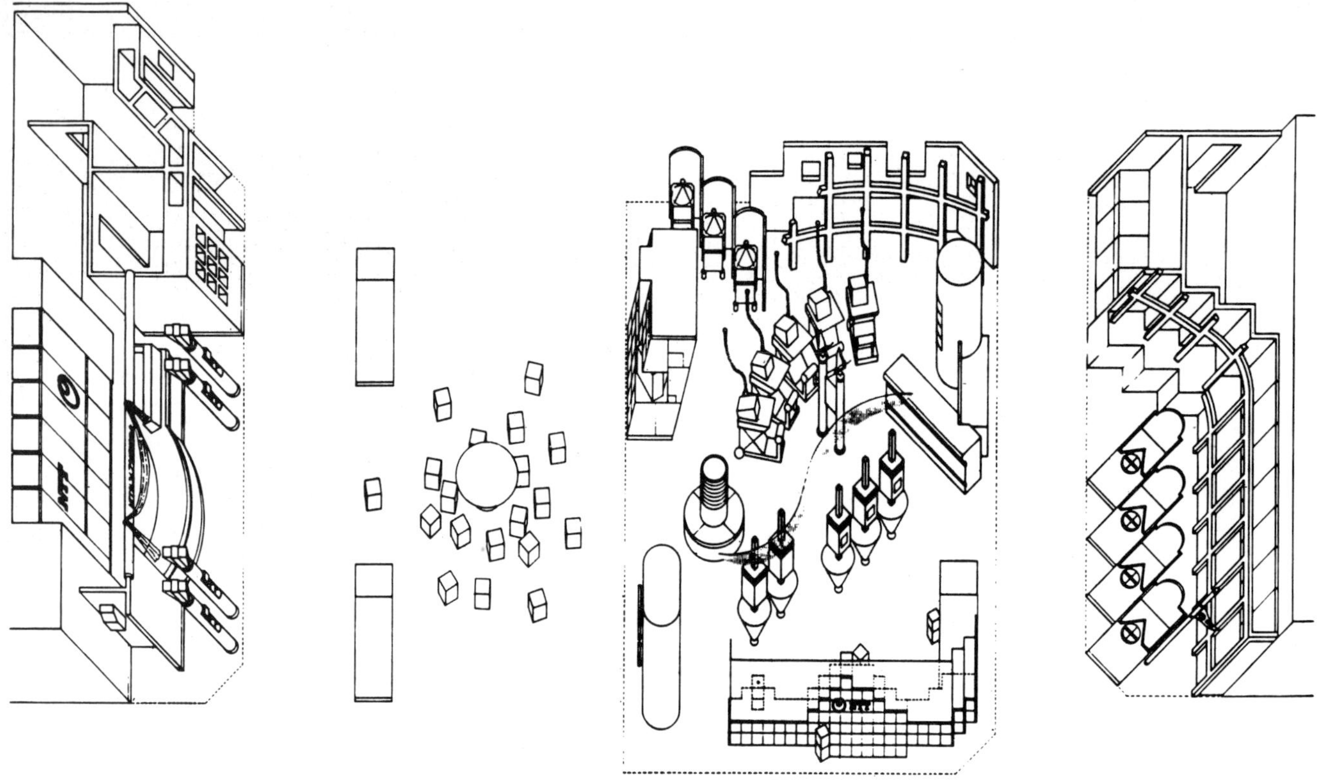

材料仕様

〈業務カウンター〉天板／大理石　見付／楢集成材染色仕上げ　真鍮ゴールドメッキ仕上げ　幅木／ステンレスＨＬ　腰／クロス貼り　内部／ポリエステル合板貼り　〈コミュニケーションタワー〉　鋼製フレーム／メタルサンドブラスト調アルキッド樹脂塗装吹付け　〈キャプテンプラス〉　モニターカバー／スチールパンチングメタルメラミン焼付け塗装　配管／ワイヤー入りフレキシブルパイプ　プリンターカバー／アクリル板　テーブル／楢集成材練付け仕上げ　下台／角パイプメラミン焼付け塗装ノンスリップシート貼り　腰掛け／ステンレス鏡面仕上げ　硬質ゴム巻付け　タイヤ／スポークタイプ　〈テレフォンテーブル〉　角パイプ及びガラリ／スチールメラミン焼付け塗装　ボックス／ノンスリップシート貼り　下台及び球体／スチールメラミン焼付け塗装　〈キャプテンブース〉　壁面／木製ラッカー塗装　見付／ステンレスＨＬ円窓　／ゴールド角パイプ　内棚／木製メラミン化粧板貼り　床／ノンスリップシート貼り　椅子／ビニークロス貼り　幅木／ステンレスＨＬ　〈アッパーライト〉　羽根飾り／真鍮ゴールドメッキ仕上げ　球／スチールクロームメッキ仕上げ　本体／スチール特殊勘圧接着シート貼り　幅木／スチールコールドメッキ仕上げ　ステンレスＨＬ　パネル／アクリル板　〈天井雲形スクリーン〉　本体／アルミパンチングメタル

営業内容

開店／1986年３月27日　営業時間／午前10時～午後７時　休日／毎週水曜日　経営者／ＮＴＴテレコムプラザ聖蹟桜ヶ丘　従業員／６人　施設内容／インフォメーションカウンター　キャプテンシステムのプレゼンテーション　テレフォンサービス　ニューメディア機器

フード＆和風の店
Foods & Japanese Style Shop

南西側進路よりみた外観

The appearance viewed from the aisle in the southwest side.

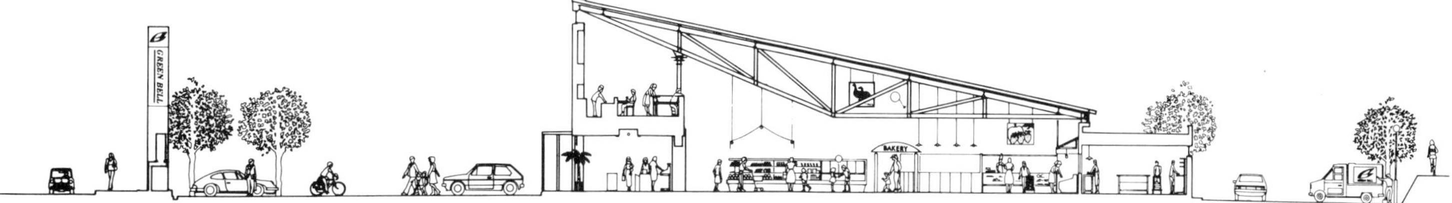

スーパーマーケットを核とした複合店
グリーンベル

富山県高岡市鐘紡1-19　Phone/0766-22-666

撮影／加斗タカオ

メインゲート広場をみる

The plaza viewed from the main gate.

スーパーのメイン エントランスホールに設けられた休憩コーナー

The rest corner provided at the supermarket's main entrance hall.

ファミリーレストラン

The family restaurant.

スーパーのエントランスホールよりフルーツ売場をみる

The fruits corner viewed from the supermarket's entrance hall.

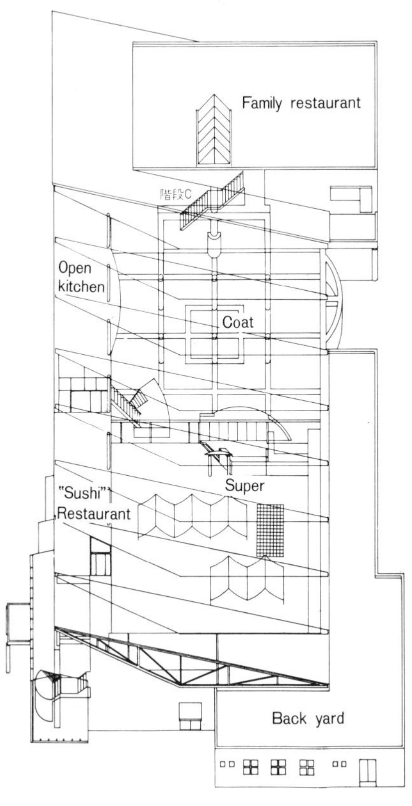

広場を媒介にした複合ショップ

高岡駅から南西へ車で約6分　カネボウ高岡工場に面した社宅跡に　この「グリーベル」は建設された。国道156号線沿い 川に挟まれた敷地は関係者の夢をかきたてた。県内は5店舗をもつスーパーマーケット「グリーンハウス」のオーナーと　そのコンサルタントが中心となり　この計画がすすめられた。"食"を中心とした単なる箱ではない　人々に親しまれる店　そして光と風を感じる店づくりがテーマとなり　深夜3時までの営業となった。

道路に並行した55mの打放しの長壁は　車に対するスケール感を表出するファサードとして　また同時に情報板として存在する。売場面積500m²のスーパーマーケットを核として　飲食4　美容　薬局各1　計6店舗を中央の広場(COURT)を媒介として複合させることで　長壁はより長く　強くなり　街区の形成へ向けて敷地いっぱいに拡がっていく。ファサードの後部は川であり　散歩やジョギングの土堤が続いている。川の復権へ向けて　川に対しての優しい表情とすべく斜めに大屋根をかけ　川沿いのプロムナードづくりへの呼びかけとしている。

〈岩佐達雄・大野文也〉(85-7)

企画／グリーンハウス　商業スペース研究所　都市建築設計事務所　ケイ(K)アトリエ

設計／都市建築設計事務所　ケイ(K)アトリエ　栗生　明　岩佐達雄　大野文也　大野　博　浜中勝美

施工／建築・グリーンハウス　内装・塩谷建設　テナント内装・日宣

構造・規模／RC造＋S造・平家　一部2階建

面積／敷地・4733.26m²　建築・1250.55m²　床・1階1095.68m²　2階403.30m²

工期／1984年10月1日～1985年3月21日

Composite Shop with Supermarket in the Main GREEN BELL

Composite shop formed round a plaza

About 6 minutes southeast by car from Takaoka Station, this "Green Bell" was constructed in the company residential site of Takaoka Factory of Kanebo. The site, along the highway (route No. 156) and facing a river, much roused the dream of those concerned, and the project was carried by the owner of the supermarket "Green House" chain (having 55 shops within Toyama Prefecture) and its consultant. The theme of shop-making was to make it not merely into a box centering around "eating," but also to have it serve as a familiar place for community inhabitants, with an atmosphere of light and wind. It is open till late at night (by 3:00 a.m.).

The long (55 m) wall of concrete as placed facing the road serves as the facade giving a spacious sense against the cars, and at the same time it exists an information board. With the supermarket whose selling area is 500 m^2 in the main, four restaurants, a beauty parlor and a pharmacy (6 shops in total) are located compositely around the central plaza (Court). In so doing, the long wall gets still longer, stronger, and fully expands across the site towards forming a street block. Behind the facade is a river with banks for walking or jogging. Aimed at rehabilitation of the river, the building has a large inclined roof to be gentle to the river, and they intend to create a promenade along the river.

1-19, Kanebo-cho, Takaoka City, Toyama Prefecture
Phone: 0766-22-6666

Design / K-Atelier
Area / Site 4733.26 m^2, Building 1250.55 m^2,
Floor: 1st floor 1095.68 m^2, 2nd floor 403.30 m^2

2階のオープンデッキより広場をみる

The plaza viewed from the open deck at the 2nd floor.

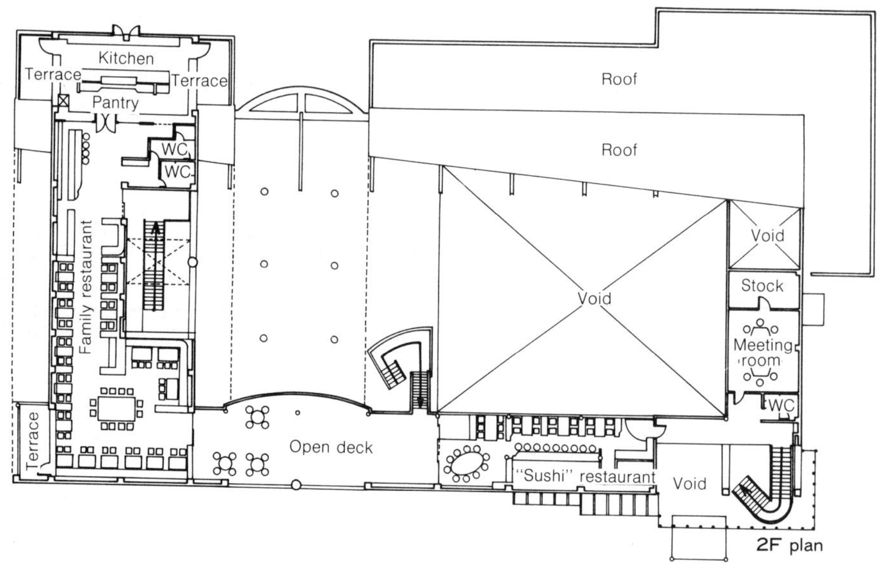

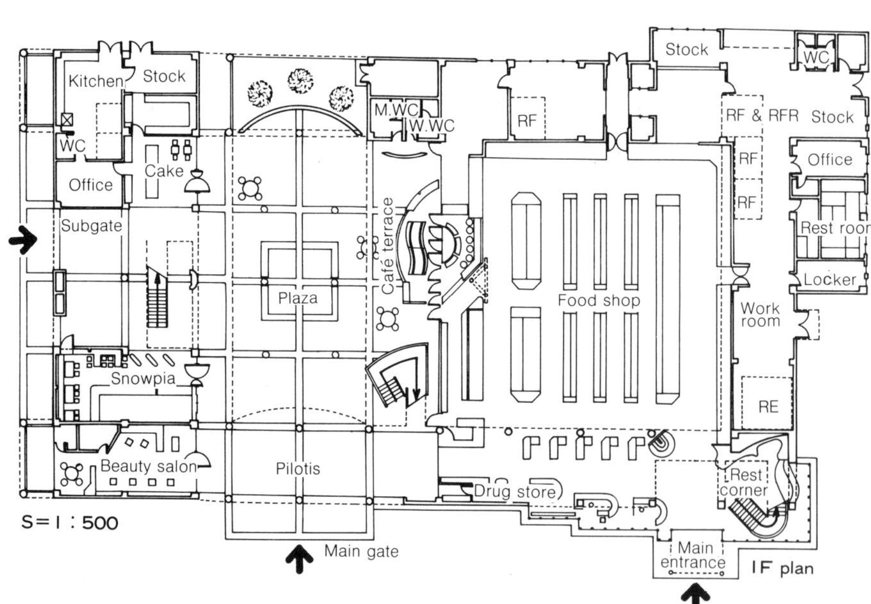

材料仕様

屋根／耐候性アルミメッキ鋼板折版　一部コンクリート　アスファルト防水砂利敷き　外壁／コンクリート打放し　アクリルクリアー塗装　鉄板サイディング　アルミカーテンウォール電解発色ステンカラー　外部床／豆砂利洗出し及び100×200炻器質タイル　サイン／ステンレス及び焼付け鋼板　〈グリーンハウス内装〉 床／テラゾタイル400角及び長天塩ビシート　一部檜フローリングウレタンCL　壁面／コンクリート打放しアクリルCL　PB下地ビニールクロス貼り　天井／不燃化粧石膏ボード

営業内容

開店／1985年3月21日　営業時間／午前10時～午前3時　休日／なし　経営者／㈱グリーンハウス　梶　登司治　従業員／10人　パート47人　合計57人

冷蔵ショーケースのディテール　集成材の上カシュー仕上げとステンレスヘアラインで構成
Details of the cold storage showcase, consisting of cashew-finished laminated material and stainless steel hairline.

京つけもの　西利

京都市中京区堀川御池上ル 京都全日空ホテル地下Ｉ階 伝統工芸ギャラリー内　Phone/075-231-1155

撮影／藤原　弘

漆黒とステンレスで構成された冷蔵ショーケースを中心にみる

The cold storage showcase featuring dark black lacquer and stainless steel.

ニューテイスト体験の場

この店は　京つけものの老舗「西利」が　新しく開発した商品・“パーティー”のために　設けた店舗である。

“パーティー”は　漬物を食卓の脇役として終らせるのではなく　オリジナルなドレッシングをあしらうことによって　ハイブリッドな味を造りだし　漬物の在り方に新しい提案を行おうとするものである。

コーナーはステージとニューテイストを体験するテーブルによって構成されている。ステージは商品の性格上　冷蔵ケースとなっている。その曲面は　とくに割り出したものではなく　たまたまこの場所に入り込んでいたギャラリー床のモザイク模様の　外周曲線をそのまま立ちあげたに過ぎない。

天板はステンレスのＨＬ仕上げ　黒曜石をモチーフとした　両袖の塊(マッス)によって支えてある。塊を貫通した鏡面仕上げの天板は破断され　あいまいな断面が　テーブルの天板へと移行される。天板は極限まで薄く造った艶消しのカシュー仕上げである。

漆黒とステンレスによって構成したこれらの装置が　ニューシーンを模索する人々にとって　既知のコードのコンバーターになることを期待している。

〈若林広幸〉(86-11)

設計／若林広幸建築研究所　若竹広幸

施工／末徳京都営業所　面積／30.8㎡

工期／1985年５月20日（１日のみ）　工費／400万円

店内全景

The entire inside scene.

材料仕様
床／橅フローリング染色塗装仕上げ　一部大理石貼り　壁面／橅練付け染色塗装仕上げ　一部ガラスモザイクタイル貼り　一部漆寒仕上げ　天井／ＰＢ下地ＯＰ仕上げ　什器／冷蔵ケース　ステージ天板・ステンレスＨＬ仕上げ及び鏡面仕上げ　ステージ腰・ステンレス仕上げ　集成材の上カシュー仕上げ　テーブル／天板・橅合板の上カシュー仕上げ　一部ステンレス鏡面仕上げ

営業内容
開店／1985年６月25日　休日／なし　経営者／㈱西利　御業員／３人　客席数／６席　客単価／800円 旬の京漬物とお茶漬セット800 旬の京漬物と宇治茶350 パーティー各種200～400

Japanese Pickles NISHIRI

A place for experiencing new tastes

This shop was provided by "Nishiri," an old established Kyoto pickles shop, for "Party," new-type pickles developed by Nishiri.

"Party" has been developed so that pickles do not merely play a secondary role on the table, but offer hybrid tastes by garnishing with original dressing, thus proposing a new style of pickles tasting. The corner consists of a stage and table for experiencing the new tastes. In view of the nature of goods, the stage consists of a cold storage showcase. Its curved surface was employed casually, simply by raising the circumferential curve of mosaic pattern on the gallery floor which *happened* to be there.

The stage's surface board is of HL(hairline)-finished stainless steel, with both ends supported by obsidian-motif masses. The mirror-finished surface board penetrating the masses is broken, and the vague cross-section is shifted to the table. The surface board, thinned to an extremity, is finished with frosted cashew.

It is expected that these units featuring dark black lacquer, stainless steel finish become a converter of the known code for those groping a new scene.

Horikawa-oike, Nakagyo-ku, Kyoto City　　Phone: 075-231-1155

Design / Hiroyuki Wakabayashi
Area / 30.8 m^2

入口側より１階洋菓子売場をみる
The 1st floor Western confectionery corner viewed from the entrance side.

和洋菓子＋和洋レストラン
＋カフェ
たちばな本店

東京都世田谷区南烏山5-14-5　Phone/03-309-2341

２つの顔をもつファサード
The facade having two faces.

撮影／本木誠一

材料仕様

屋根／モルタル金鏝目地切り　シート防水仕上げ　一部化粧屋根(カラーベスト)ｒ壁／黒御影石　二丁掛タイル　ＡＬＣ版吹付タイル　床／1階･〈和菓ｺ　塩ビタイル貼り　〈茶室〉磁器タイル貼り300角　〈洋菓子〉塩ビタイル貼り　〈パン売場〉楢パーケットフローリング　２階･〈カフェ〉楢フローリングｔ＝10カーペット敷き　〈和食〉ｔ＝10カーペット敷き　壁面／１階･〈和菓子売場〉聚落仕上げ　〈洋菓子〉大理石貼り　ビトロガラス貼り　漆喰仕上げ　〈パン売場〉ビトロガラス貼り　２階･〈カフェサロン〉レンガタイル貼り　一部ミラー貼り　〈レストラン〉漆喰仕上げ砂岩貼り　柱型・白ラワン練付け　天井／１階･〈和菓子〉光天井　アクリル板和紙貼り　一部赤松練付け合板目透し貼り　〈洋菓子〉漆喰仕上げ ビニールクロス貼り　〈パン売場〉ビニールクロス貼り　２階･〈カフェ〉タモ合板透し貼り　一部光天井　すりガラス　〈レストラン〉漆喰仕上げ　梁型･白ラワン練付け　〈和食〉白ラワン練付け合板目透し貼り　上り天井・漆喰仕上げ

営業内容

開店／1984年11月15日　営業時間／売店・午前９時30分～午後８時(日～木曜日)　午前９時30分～午後９時(金～土曜日)　カフェ・／午前９時30分～午後11時　レストラン及び和食／午前11時～午後11時　休日／毎月第３水曜日　経営者／橘　順三　従業員／80人　客席数／カフェ40席　レストラン62席　和食37席　客単価／和菓子1700円　洋菓子1200　パン600円 カフェ600円　レストラン2000円　和食2500円

入口側より１階和菓子売場をみる

The 1st floor Japanese confectionery corner viewed from the entrance side.

２階レストラン

The 2nd floor restaurant.

2階カフェサロンの中庭に面した客席をみる

The guest seats at the 2nd floor cafe salon facing the courtyard.

2つの顔を持つ外観

外観は2つの顔を持たせることにした。1つは和菓子の老舗として格調の高い和の外観。1つは洋菓子らしい夢のある　親しみ易い洋の外観である。和菓子の外観及び入口廻りのあり方　洋菓子の外観及び入口廻りのあり方2階レストランへの導入路等も　かなりうまく解決できたと思う。

和菓子における生菓子　贈答　煎餅等のレイアウトの仕方　洋菓子の生菓子　アイスクリーム　ケーキ　チョコレート　贈答　工場等のレイアウトの仕方等は　客の購買心理を十分考慮して配列した。また　ショーケースの高さ　幅等は客の店員に対する親しみ易さの度合で決定された。和菓子　洋菓子共　あえてコストの安いファッションタイルを使ったことにも多く理由がある。

〈小池　晩〉(85-8)

設計／ワイケイ(Y.K.)都市・建築研究所
　　小池　晩
施工／清水建設
構造・規模／S造・地上2階建
面積／敷地・524.78m² 建築・442.048m²　床・地下ピット37.037m² 1階435.725m²　2階422.174m² 屋上36.223m² 合計931.159m²(うち厨房288.7m²)
工期／1984年4月27日～10月31日
工費／2億6500万円

Confectionery + Restaurant + Cafe TACHIBANA

The appearance having two faces

We designed the appearance so that it has two faces: the one is a dignified Japanese appearance of a time-honored Japanese confectionery shop, while the other is a familiar Western appearance full of dreamy elements. It is believed that we could somewhat successfully design the appearance and entrance area of the Japanese-style shop, as well as the appearance, entrance and passage leading to the 2nd floor's restaurant of the Western style confectionery shop.

The layout of fresh confectionery, gift items, rice crackers, etc. in Japanese style, and fresh confectionery, ice cream, cakes, chocolate, gift items, factory, etc. in Western style, were arranged with due consideration given to the purchasing psychology of guests. The height, width, etc. of the showcases were determined in terms of guests' familiarity with shop

中央入口ホールの中庭を通して洋菓子売場をみる
The Western confectionery corner viewed across the courtyard at the central entrance hall.

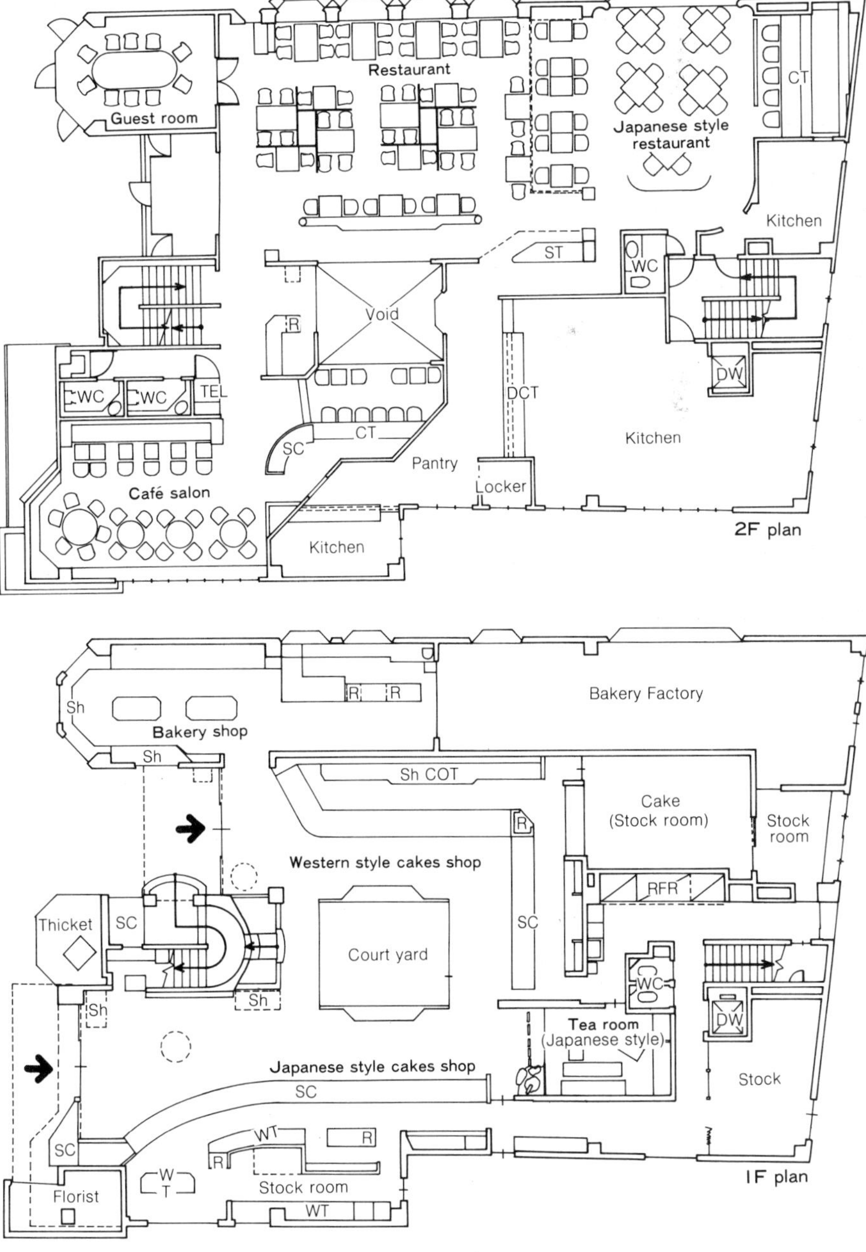

staffs. By this reason we were motivated much to employ cheap fashion tiles for both Japanese and Western confectionery corners.

5-14-5, Minami-karasuyama, Setagaya-ku, Tokyo Phone: 03-309-2341

Design / Ban Koike
Area / Site 524.78 m², Building 442.048 m²,
Floor: Basement pit 37.037 m²,
1st floor 435.725 m²,
2nd floor 422.174 m²,
Roof floor 36.223 m²;
Totalling 931.159 m² (kitchen 288.7 m²)

正面入口廻りをみる

The front entrance area.

リカーショップ ヤマノウチ

京都市南区西九条藤ノ木町21-2　Phone／075-681-9546

撮影／平井広行

単純で抽象的なボックス空間

「ヤマノウチ」はこの同じ場所で長い間　近所の人々に親しまれてきた店舗であるため　それまでの顧客にとっては　新しい「ヤマノウチ」の展開を感じさせるものであり　同時に　この新しい店舗が　新たな顧客を掘りおこすことを意図した。

この店舗は　外壁からつながっている白いレンガタイル貼りの壁――室内では棚　リーチ　イン　クーラー等がビルトインされる――によってつくられるボックス状の空間及びその内部に点在する　レジカウンター　可動のディスプレイ家具からなっており　特別に存在を主張してくれるモノや形態もなく　単純な構成となっている。ただ　ここでは　それぞれの面や単純な形態が抑制された素材感を与えられた時　何を語り始めるか　そして単純で抽象的なボックス状空間が　どう変化するかということがテーマであった。

〈岸　和郎〉(85.5)

設計／岸　和郎＋匠設計室　施工／中央建設

構造・規模／S造・地上2階建

面積／78.42㎡　工期(内装)／1984年8月30日～10月23日

工費／1800万円

Liquor Collection YAMANOUCHI

A simple, abstract box space

For a long time "Yamanouchi" has been patronized by the neighboring people at this same place. The new shop, however, will make the conventional clients feel a new development of "Yamanouchi," while the same shop is intended to catch new guests.

This shop consists of a box-like space created by white brick-tiled walls continuing from the outer wall – inside the shop are built-in shelves, a reach-in cooler, etc. – and a register counter and movable display furniture dotted here and there. There are no particular things or shaping asserting their own special existence, and they are simply arranged. Here, however, we wished to pursue what those planes and simple shapes begin to talk when given a restrained sense of material, and how this simple, abstract box-like space changes.

21-2, Nishikujyo Fujinoki-cho, Minami-ku, Kyoto City
Phone: 075-681-9546

Design / Waro Kishi
Area / 78.42 m^2

材料仕様

外壁／レンガタイル貼り(白)　二丁掛け　アルミパネル貼り　外部床／真鍮切り文字　床／ゴムタイル貼り　壁面／レンガタイル貼り(白)　二丁掛け　天井／ＰＢｔ＝９全面寒冷紗貼りパテしごきの上ＶＰ　家具／コールテン鋼錆仕上げ　フロートガラス　レジカウンター／黒御影石ジェット仕上げ　コールテン鋼錆仕上げ

営営内容

開店／1984年11月６日　営業時間／午前11時～午後７時　休日／毎週日曜日　祭日　経営者／㈱ヤマノウチ　従業員／サービス１人　パート及びアルバイト２人　合計３人　客単価／3500円

入口部より店内をみる

The inside scene viewed from the entrance area.

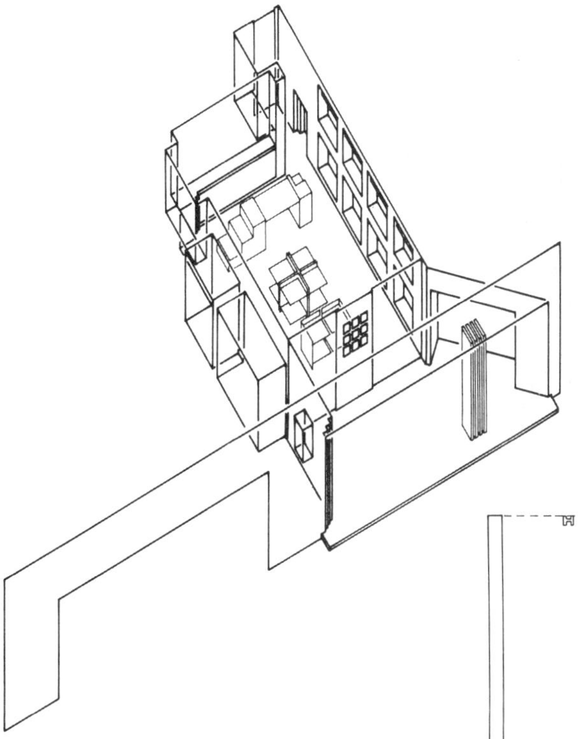

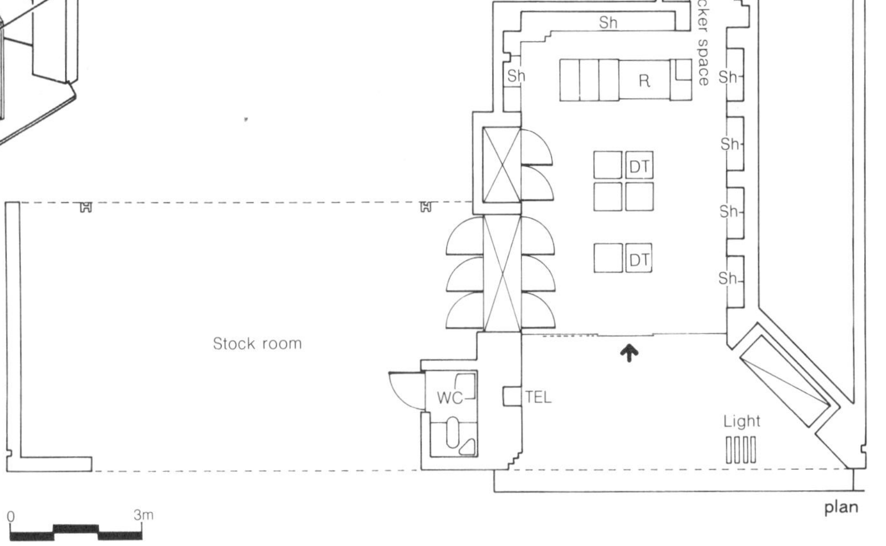

WT
Ice stocker space
Sh
Sh
R
Sh
Sh
DT
Sh
DT
Sh
Stock room
WC
TEL
Light
0
3m
plan

リカーショップ　イヌイ

徳島市大道1-28　Phone/0886-52-8090

彫塑的な建築物

ＲＣラーメン構造＋ヴォールト屋根と　曲面熱線反射ガラスブロックの組み合せで　建築に彫塑的な形態を与えた。素材のもつ質感を最大限に引き出すことにより　小規模だが　通りに対して強いインパクトを与え　天体の移行する光の変化を　建築の内外に印象づける構想を描いた。店舗の２階に至る段階を吹抜け部分において視覚化し　陳列棚として利用し　商品の展示と空間的な遊びが一体となって　アプローチから２階へと　人が楽しみながら　サーキュレートできるように計画した。
また　ＲＣ打放しの構造的な造形と　曲面ガラスブロックや　入り組んだガラス面との複合的な組み合わせが　構造的には明確に　表情としては変化に富んだ空間を内包するようにデザインした。
酒類という商品の性質上　西に面して直射光を防ぎながら　内部を通りから見えるようにするという相反した条件を　解決するのが困難であった。　〈武市義雄〉(84-12)

設計／ＲＥＡ建築工房　武市義雄　武市啓子
施工／牧野工務店
構造・規模／ＲＣ造・地上３階建
面積／敷地・198.67m²　建築・66.05m²　床・146.06m²
工期／1982年５月１日～９月30日
工費／2348万円

Liquor Shop INUI

A plastic artistic building

By combining RC rahmen structure with a vaulted roof and curved surface in heat rays reflective glass blocks, a plastic artistic image was given to the building. By maximally drawing the quality sense of each material, the building was designed to give a small but strong impact, and impress the inside and outside of the building with changing celestial light. The staircase leading to the 2nd floor was visualized at the stairwell area, and utilized as display shelves. Thus, with the commodity display and spacial play being united, people are allowed to circulate from the approach to the 2nd floor, while amusing themselves.
Additionally, the structural feature of RC as placed is compositely combined with curved glass blocks and complicated glass surfaces so that a structurally definite space having varied features may be contained.
In view of the nature of liquor, the direct sunlight had to be prevented though the building faces west, while it was necessary to make the inside visible from the outside. It was difficult to solve these problems.

1-28, Omichi, Tokushima City
Phone: 0886-52-8090

Design / Yoshio Takeichi
Area / Site 198.67 m², Building 66.05 m², Floor 146.06 m²

ファサード　ＲＣラーメン構造の造形性とヴォールト屋根やガラスブロックの曲面壁が複合的表情の変化をみせる
The facade. RC rahmen structure, vaulted roof and curved surface in glass blocks constitute a composite expression that changes.

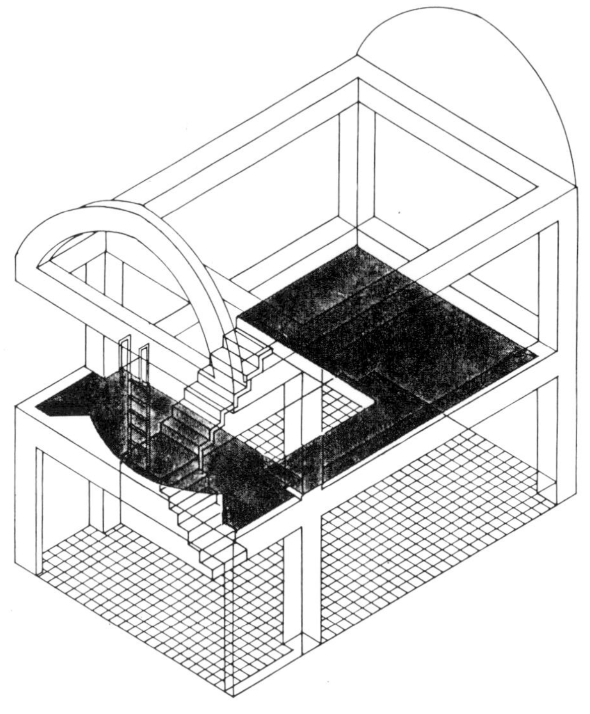

撮影／村瀬武男

２階売場より吹抜けを通して見返す　夜はドーム天井のスリットから外部へ光が漏れる

Looked back from the 2nd floor's selling corner through the stairwell. At night, light leaks outside through the dome ceiling's slits.

材料仕様

外壁／スチール及びガラス　スチール及び熱線反射ガラスブロック145×145×95　柱及び梁天井／ＲＣ打放し　アプローチ天井／パンチングメタル　床／磁器質タイル200角貼り

ランドマーク的な要素を採り入れた外観

The appearance employing a landmark-like element.

ミートショップ タニヤマ

愛知県豊橋市花田二番町 3　Phone/0532-31-8535

撮影／斎部　功

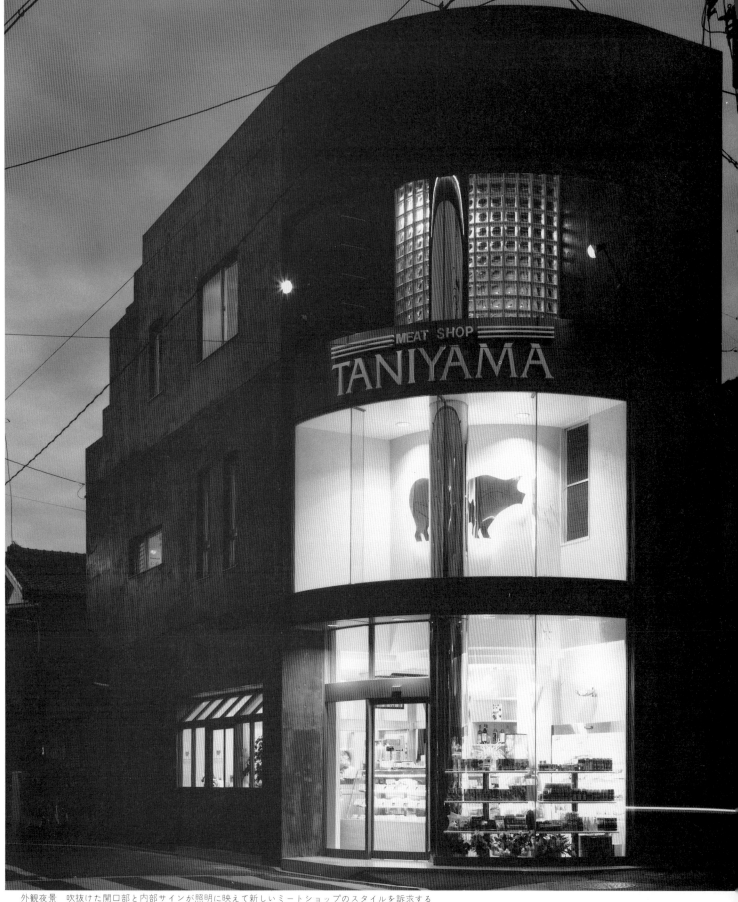

外観夜景　吹抜けた開口部と内部サインが照明に映えて新しいミートショップのスタイルを訴求する
The night scene of the appearance. Pursuing a new meat shop style having the opening with a stairwell and inside sign reflecting the brilliant lighting.

材料仕様
屋根／コンクリート直均しの上に露出シート防水　外壁／コンクリート打放しの上にウレタンクリアー　外部床／人造大理石　サイン／スチールパネル　メラミン焼付け　〈店舗部分内装〉　床／人造大理石及びクリンカータイル　幅木／モルタル目地幅木　ＶＰ　壁面／外部用ラフトン吹付けの上にトップコートローラー塗装２回　天井／ＰＢｔ＝９パテしごきサンダーがけの上にローラー塗装２回
家具／楢合板ウレタンラッカー塗装

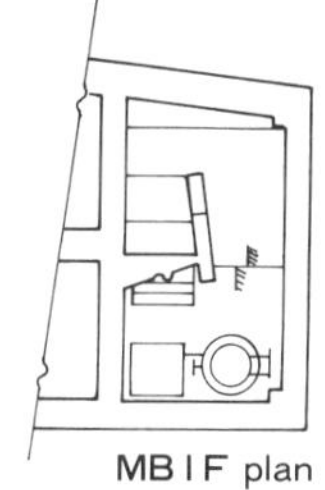

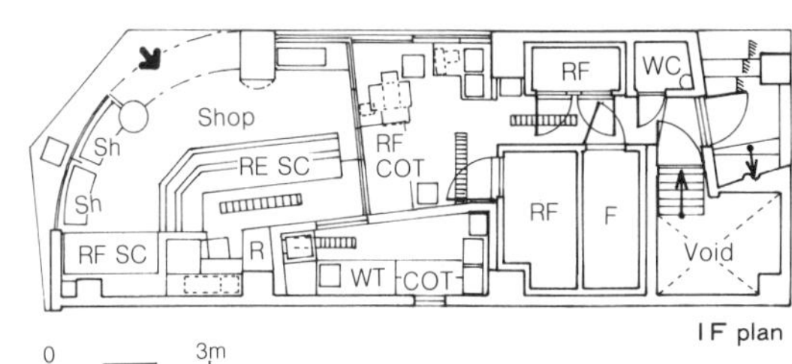

デリカと惣菜で奥行を持たせた商品構成

豊橋駅西口より徒歩10数分。背後に広々とした古くからの住宅街を控え　申し分のない商圏である。従来の木造２階建ての後に　鉄筋コンクリート造　地上３階　地下１階建ての新築工事となった。

設計にあたっては　次のような設定で行った。

- ●豊橋で伸びつつある高級和牛や骨付肉を軸に　デリカ惣菜で奥行きと幅をもたせた商品構成をとり　30代の主婦を中心にした食肉専門のイメージを追う。
- ●そのために　従来の食肉店のイメージを一新して　ファッション性の強い食肉店とする。
- ●店舗のファサード　平面　断面計画等は　新築のメリットを最大限に生かして　すべて店中心の計画とする。
- ●２本の正面道路に面した壁面を店舗のための看板とし概念化したデザインとする。
- ●建物は　銀杏並木が終る四辻のランドマークの役割を果たすようにする。
- ●インテリアの構想は　秤量売り　対面販売の空間化の象徴として　機能的な冷蔵ショーケースを中心に組み立てる。

〈大岩剛一〉(85-1)

設計／大岩剛一＆ジグ設計工房　大岩剛一　高浜誠一

施工／小野工務店

構造・規模／ＳＲＣ造・地上２階　地下１階建

面積／敷地・75.16m² 建築・60.11m² 床・地下１階10.04m²
　１階50.15m²　２階43.82m²　３階41.05m²
　合計145.06m²(うち厨房28.0m²)

工期／1984年２月12日～７月31日

工費／3500万円

Meat Shop TANIYAMA

A commodity lineup varied with delicatessen and daily dishes

10 odd minutes by walk from the west exit of Toyohashi Station. Behind this shop exists an old extensive residential quarter, and constitutes an ideal commercial area. At the back of the conventional two-storied wooden building, this ferroconcrete building, three-storied above and one-storied under the ground, was newly constructed.

In designing it, the following considerations were given.

- With quality Japanese beef and rib, etc., which are increasingly demanded in Toyohashi, in the main, this shop offers a commodity lineup varied with delicatessen and daily dishes, pursuing an image of the shop specializing in meat intended for housewives in their 30's.
- For this purpose, by completely wiping out the conventional meat shop image, create a very fashionable meat shop.
- To maximize the merits of new construction, the facade, plan, cross-section, etc. are all designed specially for this shop.
- The wall facing two front roads is used as a shop sign which is symbolic of this shop.
- The building is designed so that it serves as a landmark of street crossing where a row of maidenhair trees ends.
- To spacially symbolize scale sales and man-to-man sales, the interior is made up, centering around functional cold storage display cases.

3, Hanadaniban-cho, Toyohashi City, Aichi Prefecture
Phone: 0532-31-8535

Design: Goichi Oiwa
Area / Site 75.16 m^2, Building 60.11 m^2,
Floor: Basement floor 10.04 m^2,
1st floor 50.15 m^2, 2nd floor 43.82 m^2,
3rd floor 41.05 m^2;
Totalling 145.06 m^2 (kitchen 28.0 m^2)

営業内容

開店／1984年８月３日　営業時間／午前８時30分～午後８時(夏)～午後７時30分(冬)　休日／毎週日曜日　経営者／谷山裕身　従業員／３人　客単価／1500円　主な取り扱い商品／和牛ヒレ　和牛ロース　豚ロース　サラダ　ハンバーグ　とりの唐揚げ　コロッケ

入口右側の調味料　関連商品コーナー
The seasonings and related goods corner in the right side of the entrance.

売場より奥の加工　調理室方向をみる
The inner processing/cooking room area viewed from the selling corner.

ファサード　道路拡幅が予定されている前庭を小広場として通りに開放している
The facade. The facade along the road whose width is expected to be broadened, is opened as a small plaza.

和洋菓子 玉木家

埼玉県秩父市東町8-2 Phone/0494-22-0810

撮影／本木誠一

客溜りより茶室をみる
The tea ceremony room viewed from the guest service area.

小広場としての前庭部とサインポール
The front garden as a small plaza and the sign pole.

街造りに即した店づくり

「玉木家」は　西武秩父駅から秩父神社へ向う番場通りに面して建っています。秩父の風土を菓子造りに取り込むことに努力しているので　本物志向の昨今　和菓子の多い秩父でも　最も評判の高い店です。

番場通りは　都市計画道路に指定されていて　拡幅が計画されています。「玉木家」は　その計画を積極的に店構えに取り込み　店の前に縁台　日傘　水鉢　筧　道標をイメージした看板などを配して通りに開放し　町角の小さな広場としています。また　植込みには　もっこく　りょうぶ　さざんか　くちなし　がまずみ　なつつばきを　下草には　ふっきそう　やぶこうじ　おおくまざさを配して　四季おりおり町角に変化を与えることを意図しています。ショーケース前のマロニエが大樹となって　広場に緑陰を落とすのが楽しみです。　〈長部　稔〉(85-2)

設計／アーキブレーン　長部　稔　恩田公雄　宮崎　直
施工／守屋組
構造・規模／ＳＲＣ造　一部Ｓ造・地下１階　地上４階建
面積／地下１階50.40㎡　1階112.35㎡　2・3階各91.44㎡　4階94.89㎡　塔屋11.74㎡　合計452.26㎡
工期／1983年10月11日～1984年８月29日　工費／１億2000万円

材料仕様
屋根／最上階・着色アルミ板ｔ＝８　元旦ルーフ　システムII　一文字葺き　1階屋根・銅板ｔ＝４　元旦ルーフ吊子止　一文字葺き　外壁／コンクリート打放し　外部床／玄昌石　一部コンクリート直均　目地・玄昌石こば立て　サイン／塔屋型付・亜鉛鉄板カッティングシート　タフカル貼り　店先自立・コンクリート打放し　店先壁付・銅板鍛金　床／玄昌石　地履／ベルファスト　幅木／杉板　壁面／白聚落塗り　付柱・桧　天井／不燃石膏ボード　ビニールクロス貼り　斜め天井・ミネラートンキューブ　ストライプ

営業内容
開店／1984年８月30日　営業時間／午前８時～午後８時　休日／なし　経営者／㈱玉木屋・浅見長次　従業員／サービス４人　工場10人　パート２人　合計16人　客単価／1500円　主な商品／だいこくずきん130　屋台ばやし最中80円　秩父従来80円　花づつみ70円　皆野羊かん250円　秩父御山1000円　秩父旅日記2000～5000円

客溜りより前庭をみる

The front garden viewed from the guest service area.

Japanese Confectionery TAMAKIYA

Shop making attuned to city-planning

"Tamakiya" stands facing Banba Street that runs from Seibu-Chichibu Station to Chichibu Shrine. Since it is endeavored to incorporate the natural features of Chichibu into confectionery making, this shop is one of the most highly reputed shops in Chichibu where there are many Japanese confectionery shops.

Banba Street is designated as a street under city planning, and will be broadened. "Tamakiya" has positively incorporated the plan into the shop making, featuring a Japanese bench, sunshade, water basin, water conduit and sign imaging a guidepost that are opened to the street to form a small square at a street corner. The grove comes with Ternstroemia japonica, "ryobu," sasanqua, gardenia, dockmackie and summer camellia, which "fukkisou," spear flower and large striped bamboo are arranged as underplants; thus, it is intended to give seasonal changes to the street corner. It is hoped that a marronier in front of the showcase grows into a large tree, casting a green shadow over the square.

8-2, Higashi-cho, Chichibu City, Saitama Prefecture
Phone: 0494-22-0810

Design / Minoru Hasebe
Area / Site 206.40 m², Building 128.03 m²,
Floor: Basement floor 50.40 m², 1st floor 112.35 m²,
2nd floor 91.44 m², 3rd floor 91.44 m², 4th floor 94.89 m²,
Roof Bldg. 11.74 m²; Totalling 452.26 m²

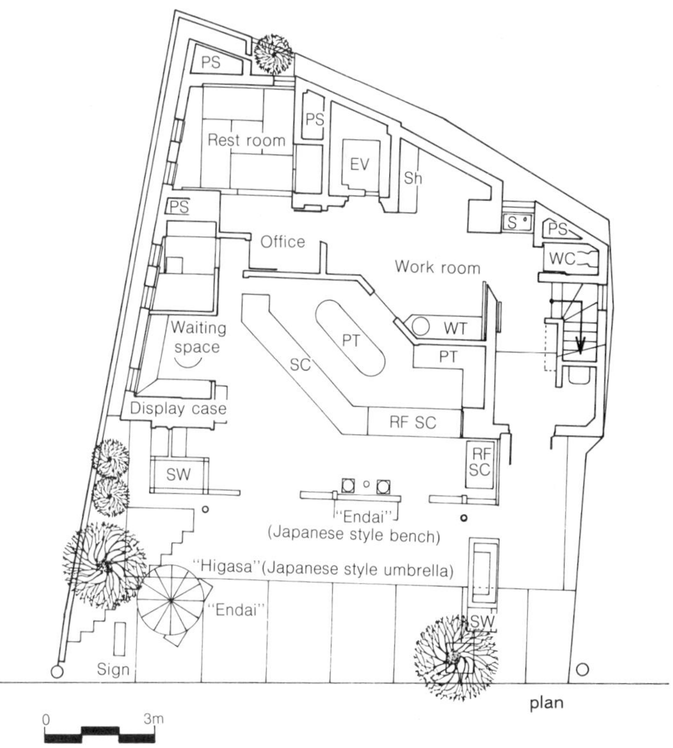

plan

商品の展示や腰掛けとしても使える茶室

The tea ceremony room that can be used also for goods display or as a seat.

外観夜景

The entire appearance at night.

和菓子

萬々堂通則

奈良市橋本町34　Phone/0742-22-2044

撮影／村瀬武雄

入口より店内をみる

The inside viewed from the entrance.

材料仕様

屋根／銅板一文字葺き　外壁／北木石磨き　外部床／北木石バーナー仕上げ　サイン／黒御影石　一部突つき彫　床／ファインスレート黒　一部白　幅木／北木石磨きｈ＝90　壁面及び天井／ＰＢｔ＝12　じゅらくビニールクロス貼り　家具／塩ジ　カシュー仕上げ　カウンター／洋桜材　ウレタン着色仕上げ　スクリーン／脚・ステンレス45角パイプ　棚・塩ジ　素地仕上げ

営業内容

開店／1983年12月17日　休日／なし　経営者／河野ヒサ子　従業員／サービス５人　パート２人　合計７人　主な商品／春日ぶと饅頭　餅飯殿　青丹よし　八重の里

視覚ポイントとしての軽快なショーケースをみる

The showcase as a visual point giving a buoyant sense.

確かな伝承性と深い情緒性の表現

御菓子司「萬々堂」は100年の歴史と伝統をもつ老舗である。
“確かな伝承性と深い情緒性の表情”これがこの店のデザインポリシーである。古都のイメージにより　作風はおのずと書院造りをベースとし原則として(一部使ってしまったが) 新しい素材は用いないという　厳しい条件でスタートした。
和菓が心地良い甘味であるなら　店舗は　このあとに続く心地良い渋味のようなものである。華美と侘びの連動の中で「萬々堂」が語る“菓子文化”を具現化するため　マテリアルの質感を一義的に彩られた黒漆に描いた朱赤の細い線。このパターンは東大寺・二月堂の文机にそのモチーフをみることができるし　また　ディスプレイ額は　東大寺　清水公照長老の御直筆によるものである。こうした格調の演出を図る一方　適度の緊張感を醸し出す空間構成を求めた。各所に配した石の表情——ケース台石の突つき彫りの黒御影は　木質との融合により　その冷たさを和らげさせた。

〈寒川　登〉(85-2)

設計／寒川　登　古川浩二
施工／寒川商業建築研究所　フジシタ工芸
面積／138.4m²　工期／1983年11月18日～12月15日

Japanese Confectionery MANMANDO

An expression of sure tradition and deep emotion

The confectionery shop "Manmando" is a time-honored shop having 100 years of history.
"Sure tradition and deep emotion" – this is the design policy of this shop. Keeping to the image of an old city, the shop naturally is styled after a study. In principle, the shop making started with a severe condition that new materials are not used (though we used in part).
If we regard that Japanese confectionery represents a pleasantly sweet taste, the shop itself is a comfortably bitter taste that ensues. In the midst of interlocking luxury and taste for the simple and quiet, "confectionery culture" as mentioned by "Manmando" is expressed by drawing a sense of material quality with fine red lines on simplistic black lacquer. We can find its motif in the desk at Nigatsudo, Todaiji

ショーケースを通して接客カウンターをみる　The guest service counter viewed across the showcase.

Temple. The display frame was directly written by Elder Kosho Shimizu, Todaiji Temple. While presenting such dignified atmosphere, we pursued a space producing an adequate tension. The appearances of stones arranged here and there – the coolness of peck-carved black granite as the case base was softened by fusion with the wooden quality.

34, Hashimoto-cho, Nara City　Phone: 0742-22-2044

Design / Noboru Sangawa
Area / 138.4 m^2

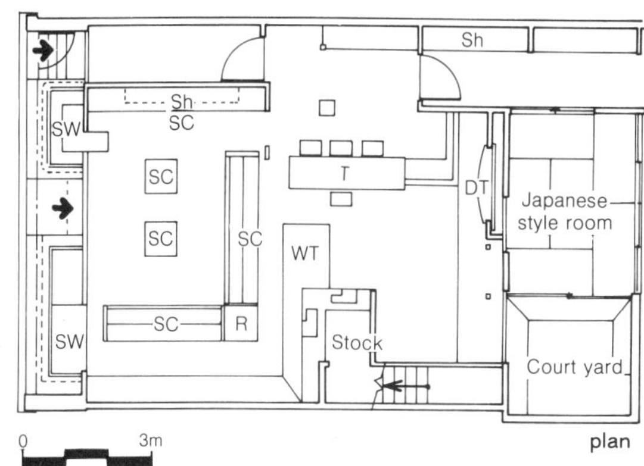

plan

ファサード

The facade.

和菓子
銀座　三万石

東京都中央区銀座6-4-8 曽根ビル1階
Phone/03-575-0007

撮影／鳴瀬　亨

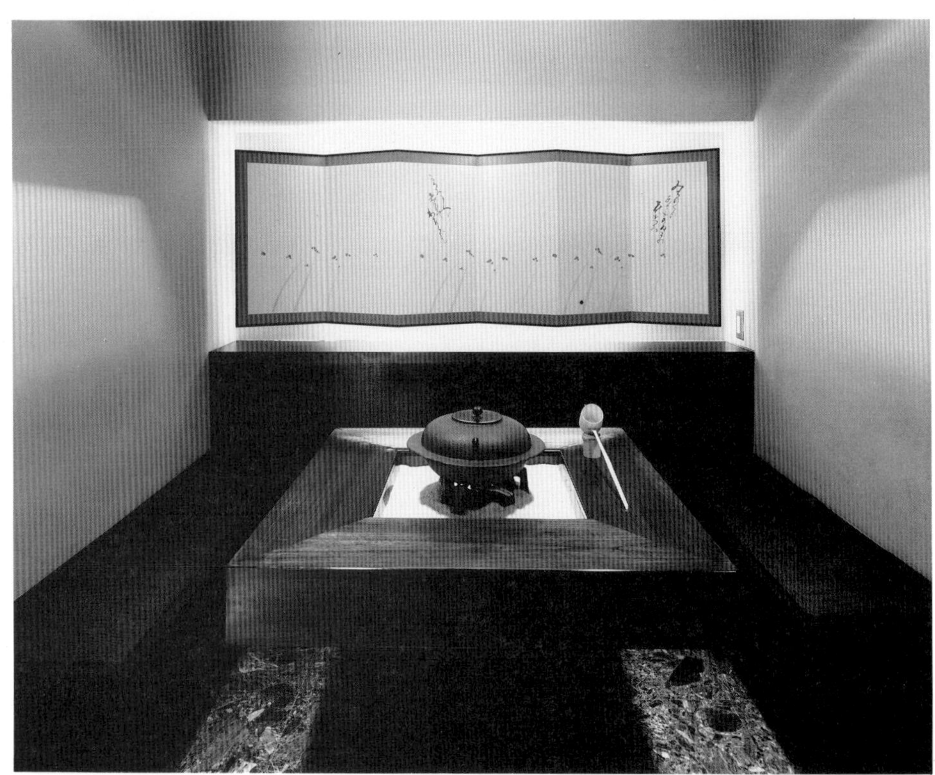

お茶を飲んで休めるスペース

The space where you can take rest while drinking tea.

材料仕様

外壁及び入口床／黒御影石バーナー仕上げ　床／テラゾブロック　壁面及び天井／ＰＢ下地　寒冷紗パテＶＰ仕上げ　家具／メラミン化粧貼り

営業内容

開店／1984年９月17日　営業時間／午前10時30分～午後10時　休日／なし　経営者／三万石不二屋　池田惣一　従業員／サービス５人　主な商品／生菓子　羊かん1200～　干菓子（箱詰）1500～

入口より店内売場をみる

The inside selling corner viewed from the entrance.

若い層にも受け入れられる店づくり

「銀座　三万石」の母体となる「三万石 不二屋」は　福島県　宮城県で和菓子の店を25店舗直営し　年間50億の売り上げがある企業である。今回の東京出店に関して　どこに出店するかが問題であった。特に銀座を選んだ理由は「西武」「阪急」の大型商業施設ができ　今後ますます情報　文化が伝達される環境ができつつある場所だからである。

そこで　和菓子が　若い層にも受け入れられるような店づくりをテーマとし　日本の伝統の形を　モダンに表現してみた。お客が来店したらすぐお茶のサービスができる機能　また　ちょっと休めるスペースをとり入れている。　〈小松健男〉(85-2)

企画・設計／三万石不二屋企画開発部　小松健男

施工／大日本印刷ＣＤＣ事業部　面積／91.9m²

工期／1984年８月15日～９月10日　工費／2700万円

Japanese Confectionery Ginza SANMANGOKU

Shop making that is acceptable also by the young

"Sanmangoku Fujiya," from which "Ginza Sanmangoku." stemmed, is an enterprise which directly runs 25 Japanese confectionery shops in Fukushima and Miyagi Prefectures, thus securing yearly sales of 5,000 million yen. In opening this Tokyo branch shop, the location was a great problem. The reason why Ginza was chosen is that there appear large commercial facilities, such as "Seibu" and "Hankyu," and is forming an environment where information and culture are increasingly transmitted.

Thus, we tried to make a shop so that Japanese confectionery may be accepted also by the young, by expressing Japanese tradition in a modern style. When guests drop in, they are instantly served a cup of tea and can take rest at ease.

6-4-8, Ginza, Chuo-ku, Tokyo　Phone: 03-575-0007

Design / Takeo Komatsu
Area / 91.9 m^2

奥より売場ショーケースをみる

The selling corner's showcase viewed from the inner part.

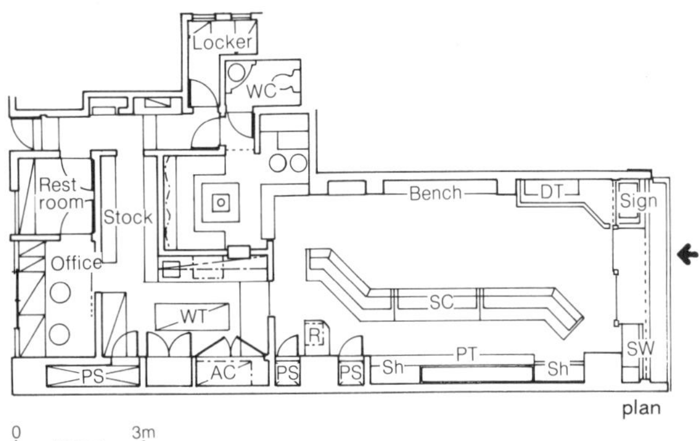

店内左側より天井を見上げる

The ceiling looked up from the left side of the inside.

和菓子 京富

大阪市北区曾根崎新地1-3-16　Phone/06-341-0025

撮影／川元　斉

入口より天井端切り込みと正面飾り棚をみる

The ceiling end check and front display shelf viewed from the entrance.

ファサード

The facade.

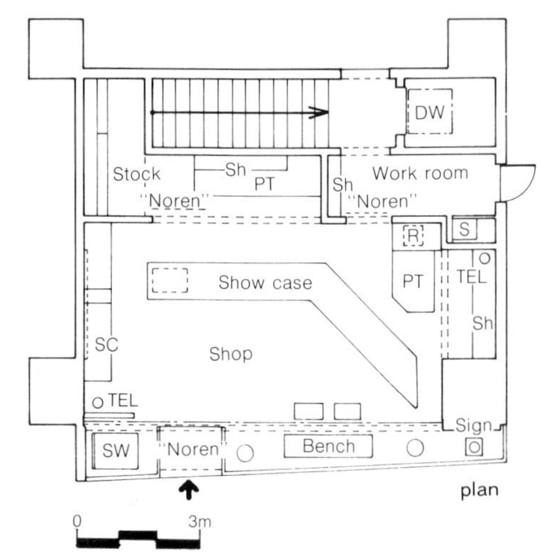

店内右側より全景をみる

The entire inside scene viewed from the right side.

湾曲ラインで柔らかさと豊かさを表現

「京富」は　和菓子の老舗であり　会社関係のお使い物や　お茶会等の注文が多い。店はお女将さんとお孫さんを中心に家族的経営をしている。以前の店が手狭になり　売場を拡張するという主旨であったが　老舗らしさを出しながら　かつ新しいイメージの店舗という要望を　いかに視覚化するかが　設計のテーマであった。それには　伝統様式を直接的に具体化するよりも　和菓子の持つ情感の中に　日本文化の結果を捕らえそれを抽象的に表現する方が　むしろインパクトが強く　より整理された形となると考えた。

天井高を高くとり　片側に大きく湾曲させ　正面の壁にそのままつなげることで　一つの流れをつくり　全体に柔らかさと豊かさを表現した。ただし　リリカルに流れないように　全体の色調はいわゆる聚落色を避けグレーに押さえた。反対に照明器具や家具のモチーフには　植物的な色や形を用いて　和菓子のテーマ性を出したつもりである。

〈浅田　環〉(85-2)

設計／竹中工務店大阪本店設計部　雲雀　稔　浅田　環
施工／竹中工務店　面積／45.1㎡
工期／1984年６月８日～７月13日

Japanese Confectionery KYOTOMI

Expresses softness and richness with curved lines

"Kyotomi" is an old established Japanese confectionery shop, and has been patronized by companies which wish to use as a gift, or by those holding a tea party, etc. It is run mainly by the manageress and her grandchildren.

The former shop had somewhat become narrow, and the selling corner had to be expanded. In redecorating it, they wished to maintain the dignity of their tradition, while giving a new shop image. Our design theme was to visualize these requests. For this purpose, we felt that, instead of directly materializing the traditional style, it would be better to abstractly express the results of Japanese culture in the atmosphere produced by Japanese confectionery, as it would have a stronger impact with a more refined style.

By securing a high ceiling curved conspicuously towards one side, the ceiling was directly joined to the front wall. By making a flow in this manner, we expressed softness and richness as a whole. However, in order to prevent the atmosphere from becoming too lyrical, we eschewed from using too showy colors, and used grey as an overall tone. In contrast to the overall tone, we used plant-like colors or shapes as a motif of lighting apparatus and furniture, to harmonize with Japanese confectionery.

1-3-16, Sonezaki-shinchi, Kita-ku, Osaka City　Phone: 06-341-0025

Design / Takenaka-komuten Osaka
Area / 45.1 m^2

材料仕様

床／瓦タイル貼り300角　壁面／コンクリート打放し　小叩き及び鋼板貼り　天井／ケイ酸カルシウム板ｔ＝10 メタリックシルバー塗装　照明器具／ダウンライト60W　カウンター　ベンチ／楓　漆塗り

営業内容

開店／1985年４月30日　営業時間／午前10時～午後７時　休日／毎週木曜日　経営者／㈱浜佐商店・望月敬三郎　従業員／サービス５人　客席数／６席　客単価／喫茶500円 店売り1000円　贈答品3000円　客回転数／５回　主なメニュー及び主な商品／〈喫茶〉　煎茶　抹茶　玉露　冷煎茶　冷抹茶より１品　菓子１品付き500　３号コース1000　〈売店〉茶35種100ｇ／1400～5000　贈答品／14種1000～２万

木目の強調された漆塗りカウンター席をみる

The lacquered counter seat accented with the grain of wood.

ギフト&グリーンティハウス 茶の葉 銀座店

東京都中央区銀座3-6-1 松屋銀座地下1階 Phone/03-567-1211

撮影／北田英治

ショップ フロント
The shop front.

カウンター席と待合席をみる　コンクリート小叩き　鋼板貼りの壁面　漆塗りのベンチとカウンターなど　素材の対比による空間構成
The counter seat and waiting seat. The space composition featuring the contrast of materials – rough concrete surface, wall surface covered with steel plate, lacquered bench and counter.

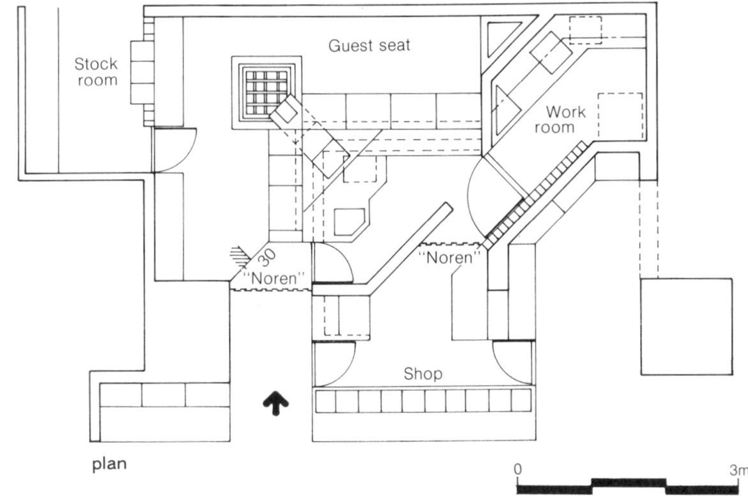

日本美の魅力を現代の目で引き出す

この店は「たまプラーザ店」（別冊商店建築No.20収録）に続く２号店である。

「たまプラーザ店」は日常生活の延長といった雰囲気を持っているが　こちらの方は銀座らしい“晴れやかさ　緊張感”が品よくまとめられている。

「銀座店」では　特にギフト商品の伸びを期待しているというが　これは茶の商品特性である高級性　嗜好性に着目し　ギフトという贈り手のセンスを代弁する物　行為に結び付けようとしたものだ。

今　日本茶は在来の和風ヘルシー商材として注目される一方　若い層への訴求性では　いま一歩の感がある。が　真の課題は表面的なファッション化を急ぐことではあるまい。

「茶の葉」の企画　設計　経営に携わった田尾宥之輔氏によれば　むしろ茶の生産　流通　消費構造のメカニズムの再検討こそが　先決問題であるという。しかも　茶舗は日本の魅力を現代に蘇生させる上で格好のモチーフなのだそうだ。

〈編集部〉(85-11)

設計／アッセンブリッジ都市建築総合研究所
田尾宥之輔
施工／井上工業
面積／44m²（うち厨房6.7m²）
工期／1985年３月１日～４月30日

Gift & Green Tea House CHA-NO-HA Ginza

Draws out the attraction of Japanese beauty with modern eyes

Following "Cha-No-Ha Tama Plaza" shop (introduced in Shotenkenchiku Extra No. 20), this is the second shop in the group. While "Tama Plaza Shop" gives an atmosphere which is something like an extension of daily life, this shop in Ginza elegantly embodies "gaiety and tension" becoming Ginza.

"Cha-No-Ha Ginza," among others, is expecting that demand for green tea as a gift may grow. They intend to connect the product characteristics of tea (high grade image and taste) with a thing or act that speaks for a person using tea as a gift.

Although Japanese tea is drawing attention as traditional healthy goods, it seems to be appealing a little poorly to the young. However, it is felt that we need not hurry up superficial pursuit of fashionable arrangement. Rather, as Mr. Yunosuke Tao, who was involved in planning, design and management of "Cha-No-Ha," stressed, it would be more urgent to reexamine the structure and mechanism of tea production, distribution and consumption. What's more, according to him, a green tea house is a very suitable motif in causing the attraction of Japan to revive in the present.

3-6-1, Ginza, Chuo-ku, Tokyo
Phone: 03-567-1211

Design / Yunosuke Tao
Area / 44 m² (kitchen 6.7 m²)

材料仕様
外壁／彩薬タイル貼り47角　銅製サッシ　外部床／花崗岩貼り　床／テラゾタイル貼り400角　幅木／ＰＢ下地　聚落サテン吹付け　照明器具／スチールメラミン焼付け（黒）＋ワーロン紙ブラケット　スパン紙　クリプトン球

営業内容
開店／1984年７月16日　営業時間／午前８時～午後10時　休日／毎週日曜日　祭日　経営者／㈱京富　従業員／10人　主な商品／生菓子150　干菓子120羊かん800　カステラ1000

1階左側面をみる

The 1st floor's left side.

スーベニール いづみや

神奈川県足柄下郡箱根町158　Phone/0460-6-6030

ファサード

The facade.

撮影／斎部　功

2階中央より正面道路側をみる　開口部の配置は伝統的な"蔵"を意識したもの

The front road side viewed from the center of the 2nd floor. The arrangement at the opening takes account of an image of traditional warehouse.

階段より2階を見上げる　The 2nd floor looked up from the staircase.

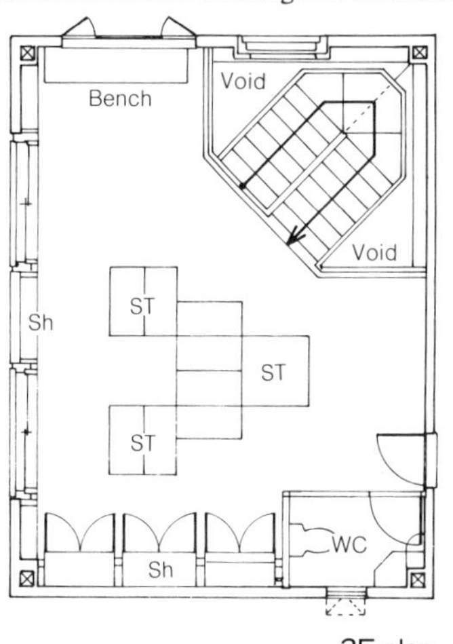

2F plan

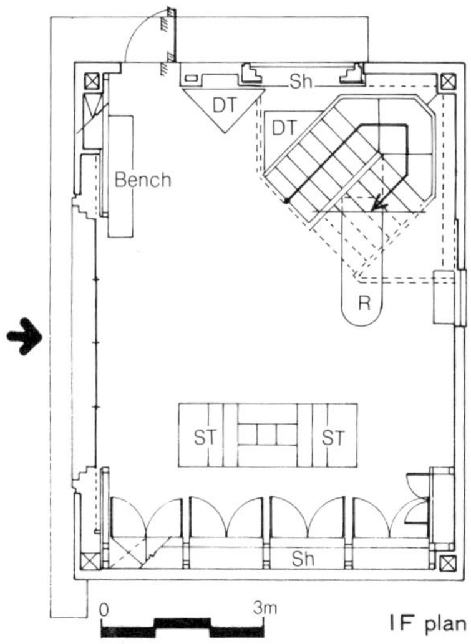

1F plan

2階階段より右側面をみる

The right side viewed from the 2nd floor staircase.

現代感覚の蔵をローコストでつくる

箱根では　シーズンオフは1月～3月と短く、この一年中で最も寒い時期に工事をしなくてはならなかった。そこで鉄骨造とし　外壁と2階床をＡＬＣ板による乾式工法をとった。ローコストを心がけたため　軽い感じになりがちであるが　蔵という重厚な形を用いることにより　落ち着きを与え　のれん　日除　檜の看板等で商家の趣を醸しだした。

内部は鉄骨の梁(色／墨色)　鉄骨の階段(色／猩々緋)を　かくさず見せることで　現代感覚の蔵を空間イメージし　鉄と木と対比させ　寄木細工が引き立つ工夫をした。

店の周囲には雑多なみやげ物店が多いが　箱根寄木細工で有名な畑宿に比べて　高級な寄木細工を売るみやげ物店が数少ない。そこで　箱根の特徴を生かした　寄木細工　組木細工　木の玩具の専門店にしたいというのが　オーナー若夫婦の希望であった。〈菅　利春〉(86-4)

設計／小暮渉建築研究所＋ＡＧＵＳ造形計画事務所
　協力　江田　登　アトリエディーイーシー(構造)
施工／石井建設　構造・規模／Ｓ造・地上2階建
面積／敷地・52.05m²　建築・41.04m²　床・1～2階各41.04m²　合計82.08m²
工期／1985年1月7日～3月27日　工費／1450万円

Souvenir IZUMIYA

Builds a modern sense warehouse at low cost

In Hakone, off-season is as short as January to March, and we had to carry out the works in the coldest period during the year. Thus, we employed a dry process with ferroconcrete structure, and ALC plates for outer walls and 2nd floor.

Since we intended to reduce the cost, we adopted the dignified shape of a warehouse to give a composed atmosphere, thereby preventing the building from giving a somewhat light image due to the low cost. In this connection, we also arranged a traditional Japanese shop curtain, sunshade, signboard made of Japanese cypress, etc., thereby producing an atmosphere of a traditional Japanese merchant's house.

The inside is designed so that steel-frame beams (China ink color) and steel-frame staircase (scarlet) are visible to give a modern sense image of a warehouse. We also tried to contrast iron with wood, thereby helping the parquetry to stand out.

Around "Izumiya" stand miscellaneous souvenir shops, and compared to Hatayado which is famous for Hakone patchwork, the number of souvenir shops selling high-grade parquetry is small. Thus, it was the hope of the young owner and his wife to open a shop specializing in parquetry, fretwork and wooden toys, by utilizing the local folk artistic features of Hakone.

158, Hakone-machi, Ashigarashimo-gun, Kanagawa Prefecture
Phone: 0460-6-6030

Design / Toshiharu Suga
Area / Site 52.05 m², Building 41.04 m²
　Floor: 1st floor 41.04 m², 2nd floor 41.04 m²;
　Totalling 82.08 m²

材料仕様

屋根／石綿スレート板瓦葺き　棟瓦・日本瓦　外壁／ＡＬＣ板ｔ＝100 下地　合成樹脂エマルジョン系吹付け仕上げ　アルミサッシ　スチール窓枠　外部床／磁器タイル貼り150角　サイン／桧　床／磁器タイル貼り150角　幅木／米松ＣＬ　一部ＯＰ　壁面／ＰＢｔ＝12下地　寒冷紗ＶＰ　天井／1階・ワイヤーメッシュ100角焼付け塗装　2階・ＰＢｔ＝12下地　寒冷紗ＶＰ　什器／米松突板　扉・デコラ貼り　のれん及び日除／木綿あいぞめ　スクリーン／和紙　アルミ　カウンター／米松突板　トップ・デコラ貼り

営業内容

開店／1985年4月1日　営業時間／午前9時～午後7時　休日／なし　経営者／中里健次　従業員／3人　客単価／5000円　主な商品／寄木細工・ひみつ箱800～8000 お盆4000～1万5000　小物タンス8000～12万　組木細工300～1万1000 木象1200～5万　木のおもちゃ300～3000

創作京履物 伊と忠

京都市下京区四条河原町東　Phone/075-221-0308

商品の美しさを支える金属素材

「伊と忠」は京履物の老舗で　優美で工夫を凝らした上質の和装履物を商っている。

女性用の装(草)履　下駄は実用機能をこえて工芸的な密度さえ感じる。装履の素材は革　織物(絹　金銀箔)が主だが　それらの加工技術の多様さと美しさは驚くほどである。佐賀錦　つづれ錦等　礼装用セット（装履　バッグ一対）に使われている素材は　布とはいえ金属的な質感をもっている。

この礼装用セットを展示するガラスケースと　店の顔であるフロントウインドの背景には　単純に商品が目立てばよいものではなく　商品の美しさを支える素材が必要と考えた。金属の中でも　硬さと柔らかさのイメージを併せもつ真鍮　丹銅プレートに多種類の繊細な表面加工を施し　切り欠き貼りすることで　京友禅の伝統的図柄を連想し　着物へとイメージが拡がっていくことを意図した。　〈石村徹之〉(84-12)

設計／スペースデザインオフィス　ビーイング　石村徹之

施工／宮崎木材工業　面積／45.8m²

工期／1984年7月21日～8月27日　工費／3400万円

撮影／藤原　弘

真鍮　丹銅などが貼り分けられたショーケース

The showcase to which patches of brass, red copper, etc. are pasted.

Japanese Footwear I-TO-CHU

Metallic materials supporting the beauty of goods

"I-To-Chu" is a time-honored Kyoto style footwear shop, dealing in elegant, elaborate and high-grade Japanese footwear.

Japanese women's sandals and 'geta' (wooden clogs) even make us feel as if they are an object of industrial art, going beyond practical functions. Japanese sandals mainly use leather and textiles (silk, gold/silver foils, etc.), but their processing techniques are amazingly varied and they are amazingly beautiful. Although Saga nishiki (Japanese brocade), figured brocade and other materials used as a formal wear set (a pair of Japanese sandals and beg) are cloth, these pieces of cloth have a metallic quality.

We thought that glass cases for displaying those formal wear sets and the shop's face – front window – must be arranged by using materials that can support the beauty of goods, as it is not enough to make goods merely noticeable.

By providing many kinds of delicate surface processing on the brass and red copper plates which have both hard and soft images, with notch pasting, we intended to remind guests of Kyoto-Yuzen's traditional patterns, and help expand their image to Japanese clothes.

Shijyo-kawaramachi, Shimogyo-ku, Kyoto City
Phone: 075-221-0308

Design / Tetsuyuki Ishimura
Area / 45.8 m²

材料仕様

スクリーン／ラワン合板ｔ＝5.6下地　真鍮　丹銅プレーｔ＝1.2コーティング仕上げ　ショーケース／ラワン合板ｔ=5.6下地　真鍮プレート梨地模様エッチング及び同　硫化いぶし及び破打ち加工及び幾何学模様エッチング加工硫化いぶし　丹銅プレート砂打ち加工及び同　草花模様エッチング加工

ファサード

The facade.

正面外観全景をみる

The entire front appearance.

オリジナルグッズ＆ブティック
釜座　二年坂

京都市東山区清水二年坂　Phone/075-531-1715

撮影／藤原　弘

1階店内奥をみる　吹抜けている中庭がこの店のポイント

The inner part of the 1st floor. This shop features a courtyard with a stairwell.

1階中庭をみる　奥の陳列棚は棚が可動式になっている

The courtyard at the 1st floor. The inner display shelves are movable.

材料仕様

屋根／日本瓦葺き　一部銅葺き　外壁／杉及び米松　カラーステイン仕上げ　外部床／御影石貼り　一部叩き仕上げ　床／1階・ラミネートビニール板ヘリングボーン貼り　2階・カーペット敷込み　幅木／ラワン下地ｈ＝50ラッカー仕上げ　壁面／ＰＢ下地クロス貼り　一部塩地染色の上ＣＬ　天井／ＰＢ下地クロス貼り　照明器具／ユニバーサルダウンライト　家具／アンティック家具　什器／塩地染色の上にＣＬ　楢材染色の上ＣＬ　米松染色の上にＣＬ　棚板／ブルーペンガラスｔ＝8

営業内容

開店／1985年12月30日　営業時間／午前9時～午後6時　休日／なし　経営者／野村泰之　従業員／6人　客単価／2万～3万　主な取り扱い商品／ギフト商品（ネクタイ　バッグ　アクセサリー　ハンカチ　組紐　陶芸工芸品等）

2階からみた吹抜け

The stairwell viewed from the 2nd floor.

2階を階段越しにみる

The 2nd floor viewed across the 2nd floor.

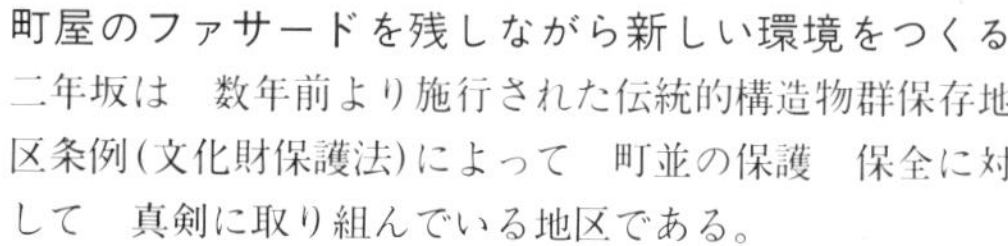

町屋のファサードを残しながら新しい環境をつくる

二年坂は　数年前より施行された伝統的構造物群保存地区条例(文化財保護法)によって　町並の保護　保全に対して　真剣に取り組んでいる地区である。

店舗は　このような地域性を生かしながら　新鮮さを感じるように　環境にとけこみながら　その存在感をもつようにすること。一見　特異と感じる商品群　商品環境の新しい訴えをもつこと。より自然に客が回遊することができて　より好感をもって滞在時間をのばせること。1階　2階の商品構成の違いを自然に訴えることができ互いに良い影響を与えられること。商品陳列や　ディスプレイだけではなく　季節感をだすこと。メーカーのアンテナショップ　イメージショップとしての店舗であるばかりでなく　全国のＦＣに対しての多方面にわたる役割を果たせること　など主に考えた。　〈菊池孝造〉(86-4)

設計／菊池孝造　施工／林工芸

構造・規模／木造＆Ｓ造　地上２階建(一部３階建)

面積／敷地・155m²　建築・130m²　床・１階130m²
　２階120m²　３階34m²　合計284m²

工期／1985年12月10日～28日　工費／3500万円

Original Goods & Boutique KAMANZA Ninenzaka

Creates a new environment while leaving intact the facade of an old tradesman's house

Ninenzaka is an area where people are earnestly endeavoring to protect and preserve their streets in compliance with the municipal ordinance for areas whose traditional structures are to be preserved (in the Cultural Properties Protection Law) which was enacted a few years ago.

In designing this shop, we took into considerations the following points: a) While making use of those regional features, the shop must give a fresh impression, so that it must assert its own existence while fusing with the environment; b) To create an appeal with a product group and a product environment that are seemingly strange; c) To allow guests to move about more naturally and stay longer with more favorable feelings; d) To assert the difference in goods lineup between the 1st and 2nd floors more naturally, so that they can mutually affect favorably; To give seasonal senses – not merely display goods; e) To have this shop serve not merely as an antenna shop or image shop of the manufacturer, but also as a center playing various roles for franchised shops across the nation.

Ninenzaka, Kiyomizu, Higashiyama-ku, Kyoto City
Phone: 075-531-1715

Design / Kozo Kikuchi
Area / Site 155 m^2, Building 130 m^2,
Floor: 1st floor 130 m^2, 2nd floor 120 m^2,
3rd floor 34 m^2; Totalling 284 m^2

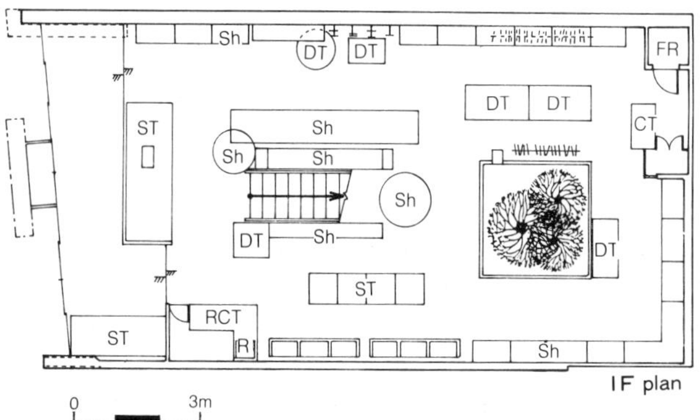

1F plan

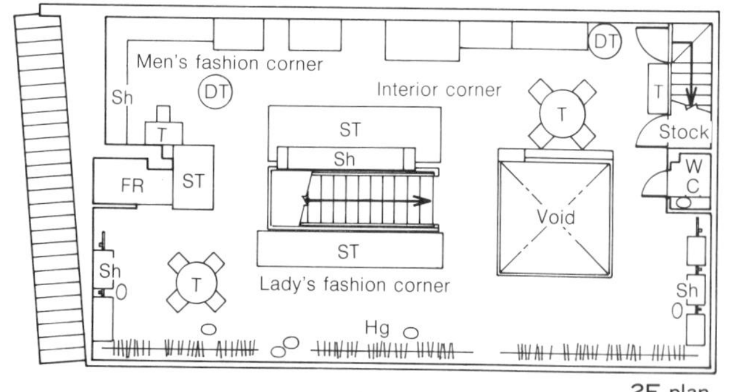

2F plan

現代的な倉のイメージの外観

The appearance comes with a modern warehouse image.

正面外観夜景

The front appearance at night.

陶器＆漆製品 陶三倉

栃木県足利市大町444-1　Phone／0284-41-4660

側面外観

The side appearance.

撮影／大竹静市郎

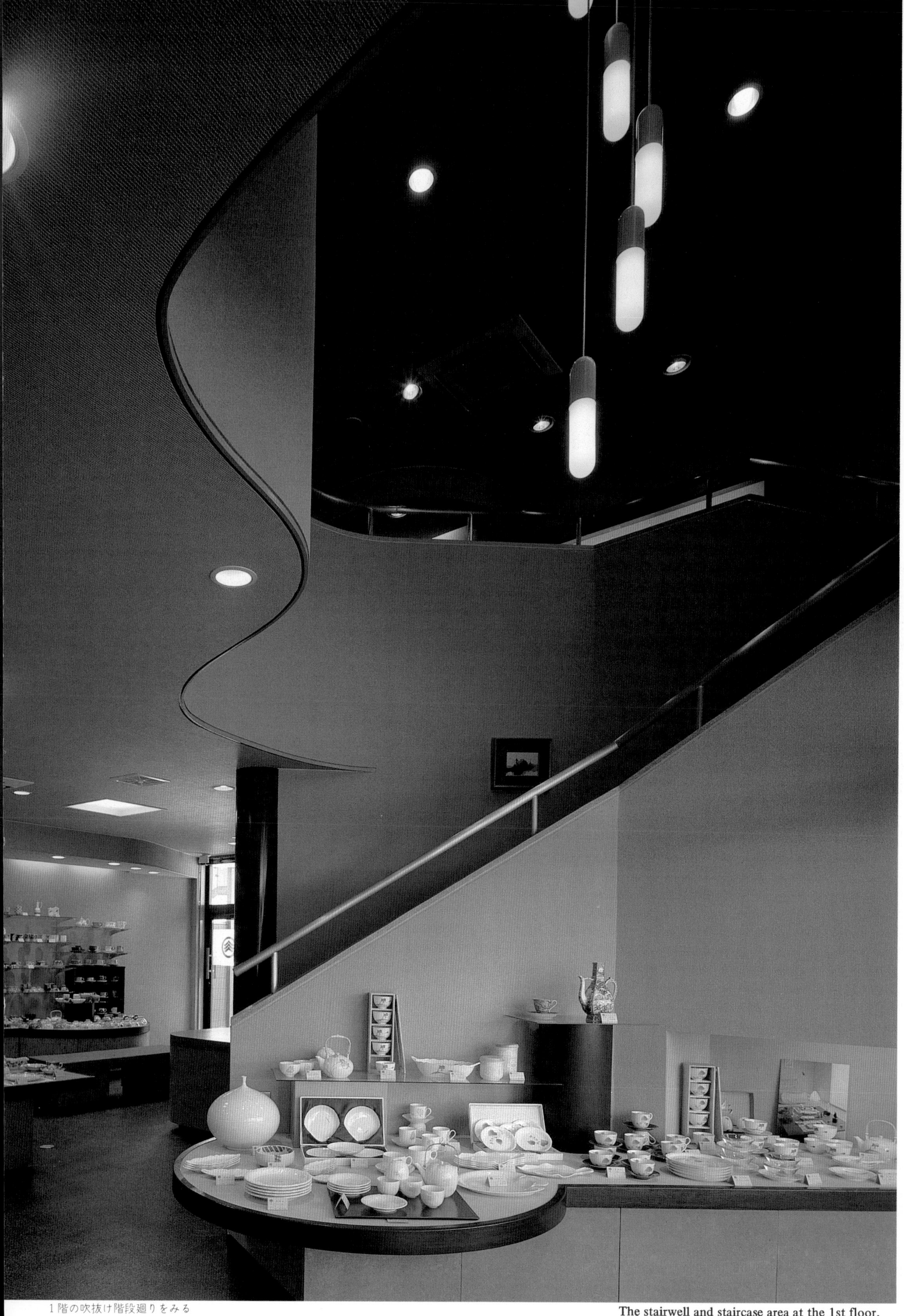

1階の吹抜け階段廻りをみる

The stairwell and staircase area at the 1st floor.

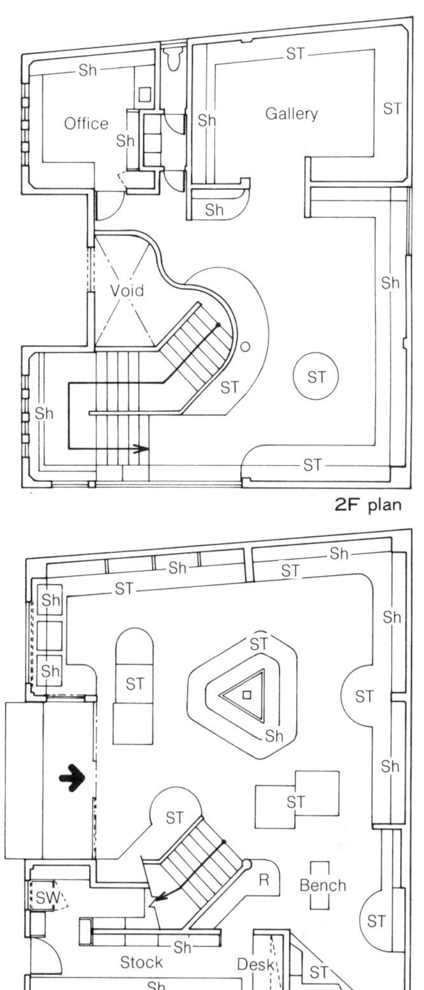

トップライトと吹抜けで開放的な２階コーナー
The open-style 2nd floor corner with the top light and stairwell.

1階入口側コーナーをみる
The entrance side corner at the 1st floor.

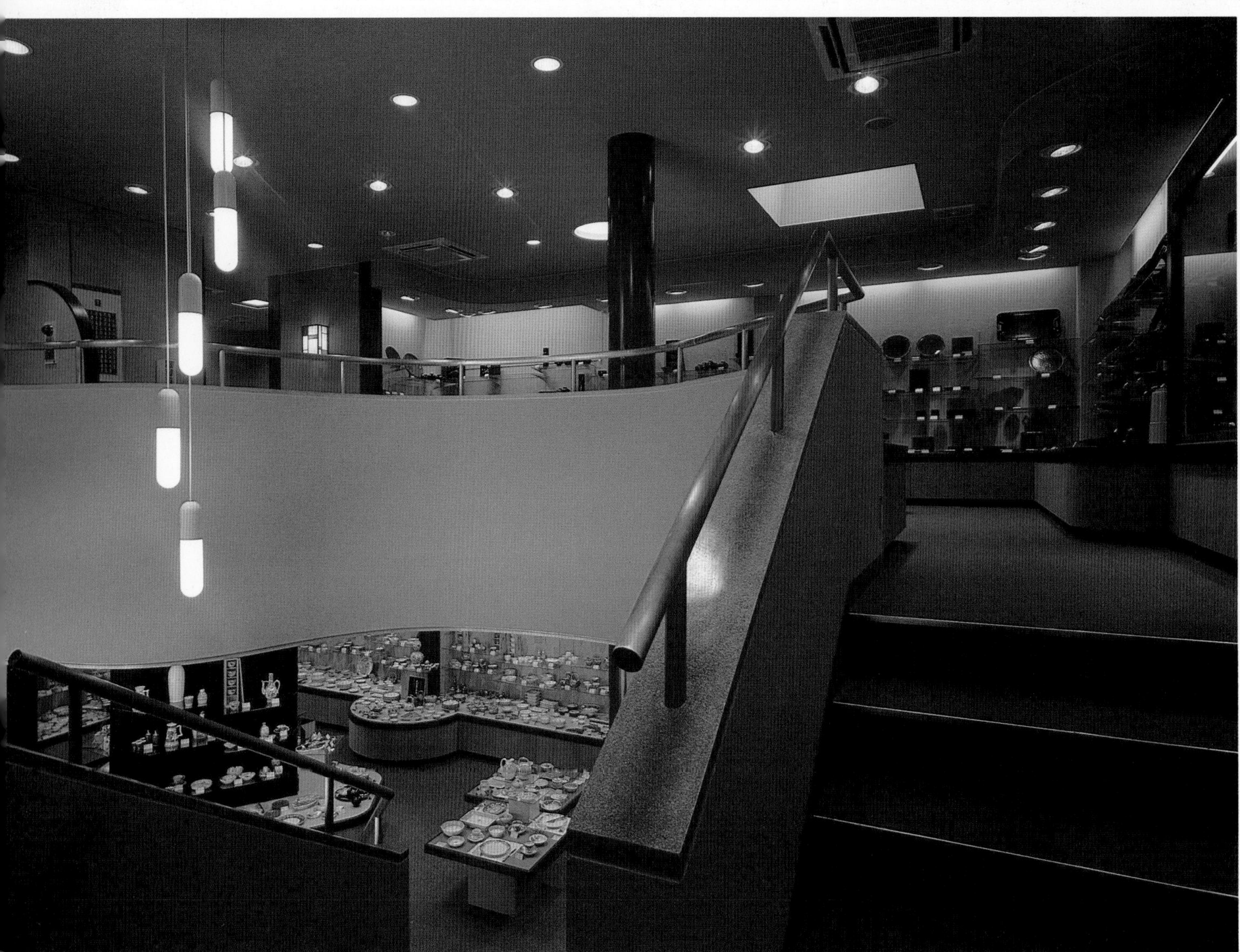

吹抜け階段の中段踊り場より1階と2階のフロアをみる

1st and 2nd floors viewed from the middle stage landing at the stairwell.

現代的倉のイメージ

外観デザインは 歴史のある街のイメージと屋号「陶三倉」ということもあり 現代的な倉のイメージとしてまとめ 屋根は和瓦を葺き 外壁材には やはり陶器を扱っている店なので グレーの陶器タイルを使用した。また タイルの壁面のもつ"かたさ""つめたさ"をなくすため 中央部分にシンプルなデザインのステンドグラスをはめ込んだ。昼間は店内に彩りと採光を与え 夕方からは 外観の一つのポイントとなった。
平面計画は 1階が陶器製品売場と倉庫 2階が漆器製品と作家のギャラリーコーナー そして事務室。ポイントは いかに1階より2階へと上がり易くするかということで 開放的な吹抜けホールを設け 1階より2階が見えるようにし また 階段幅を広くとり 中段踊り場部分にステージ棚を置き 製品を見ながら 2階へといけるようにした。

〈石井道男／バンナ建築設計室〉(86-11)

設計／バンナ(VAN-A)建築設計室 石井道男
施工／野口建設 構造・規模／重量S造・地上2階建
面積／敷地・158.022m² 建築・124.42m² 床・1階116.68m² 2階109.98m² 合計226.66m²
工期／1985年7月20日～11月20日 工費／2293万円

China Shop TOMIKURA

Gives an image of modern warehouse

In view of an image of a historical street and time-honored shop name "Tomikura," the appearance was designed to give a modern warehouse's image. The roof is covered with Japanese tiles, and the outer wall was finished with grey porcelain tiles to harmonize with the shop image. In order to wipe out "hardness" and "coolness" of the tiled wall surface, simply designed stained glass was set in the center. In the daytime, the inside is provided with coloring and lighting, while at night the appearance serves as an accent.
As for the plan, the 1st floor consists of chinaware selling corners and a warehouse, while the 2nd floor consists of a gallery corner for lacquered ware and artists, and an office.
The point of design lay in how to secure an easier access from the 1st floor to the 2nd floor. So, by providing an open-type stairwell hall, the 2nd floor was made visible from the 1st floor. Also, by broadening the stairs, a stage shelf was provided at the middle landing so that you can go up to the 2nd while viewing the goods.

441-1, Omachi, Ashikaga City, Tochigi Prefecture
Phone: 0284-41-4660

Design / Michio Ishii
Area / Site 158.02 m², Building 124.42 m²,
Floor: 1st floor 116.68 m², 2nd floor 109.98 m²;
Totalling 226.66 m²

材料仕様
屋根／三洲陶器瓦 外壁／磁器質タイル貼り100角 外部床／セラミックプレートデラックスタイル貼り300角 サイン／スチール焼付け加工塗装 床／ビニールタイル貼り 幅木／ソフト幅木 壁面／クロス貼り 天井／ビニールクロス貼り

営業内容
開店／1985年12月7日 営業時間／午前10時～午後7時30分 休日／毎週木曜日 経営者／津久井利・ 従業員／2人 客単価／8000円 主な商品／食器 花器 漆器など和陶器全般

モンドリアン パターンのファサード

The facade in mondrian pattern.

漆製品 うるし オータキ

新潟県村上市片町2-32 Phone/0254-52-2695

撮影／寺井幹郎

1階店内をみる

The inside at the 1st floor.

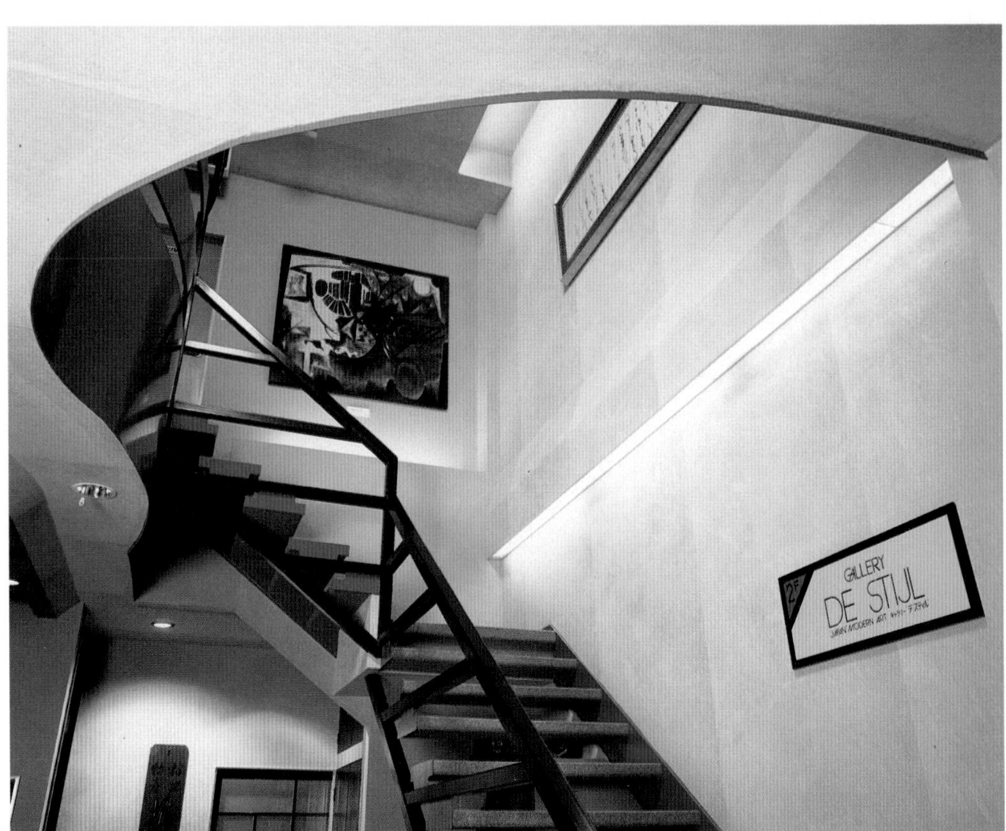

2階への階段廻りを見上げる

The staircase area up to the 2nd floor.

材料仕様

屋根／長尺カラー鉄板瓦棒葺き t =0.4 外壁／アルミパネル t = 2 電着塗装　一部乾式サイディング貼り　床／磁器タイル　サイン／アクリル　床／カーペット敷き　幅木／カーペット立上げ　壁面及び天井／ＰＢ t = 9 下地クロス貼り　照明器具／ＤＬ　スポットライト　什器／メラミン化粧合板　トップ・クロス貼り

営業内容

開店／1986年２月22日　営業時間／午前９時～午後７時　休日／毎月第４木曜日　経営者／大滝源一　従業員／６人　客単価／１万円　主な取り扱い商品／器　花器　額　アクセサリー　家具　漆オブジェ

2階ギャラリーをみる

The gallery at the 2nd floor.

妙を織りなす“はれ”と“くすみ”の空間

この地には“村上唯朱（ついしゅ）”という　使い込むうちに“はれ”を持つ伝統工芸がある。この工房では　日常使いこんでいけるような　身近な漆製品を提供している。

また「JAPAN(漆)MODERN・ART」の作品も制作しており　その展示スペースとして　ギャラリーの併設となった。2階壁面を1つのパネルと見立てて　この工房の兄弟にデザインをお願いした。それが　明快な壁面構成をもちながらも　鉛色の空に一条の光を散らす　風土性の彩によるモンドリアンパターンである。これは単純なる平面処理ではあるが狭い間口に接するファサードとしてフォルムの追求は　この町並の表面的なファサードと路面によって形づくられる連続的フレームを失うと考えられたし　建築することによって失われる物を　再構築するには適当と思われた。内部空間においても　ファサードのモンドリアンを立体的に引用している。内装はモノトーンで覆い　照明も雲から漏れるようにし　その“くすみ”の中に製品である朱のもつ“はれ”を散らし　風土性の彩を意識している。また　外部の散漫な視界を遮断するため開口部は視線から上部を閉じている。

〈野澤　繁／空間舎〉(86-11)

設計／空間舎　野澤　繁　野口幸輔
　　協力　アートデザイン　大滝　豊　大滝　聡
施工／山口工務店　構造・規模／S造・地上2階建
面積／敷地・374.38m^2　建築・83.75m^2　床・1階75.38m^2　2階83.75m^2
　　合計159.13m^2
工期／1985年10月10日～1986年2月22日

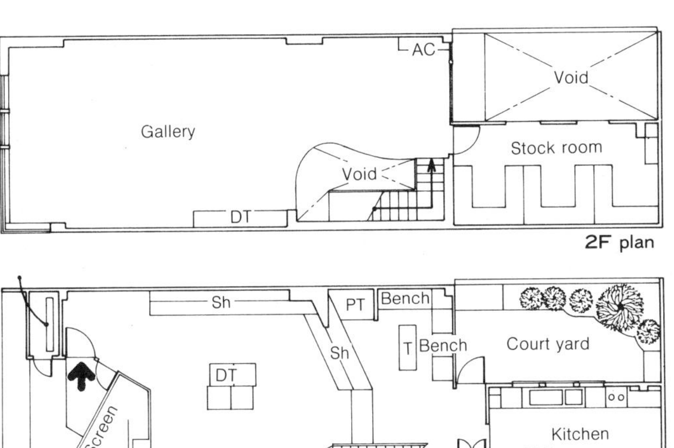

Lacquered Ware OHTAKI

“Bright” and “dark” spaces harmonizing melodiously

In this land there is a traditional piece of artistic work called “Murakami Tsuishu” which has “brightness” as you go on using it. At this workshop, daily lacquered ware is offered to help in your daily life. It also is producing the works for “Japan modern Art,” and a gallery was provided as an annex as their display space. Regarding the 2nd floor’s wall surface as a panel, we requested the workshop’s brothers to undertake its design. The result was a Mondrian pattern which is very clear in composition, but locally colored with a streak of light scattered over the leaden sky. Although this is a simple plane treatment, since it was felt that the form as the facade facing the narrow frontage might interfere in the continuous frame shaped by the street’s superficial facade and road surface. It was thought reasonable to reconstruct the disappearing one by building this shop. Even at the inside space, the Mondrian pattern of the facade was solidly cited. The interior was covered with a monotone, and it was arranged to have lighting leak from clouds, and within the “darkness,” “brightness” of the red ware is scattered to express local coloring. Additionally, in order to intercept the external diffusive sight, the upper part of the opening is shut out from your eyes.

2-32, Kamikatamachi, Murakami City, Niigata Prefecture
Phone: 0254-52-2695

Design / Shigeru Nozawa
Area / Site 374.38 m^2, Building 83.75 m^2,
Floor: 1st floor 75.38 m^2, 2nd floor 83.75 m^2;
Totalling 159.13 m^2

展示室より和室をみる

Japanese style room viewed from the display room.

陶器 陶耕庵

北海道札幌郡広島町大曲251　Phone/01137-6-2577

撮影／安達　治

ファサード

The facade.

ホーチより入口扉をみる

The entrance door viewed from the porch.

陶器を包み込む大きな木の箱のイメージ

〈炎の洗礼を受けて世の中に生まれてくる我が子のような器たちに　納める空間を与えることが生んだ人間としての責任である〉と　言い続けてきた女流陶芸家・高橋千弥先生の展示室である。

札幌市近郊の大曲という地名のついているこの辺は　まだ自然の姿が残り　季節の移り変わりを感じさせてくれる静かなところである。美しい陶器が　桐箱の中に入っているように　ここに置かれる器たちを包み込む大きな木の箱を作るという空間イメージから　内外装とも　米松の厚板を仕上げ材として使用している。

路と建物とを結ぶ　目に見えない空間を大切にしなければならないと考えているが「陶耕庵」では　路から器たちまでを結ぶ空間を大切に考えた。

単純な四角い箱の中での　器と人とのいろいろな出合いに期待している。　〈村上憲一〉(85·5)

設計／村上建築設計室　施工／竹内組
構造・規模／W造・平家建
面積／敷地・735m²　建築・127.24m²
　　床・112.77m²
工期／1984年5月8日～7月26日
工費／1300万円

Chinaware TOKO-AN

An image of large wooden box encasing chinaware in

This is a display space of Ms. Chiya Takahashi, a woman potter who has kept asserting: It is the responsibility of us man to give a space to encase ware which is like my child who is born in this world baptized with flames."

This area named Omagari in the suburbs of Sapporo City still has natural elements where you can feel seasonal changes in a quiet atmosphere. Just as beautiful chinaware is in a paulownia box, we employed a space image by making a large wooden box encasing chinaware placed here, using the Oregon pine planks as the finishing material in both interior and exterior.

We felt it important to carefully treat the space that connects the road with the building. In the case of "Toko-An," we made much of the space connecting the road to "ware."

It is expected that in this simple square box, ware and man meet in different ways.

251, Omagari, Hiroshima-cho, Sapporo-gun, Hokkaido　Phone: 01137-6-2577

Design / Kenichi Murakami
Area / Site 735 m^2, Building 127.24 m^2,
Floor 112.77 m^2

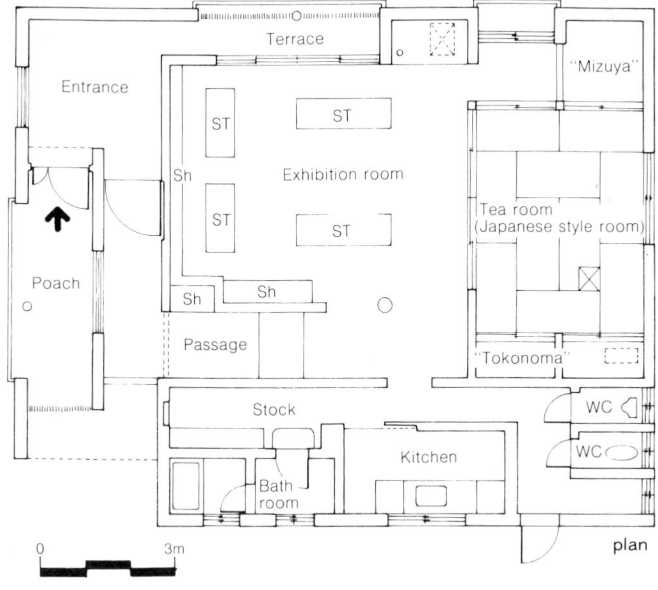

材料仕様

屋根／ガルバリウム鋼板 t＝0.4　外壁／米松 t＝30たて貼り　外部床／那知石洗出し　床／那知石洗出し　幅木／黒モルタル金鏝押え　一部米松 t＝21　壁面／米松 t＝21　本実継ぎ
天井／米松 t＝21　本実継ぎ

営業内容

開店／1984年8月1日　営業時間／午前9時～午後5時　休日／なし　経営者／高橋千弥　従業員／2人

●この索引の店名 所在地 電話番号等は本書初版発行時のものです。変更されている場合もありますので ご了承ください。

1989年6月／商店建築社

別冊商店建築36
秀作ショップデザイン／物販店 & ショールーム
1988年3月31日初版発行
1989年6月10日第2刷発行
編集発行人　村上末吉

編集●辻田　博
制作●菅谷良夫

協力スタッフ
表紙デザイン●ウィークエンド
本文レイアウト●ぱとおく社
英文●海広社
印刷●三共グラビヤ印刷
写植●福島写植
製本●山田製本

発行所　株式会社商店建築社©
本社　東京都新宿区西新宿7-22-36-2
〒160 Phone(03)363-5770(代)
支社　大阪市中央区西心斎橋1-9-28　第3大京ビル
〒542 Phone(06)251-6523(代)

ISBN 4-7858-0097-6